Economic Interdependence
in Southern Africa

Economic Interdependence in Southern Africa:

From Conflict to Cooperation?

Jesmond Blumenfeld

Pinter Publishers, London
St. Martin's Press, New York
for
The Royal Institute of International Affairs,
London

© Royal Institute of International Affairs, 1991

First published in Great Britain in 1991 by
Pinter Publishers Limited
25 Floral Street, London WC2E 9DS

British Library Cataloguing in Publication Data
A CIP catalogue record for this book is available from the British
Library
ISBN 0 86187 044 1

First published in the United States of America in 1991 by
St. Martin's Press Scholarly and Reference Division.
175 Fifth Avenue, New York,
N.Y. 10017

Library of Congress Cataloging in Publication Data
A CIP catalog record for this book is available from the Library
of Congress.
ISBN 0-312-07562-6

Printed and bound in Great Britain

Contents

Preface   vii
Introduction   1

Part One: Historical Background

1   Early political economy   13
2   From colonization to economic interdependence   26
3   From political independence to economic conflict   42

**Part Two: The Political Economy of Dependence
and Interdependence**

4   Economic dependence and interdependence: an introduction   61
5   The theory of global 'dependence'   63
6   Measuring economic dependence   70
7   The costs of economic dependence   81
8   The analysis of economic interdependence   88
9   Economic interdependence, economic power
    and political leverage   95

Part Three: The Dynamics of Economic Conflict in Southern Africa

10   Dependence, destabilization and sanctions   107
11   Evaluating economic relations   122
12   The economic role of SADCC   135
13   Dependence and interdependence revisited   147
14   From economic conflict to economic cooperation?   156

Notes   166
Bibliography   178
Index   182

Preface

The main purpose of this study is to seek to re-examine and reinterpret some of the conventional wisdoms concerning contemporary economic relations among the countries of Southern Africa. The starting-point of the analysis is that, regardless of the specific problems of Southern Africa – including, of course, the issues of apartheid and of South Africa's relative economic size and power – exchange relations in the region cannot sensibly be discussed in terms wholly different from those applicable to the study of the international political economy in general, and of comparable situations in particular.

The project on which this work is based has two major components – one conceptual, the other empirical. In an ideal world, the two would be closely integrated. In practice, it has been necessary to separate out the two components, not least because of the difficulties of obtaining recent and usable data on economic interrelationships between the countries of Southern Africa. The present study primarily reflects the results of the conceptual analysis; the empirical material will follow at a later stage.

The study is divided into three main parts. Part One analyses the historical origins and development of interstate economic relations in Southern Africa. Part Two offers a systematic theoretical analysis of the political economy of the two key concepts of dependence and interdependence which underlie most discussions of the subject. Part Three draws on the conclusions of the preceding work to challenge some of the conventional interpretations of the nature of contemporary economic relations in Southern Africa and, in the light of this reinterpretation, offers a preliminary assessment of the prospects for such relations in the future. The main body of the study is preceded by an introductory chapter which explains why a reinterpretation is needed, and which outlines the approaches adopted and summarizes the conclusions reached in each of the three succeeding parts.

This work has been funded by grants from the Leverhulme Foundation, the Le Poer Power Trust, the Dulverton Foundation and the Department of Economics at Brunel University, West London. Some of the work was undertaken during a period when I was seconded to the Royal Institute of International Affairs at Chatham House, London, where I have been an Associate Research Fellow on Southern Africa since 1987, and where I was Convenor of the Chatham House Study Group on Southern Africa from 1985 to 1989. I am grateful for all the facilities afforded me by the Institute.
The work has benefited immeasurably from the deliberations of the Study

Group, several members of which commented in detail on an earlier draft. Professor Walter Elkan gave me the benefit of his sage advice at various stages. I owe a particular debt of gratitude to Professors Jack Spence and James Barber for their constant support and encouragement of my efforts in the prosecution of work which, by virtue of its subject matter, was unavoidably controversial. No one other than myself, however, bears any responsibility whatsoever for the views expressed herein.

Finally, I offer my apologies to my family for the extensive disruptions which this work has occasioned to normal family life and my unending appreciation for their forbearance.

Oxford, February 1991

J.P.B.

Introduction

From the outside Southern Africa looks like a basket-case, especially when measured against the Pacific Rim and Europe which have not only found the formula to settle differences, but are called economic miracles. – Peter Vale (1989), p. 96.

Economic conflict in Southern Africa

For more than thirty years now, the countries of Southern Africa have been beset by a series of long-running national liberation struggles, internal conflicts and civil wars. As elsewhere in the developing world, the sources of these conflicts were to be found predominantly in opposing ideologies, nationalisms and ethnicities, as well as in external powers and interests, which have all been in contention for political and economic power and influence.

These conflicts proved particularly prone to spill over national boundaries to involve and engulf other states in the region. A major reason for this was the racial dimension to many of the conflicts. Initially, this dimension arose out of struggles for national independence from (white) colonial rule. In the 1960s and 1970s this was particularly true in Angola, Mozambique and Rhodesia (Zimbabwe), where white-dominated minority regimes manifested a dogged – if ultimately futile – determination to resist the trend towards majority rule and to cling to political power. From the mid-1970s onwards, the focus shifted to Namibia and South Africa, where the issue was not simply white minority rule, but more specifically the racist system of apartheid. The solidarity which these varying circumstances generated between groups of states in the region, either in defence of minority rule or in support of efforts to overthrow it, rendered it virtually inescapable that internal conflicts would become externalized and the damage more widely distributed.

In any circumstances of prolonged and violent conflict, economic life inevitably suffers. Physical productive capital is destroyed, production is disrupted, infrastructures deteriorate, new investment is discouraged, market processes and exchange relations are inhibited and living standards decline. In addition, human lives are lost, or irreparably damaged, and all too often large numbers of people are made homeless and rootless, thus impoverishing the stock of human capital and diverting already scarce investible resources away from productive activities towards emergency consumption needs.

In all these respects, too, Southern Africa has been no exception. The climate of hostility and instability which has obtained during the past three decades has certainly been inimical to economic growth and development. In consequence, poverty and unemployment have been significantly increased throughout the region. Indeed, though economic conditions and performance vary markedly from one country to another, the overall picture has been – and remains – one of deepening economic decline, reflected in rising foreign indebtedness, in falling real investment, in declining real exports and, most generally, in continuously falling living standards for the more than 100 million inhabitants of the region.

Though the racial dimension to the region's conflicts has undoubtedly been important, it has not been their only distinguishing feature. In some instances, added impetus was given to the contending forces both by the region's rich and varied resource endowments and, at times, by its strategic geopolitical location. But an even more important element in some of the conflicts has been the nature and scale of economic relations among the countries concerned. This has been especially true of the Rhodesian and, more recently, the South African conflict.

When neighbouring states regard each other with hostility and suspicion, commerce between them is put at risk. At best, the mutual gains from bilateral trade and investment are reduced; at worst, cross-border economic relations come to be viewed, not as the basis for raising economic welfare between trading partners, but rather as instruments for the conduct of international economic warfare. Again, evidence of this abounds in Southern Africa. Apart from the two which were fuelled by the issue of intra-regional economic linkages, all of the region's conflicts have had consequences for such linkages. In some instances, the conflicts have actually proved to be a stimulus to certain aspects of intra-regional relations. More generally, however, the effect on cross-border exchange relations has been to distort and inhibit them, sometimes in the most profound ways.

Dependence *vs.* interdependence

In recent times, the important role played by economic relations in the region's conflicts has rendered the content and the consequences of these relations highly contentious issues. This has been especially true of economic relations between the dominant regional power, South Africa, and its less powerful neighbours.

Prior to the 1970s, the accepted – and uncontested – view of Southern Africa was that it was an economically coherent region, with the South African economy at its core. The link between South Africa and the other

regional economies was thus seen as being one of mutual – and, by implication, beneficial – interdependence. This view was subsequently challenged
by the argument that the region has been characterized by 'one-sided' –
and, by implication, undesirable – economic dependence of the neighbouring states upon South Africa.

Economic dependence and economic interdependence in international
relations are terms which refer to the political, as well as to the economic,
characteristics and consequences of economic linkages across national
boundaries. They therefore raise issues – such as the nature of power and
influence in the international political economy – which are not readily
amenable to economic analysis. Perhaps largely for this reason, analyses of
economic dependence and interdependence have tended – some notable
exceptions notwithstanding – to feature more in the domain of political
scientists interested in international economic relations than of economists
interested in international politics.

An important consequence of this situation is that political scientists tend
to employ these concepts with relatively little understanding either of their
economic theoretic foundations or of their policy implications; equally,
economists are wont to employ them with limited appreciation of the
political implications of international economic linkages.

Nowhere has this been more true than in Southern Africa, where (as we
have already implied) the normative characteristics ascribed to cross-border
economic relations, and the policy implications adjudged to flow from
them, have been more important than the descriptive terms used to categor-
ize them. In the view of the dependence school, the structures of these
relations have been unambiguously disadvantageous, both politically and
economically, for the neighbouring states and correspondingly advan-
tageous for South Africa. Moreover, the behavioural constraints were also
seen as one-sided: South Africa had almost total freedom of action; the
neighbouring countries had virtually none. This pointed to the need for a
fundamental restructuring of regional economic relations involving, at the
minimum, a significant reduction in the neighbours' dependence upon South
Africa; at the limit, it implied total disengagement from South Africa.

The alternative approach has generally taken a more benign view of the
situation: interdependent exchange relations involve mutual benefits for all
the countries of the region. In policy terms, this seemed to imply, at the
minimum, the need for more of the same: South Africa was the 'powerhouse' of the region, and it was as much in the neighbours' economic
interests as in South Africa's to extend the economic linkages between them.
For some, the argument pointed ultimately towards the desirability of a
common market (or other form of institutional economic unification) centred on South Africa and embracing most, if not all, of the regional states.

In one sense, these differences of opinion about economic relations
in the region were relatively unremarkable. Conflicting theories and

explanations for different phenomena, and conflicting policy conclusions, are as prevalent in the literature on the international political economy as in any other domain of academic debate. These differences are usually due to alternative analytical starting-points, ranging from differing behavioural assumptions to divergent ideological positions. Moreover, in this general literature, international economic relations have also been widely characterized either as dependent or interdependent. Ideological differences have certainly been prevalent in the Southern African debate: the dependence school drew its inspiration primarily from radical, neo-Marxist approaches to international economic relations, whereas the antecedents of the alternative approach were, at least nominally, liberal economic theory.

In another sense, however, the debate about Southern Africa appeared to be unusual, even unique, for two reasons. First, the policy implications of the two approaches seemed naive. Not least because of the constraints of geography and the accidents of geology, there had already been extensive economic interactions between South Africa and its neighbours ever since the mineral discoveries of the late nineteenth century. The disengagement arguments of the dependence school thus seemed to fly directly in the face of economic realities and of the economic, if not also the political, self-interest of the neighbouring states.

But the policy implications of the interdependence argument appeared no less naive in political terms, for they overlooked the political relevance of the extreme asymmetries in the structures of regional economic relations, and of the neighbouring states' consequent fears of South African domination. The thrust of the argument tended to be that economic relations were mutually beneficial, that only irrational political considerations stood in the way of extending them, and that all that was required to unleash a wave of prosperity in the region was for the neighbours to set aside these artificial impediments to greater interdependence.[1]

Second, and more important, the issue went far beyond normal analytical differences. This was particularly true for the neo-Marxist school, for whom the dependence of the neighbouring states upon South Africa was not simply a matter of analytical 'truth' or an article of faith. In effect, it became a litmus test of the bona fides of any analysis of the political economy of Southern Africa.

The explanation for this is to be found in the belief among adherents of the radical school that the fundamental problems of Southern Africa, whether political or economic, are indeed unique and that the reason lies in the specific features of South Africa's racist apartheid system. In this view, all intra-regional relations, including economic relations, have been conditioned and determined by the imperatives of apartheid, and in effect are integral to the perpetuation of South Africa's system of white domination. This belief has been reinforced by the events of the past ten to fifteen years, a period which is widely known as the era of regional destabilization, since it was a time during which South Africa, seeking to defend its interests, and particularly its capacity to sustain white minority rule, projected its military, political and economic power in the wider region in a number of ways. Although one of the effects of destabilization was to disrupt and damage intra-regional economic relations, South Africa's capacity to engage in this strategy was, in part, facilitated by the structure of these relations.

Destroying this structure has thus come to be seen as an essential part of the international struggle to end apartheid. Consequently, any analysis which implied that there was anything beneficial, normal or even defensible in the structure and content of regional economic relations was to be denounced, not merely as analytically invalid, but as morally reprehensible and politically unacceptable. In short, the inhibition of economic linkages between South Africa and its neighbours became, by definition, directly related to the prospects for eliminating the apartheid system; conversely, their promotion implied a wish to perpetuate the system.

This situation has had unfortunate consequences for the analysis of, and for policy towards, economic relations in Southern Africa. For more than a decade, it has effectively foreclosed the possibility of constructive arguments about the validity of alternative theoretical frameworks for analysis of the region's economic relations, and for the formulation of rational policies towards these relations. It has allowed only for policy conclusions and initiatives which have accorded with the prevailing – and politically 'admissible' – preconceptions.[2] More specifically, it has resulted in the two concepts of economic dependence and interdependence being employed, with little regard for academic and analytic rigour, to bolster differing ideological and political positions and prior assumptions regarding the nature and structure of international economic relations in the region. Most unfortunate of all, it has been responsible for giving rise to policies which have been, at best, inappropriate, and which – in the mid–1980s – brought the region to the brink of outright economic warfare between South Africa on the one hand and at least some of the neighbouring countries on the other. Although, in many respects, economic relations between the countries concerned in fact persisted at relatively high levels, even in the face of growing confrontation, there can be no doubt that, on balance, this atmosphere was destructive of the prospects for economic prosperity in the region.

Outline of the present study

In fact, the sources of Southern Africa's economic difficulties, and of the problem posed by and for intra-regional economic relations, are much wider and deeper than those resulting from the specific forms which white minority rule has taken in South Africa itself and in which the consequences of apartheid have manifested themselves in the wider region. It has already been made clear that, prior to the advent of destabilization in the second half of the 1970s, most of the region's conflicts had little or nothing to do with the existence and consequences of the system of apartheid.

More generally, the political and racial conflicts that have pervaded the region for the past thirty years have by no means been the only, or even the main, source of economic decline, even in those countries which managed to eschew or escape the ideological strait-jackets seemingly demanded by Marx and by Lenin. In common with the rest of sub-Saharan Africa – and, indeed, with many other parts of the non-industrialized world – economic mismanagement and the employment of highly inappropriate economic policies have been rife in most of the countries of the region (not excluding South Africa). As a result, opportunities for economic progress have been dissipated and the historical legacy of underdevelopment, far from being overcome, has merely been reinforced. Seen in this light, too, the further implication of the conventional wisdom that the ending of apartheid will be instrumental in resolving all the region's economic problems is patently false.

It necessarily follows that the relevance of the apartheid issue for cross-border economic linkages needs to be placed in its proper context. That context is the full range of variables which determine any set of intra-regional economic relations, and specifically those factors relevant to regions in which there are major imbalances of power and in which economic relations between the regional states are infused with hostility and suspicion. As stated in the Preface, providing this context, and re-evaluating regional exchange relations within it, is the primary purpose of the study.

One precondition for achieving such an objective is an understanding of the historical development of economic exchange relations in Southern Africa. The contemporary tendency to focus primarily on the destabiliz-ation period is inappropriate for two reasons. First, the interconnection between regional conflict and cross-border economic relations did not begin with South African destabilization or the 'export' of apartheid; its origins extend back some thirty years. Second, and more important, the context has not always been a conflictual one. The region's exchange relations had their origins over 100 years ago in the minerals revolution. Although the minerals discoveries were followed initially be a period of considerable upheaval, culminating in the Anglo-Boer War at the turn of the century, the countries and territories of Southern Africa subsequently enjoyed a sustained period of peaceful coexistence. During this period the underlying structures of economic relations were both consolidated and elaborated in a manner that generated a substantial degree of functional unity and coher-ence in the regional economy.

The first major focus of this study is thus to explain the conditions and processes, both political and economic, which first promoted this increasing integration of the regional economy, and which subsequently caused economic relations to become the source of conflict and potential disintegration. This historical examination, which constitutes Part One of the study, reveals clearly that, from the outset, there has been a perpetual tension between the potentially integrative impulses emanating from the underlying unity of the regional economy and the relative lack of political impulses towards any form of unified political authority over the wider region. Economic cooperation and integration have fared best in periods when there has been an overriding, and widely shared, political interest in the potential benefits. However, these conditions have never pertained either long enough or widely enough to carry the region decisively towards economic union, let alone political union. In periods when the political interests of the regional states have strongly diverged, the structural imperatives for economic cooperation have come under increasing strain, leading to heightened conflict over the nature and terms of the exchange relations between them. The tension between economic and political interests in the region has always been complicated by the contradictory influences which arise from the fact of the economic dominance exercised by and from the economic heartland centred on the Witwatersrand.

A second precondition for generalizing the context of regional economic relations must be an improved understanding of the concepts of economic dependence and interdependence. Part Two thus comprises an attempt to elucidate systematically both the analytical content and the policy implications of these two concepts. This work is grounded in the basic principles of economic theory. However, it seeks throughout to preserve an awareness that economic variables – and particularly those which are relevant to international exchange relations – are conditioned by, and evaluated within, the political and institutional environments in which they exist.

This exploration demonstrates the extent to which the analytical connotations of the two terms are frequently misunderstood or misrepresented in popular usage. In part, this is because neither concept can be uniquely defined; both are open to a range of interpretations. However, this fact in no way precludes systematic analysis of their alternative meanings. Such analysis shows that both concepts represent very complex, multidimensional phenomena, the nature of which is not always reflected in their application to concrete situations.

In the sense in which it is most widely employed, economic dependence is shown to be a largely meaningless theoretical concept. Consequently, in this sense it has little, if any, policy relevance. One contribution which this study hopes to make is to demonstrate that dependence can be given more explicit economic analytical content, which – at least in principle – renders it a measurable phenomenon with clearer policy implications. Unfortunately, however, the analysis also discloses that the data requirements for making the concept operationally useful are exceptionally demanding, and not widely available.

Analysis of economic interdependence, in turn, is shown to be bedevilled by the tensions between its positive and its negative economic and political connotations. Interdependence simultaneously brings mutual benefits and mutual costs. To this extent, it is amenable to standard economic analysis. However, the (net) mutual economic benefits which countries derive from their interdependence are no less likely to generate political conflict than political cooperation between them. An additional problem arises when the benefits are asymmetrically distributed, in that the economically 'stronger' country is commonly perceived to be able to exercise political leverage over its 'weaker' partner. In policy terms, this could be expected to generate some aversion on the weaker country's part to greater interdependence. However, the analysis suggests that this conventional wisdom may also be misleading in that it conflates two distinct issues.

Part Three of the study draws on the preceding materials to re-examine the conventional wisdoms of the past decade concerning economic relations in Southern Africa. It demonstrates that the two standard – and opposing – approaches to analysis of these relations have contributed to the conflictual atmosphere in the region, especially by creating misunderstandings about the nature and value of cross-border economic exchanges. By overlooking the basis on which international economic relations are evaluated, the 'dependence' hypothesis led to a questioning of the political legitimacy of economic links with South Africa and generated misleading policy implications. The consequent mutual hostility and suspicion created an adversarial relationship in which trade and other economic relations were viewed, not as a positive-sum game between trading partners with mutually beneficial outcomes, but as manifestations of economic strengths and weaknesses to be exploited and manipulated in the cause of disadvantaging opponents. These outcomes undoubtedly have been detrimental to all the peoples and economies of the region.

The impact of recent developments

In the wake of the remarkable political changes which have recently occurred in the region, the belief has grown that, after so many years of conflict and instability, Southern Africa may at last be in sight of political peace and economic prosperity. Collectively, the changes are being viewed by many as steps towards a wider regional political and economic accommodation, offering the prospect of regional economic renewal driven by the oft-styled 'powerhouse' of the South African economy. In short, on this view, the Southern African economies, hitherto believed to have been constrained by their unnatural, destructive and divisive economic 'dependence' on apartheid South Africa, are now on course for an era of natural, constructive and cooperative economic 'interdependence'.

Leaving aside the fact that the changing regional climate still begs many questions about internal political and economic stability in almost all the regional states, such a reversal of attitudes towards intra-regional economic relations in the region will not easily be achieved, even when the fundamental political problem of apartheid has ultimately been resolved. The message of this study is that it is not apartheid *per se* which constitutes the core inhibition for closer economic relations in Southern Africa, but rather the lack of any overriding common political interests in real economic integration. As we have indicated, even when the political conditions were relatively propitious, the historical thrust towards economic cooperation stopped well short of full economic union. Rhetoric apart, there are few objective grounds for believing that this inhibition will be significantly eroded if and when South Africa achieves a system of government which is genuinely responsive to the political and economic aspirations of all its peoples. As the countries of Western Europe are discovering, real economic integration involves the overt surrender, to a greater or lesser extent, of political sovereignty over those issues, policies and processes where sovereignty is (or is perceived to be) most crucial. The purpose of this work, it should be emphasized, is not to argue against any moves towards closer economic union in the region. If there is anywhere in sub-Saharan Africa where the continental drift towards economic collapse is not merely avoidable but also reversible, it is surely in Southern Africa. By comparison with the rest of Africa, the region is well-endowed with resources, both natural and human, and – the ravages of war and neglect notwithstanding – much of the basic economic infrastructure remains sound or capable of early rehabilitation. Moreover, since Southern Africa always has been, and still remains, an economically coherent region, it is potentially capable of benefiting from the motive force of economic cooperation among all its constituent states. Most particularly, of course, there is the potential contribution to be made by the richest and most powerful economy south of the Sahara, namely that of South Africa itself.

However, this study suggests that, if the regional states do genuinely seek closer economic integration and cooperation in the post-apartheid era, the extent to which, and the success with which, they will achieve this objective will depend significantly upon their capacity to comprehend the nature of economic dependence and interdependence and to handle the relevant issues in appropriate analytical and policy terms. The primary motivation for the study is therefore to help provide a better understanding of the determinants of international exchange relations in Southern Africa. If, in so doing, it also makes some small contribution to a reversal of the trend towards economic decline in the region, that would be a prize beyond any academic satisfaction.

PART ONE
HISTORICAL BACKGROUND

An economic heartland exercises political magnetism. A zollverein, a customs union, a common market must go forward to an empire, a federation, a community of centralized authority – or the single market will be broken up. – Ralph Horwitz (1987), p. 65.

1 Early political economy

For the purposes of this study, Southern Africa has been defined (broadly) as South Africa plus the ten countries of the Southern African Development Coordination Conference (SADCC). These are Angola, Botswana, Lesotho, Malawi, Mozambique, Namibia, Swaziland, Tanzania, Zambia and Zimbabwe. Despite some incongruities, this definition is widely accepted as adequate for most practical purposes.[1] A comprehensive history of the political economy of Southern Africa is beyond the scope of this study. However, a précis of some of the key elements which have both bound the countries of the region together, and given rise to the conflicts between them, will be helpful in understanding the determinants of economic relations within the region.

Any such discussion must start, of course, with the emergence of South Africa itself as the dominant regional state following upon the minerals discoveries in the second half of the nineteenth century. But account must also be taken of the fact – not always fully appreciated – that economic relations between states cannot be considered properly in isolation from their non-economic context. The political, military and strategic climate in which international economic relations take place both affects, and is affected by, the economic linkages themselves. More specifically, some political factors exercise an integrative influence over economic relations; others tend to be responsible for the emergence of differing 'national' interests which can lead to the exercise of conflicting influences over such relations.

This political context for interstate economic relations has always been of critical importance in Southern Africa in two broad respects. First, all of the above-mentioned countries were subject to a greater or lesser degree of formal external political and economic control or influence for much of the period up to the 1960s – in some instances, well beyond that period. The fact of such external control, particularly as reflected in British colonial rule, played a major role in shaping the development of the regional economy. Second, the political context has also been crucial for economic relations in the region in that, at certain stages, there have been sharply divergent political interests in sharing both the benefits and the costs of economic development. As already noted, such divergences brought the region to the brink of war in the post-colonial era. They were also – as will be seen – a major *casus belli* in pre-Union South Africa.

The pre-minerals era[2]

Prior to 1815, when the British finally supplanted the Dutch as the colonial administrators of the Cape of Good Hope, economic development in Southern Africa was largely restricted to the area surrounding the harbour at Cape Town, which serviced and supplied the passing shipping trade and the Dutch administration. For the rest, economic life in Southern Africa was based predominantly on subsistence, largely pastoral, agriculture.

The first half of the nineteenth century brought an influx of white settlers both to the Cape and the Natal, largely as a by-product of the great waves of emigration from Europe to the New World. The growth in the total number of settlers, from some 35,000 in 1815 to around 200,000 by the 1850s, and the dispersion of white settlement well beyond the boundaries of the Cape and of Natal (especially following the Boers' Great Trek in 1836–8), undoubtedly provided some stimulus to the development of both commerce and commercial agriculture. The latter, though mainly small-scale in character, did include the development of some rapidly expanding and highly profitable export trade, especially wool from the Cape. But this growth – both in commodity exports to, and in imports of consumer goods from, Britain – had very little multiplier impact on the development of indigenous exchange activities.

Hence, by the 1860s, outside of the harbours at Cape Town, Port Elizabeth and Durban, urban settlement and commercial activities were still confined largely to a number of small farming service centres, trading posts and administration points scattered throughout present-day South Africa. Furthermore, given that the ox-wagon was still the predominant mode of transport, all these settlements had decidedly limited growth potential and, except via coastal shipping, there was little in the way of trade between them. In many parts, particularly of the hinterland, neither a market system nor a cash economy were much in evidence. Instead, economic stasis and lack of exchange relations was the norm.

The impact of the minerals discoveries

Diamonds were found at Kimberley in East Griqualand in 1867, and gold was discovered in the eastern part of the then Boer Republic of the Transvaal in 1884 and subsequently on the Witwatersrand in 1886. The consequences, for both economy and society throughout the whole of Southern Africa, of these and of the other mineral discoveries of the late nineteenth and early twentieth centuries, were, to say the least, revolutionary.

First, foreign capital flooded in both to the Cape and to the Witwatersrand, accompanied by large numbers of skilled immigrants, speculators, traders, indentured labourers and fortune-seekers from all over the world.

Mining conglomerates were established to finance the huge investments needed to mine the rich subterranean diamond deposits and the deep-level (and low-grade) gold ores. Between 1886, when the gold fields were proclaimed, and 1913, the gold mines alone attracted capital investments amounting to £125 million.

Second, the new settlements which sprang up around the mining centres to accommodate the flood of immigrants became the nuclei of the major urban centres of the future. This was especially true in the Witwatersrand region, where the pace of change was phenomenal: for example, within four years of the discovery of gold, 100,000 people were working in the gold mines, and Johannesburg – a mere farm before 1886 – had grown to a modern city of 166,000 by the turn of the century.

Third, and of particular importance for the subsequent pattern of development throughout Southern Africa, came the beginnings of railway systems to supply the mines and the mining populations with machinery and consumer goods imported from abroad. Financed mainly by British capital and by the Cape colonial administration, railways were built from both Cape Town and Port Elizabeth to reach the diamond mines at Kimberley in 1885.[3] With the opening of the gold fields, these railways were quickly extended northwards through the Orange Free State – then also a Boer Republic – towards the Witwatersrand, with another being built from Durban to Natal. At the same time, the Transvaal government, seeking to preclude a British stranglehold over its transport links with the outside world, financed (by agreement with the Portuguese authorities) the construction of another line eastwards through Mozambique to Lourenço Marques (Maputo). This line in fact was far and away the shortest route from the Witwatersrand to the sea. These lines had all been completed by 1895.

Together with the roads which generally paralleled them, the railways naturally proved to be, at one and the same time, both the great facilitators and the great constrainers of the patterns of urban settlement and of economic development. New settlement areas and economic activities, including commercial farming, were, of course, generated at numerous points along the developing transport corridors and in the vicinity of the major junctions and railheads. Equally, settlement and development continued around the various harbours, which benefited from the greatly increased demand for their entrepôt and service functions. None the less, the centre of gravity had shifted decisively to the Witwatersrand and it was in and from the Witwatersrand that the primary impulses for development emanated.

Fourth, the difficult mining conditions, combined with a shortage of capital equipment and skilled labour, created an unprecedented demand for unskilled labour. This led, in turn, to a stick-and-carrot approach to the large-scale recruitment of African labourers away from their subsistence-style, traditional tribal existence and towards their (partial) absorption into the cash economy – an approach which included the cooptation by the

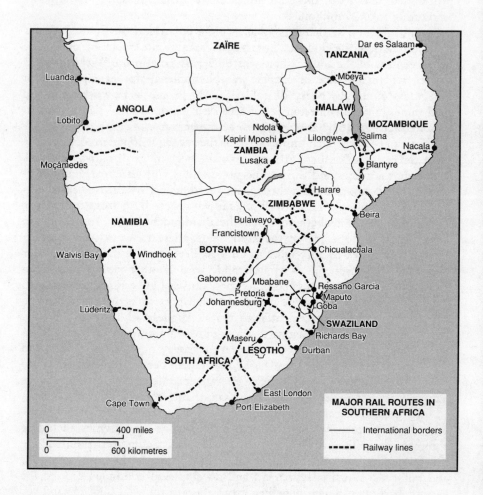

MAJOR RAIL ROUTES IN
SOUTHERN AFRICA

—— International borders
- - - - Railway lines

mining corporations of the political system in furtherance of the industry's objectives. In the process, there was created the host of legal, social and economic institutions – such as the migrant labour system – which were to become the foundations of the 'South African way of life' with all its well-known and much-debated, social, political and economic characteristics and consequences.

From the outset of the new order, the distribution of the ownership of economic assets – whether real assets (including land and physical capital), mining rights, financial capital, or human capital (education and labour skills) and, not least, political influence – was highly unequal. Those who had access to these assets were almost exclusively white and 'English' (i.e. European immigrants), whereas most Afrikaners possessed few of them, and few blacks possessed any of them. Thus were laid the foundations for the exceptional racial and language-related inequalities in living standards which were to become the most controversial economic characteristics of South African society and which, reinforced by the creation and perpetuation of political inequalities, ever since have been the source of great division and seemingly irreconcilable conflict.

In short, the main socio-economic consequence of the minerals discoveries was that an essentially feudal and traditional society underwent extraordinarily rapid transformation into a modern industrial society, but in a manner which generated gross inequalities of equally extraordinary proportions in the distribution of the benefits – and the costs – of economic development among its constituent populations and interest groups.

No less unequal than the racial distribution of economic development was its geographic distribution. From the earliest days onwards, the spatial distribution of economic activities conformed to the pattern determined largely by the geographical locations of mineral resource endowments and discoveries, and by the radial pattern of transport routes from the coasts to the interior. Subsequently, the political and economic policies of various governments sought to modify these spatial patterns, in some cases in the direction of greater equity, in other cases not. Inevitably, however, the accidents of geology meant that some areas were exceptionally favoured and some severely disadvantaged.

Much analytical attention has been given – quite rightly – to the origins and development of South Africa's economic and political systems. From the point of view of the present study, however, there are two other issues which are particularly relevant. The first is that the consequences of the minerals revolution were not confined to the boundaries of what was to become South Africa itself. The second is that, largely as a corollary of the minerals discoveries, British colonial rule came to be extended over much of Southern Africa – a fact which was to have significant implications for economic development in the region.

The regional impact of the minerals revolution[4]

There were four main reasons why the minerals revolution had a wider regional impact. First, the economic and social consequences outlined above knew no national boundaries. This was partly because, at this early stage, many boundaries were still largely non-existent, but largely because the transformations engendered by the discovery of gold were of such seismic proportions that they engulfed virtually the whole of the sub-continent. In the process was created a complex set of interdependent relations which were to endure far into the future and which were to have profound implications for the wider political economy of the entire region.

Second, the mineral wealth of Southern Africa was not, in fact, confined to the Kimberley and Witwatersrand areas. Certainly, it was heavily concentrated in the latter area and, more generally, in the Transvaal, which eventually proved to contain a virtually unparalleled array of minerals in addition to gold. However, valuable mineral deposits were soon also found elsewhere in the region. Though expectations that gold deposits on the scale of the Witwatersrand were to be found north of the Limpopo quickly proved to be something of a chimera, their actual value was not insignificant. In addition, around the turn of the century extensive coal deposits were found in Southern Rhodesia (Zimbabwe) and copper deposits were found on the Northern Rhodesian (Zambian) side of the already well-established Katangan copperbelt in the southern Belgian Congo (Zaire). (For technical reasons, however, copper was not to prove commercially exploitable for another quarter-century.)

Third, these new mineral discoveries necessitated extension of the railway system further into the interior. By the turn of the century, in pursuance of Cecil Rhodes' dream of a Cape-to-Cairo railway, the line from Kimberley had already been extended to Bulawayo in Southern Rhodesia (Zimbabwe). A separate line, constructed with the agreement of the Portuguese government, had by then also been built from the port of Beira in Mozambique to Salisbury (Harare), again in Southern Rhodesia. Like the line from the Witwatersrand to Lourenço Marques, the Beira line was significantly shorter than the Cape routes. Bulawayo and Salisbury were then also connected, via the incipient mining area of Gwelo (Gweru). Further extensions soon followed from Bulawayo to the richly-endowed Wankie coal-mining areas, then across the Zambesi and into Northern Rhodesia, via the Victoria Falls, to pass through the copperbelt around Ndola and thence across the Congolese border into Katanga.

Fourth, in the same way that the location of the minerals discoveries and of the transport routes in the Transvaal and the Cape were instrumental in determining the nature of development within South Africa itself, so the pursuit of mineral wealth further afield gave rise to similar social and economic processes in the rest of the region. Thus, the phenomenon of rapid urban development which had been witnessed on the Witwatersrand was soon repeated on a smaller scale in Southern Rhodesia and, somewhat later, in the Northern Rhodesian copperbelt. Similarly, the other socio-economic consequences, including the determination of the economic and physical infrastructures, the geographic and spatial structure and distribution of economic development, the emergence of a migrant labour system and the generation of racial inequalities in relative living standards were all repeated elsewhere in the region.

The extension of British colonial rule

Although the initial discoveries of both diamonds and gold occurred in areas which were beyond British colonial jurisdiction – namely East Griqualand and the Transvaal – they acted as a spur to the extension of that jurisdiction over much of Southern Africa by the turn of the century. There were two distinct – though closely interrelated – dimensions to this process. One of these – which will be discussed shortly – was the need to dispense with the problem of the Boer Republics in the Transvaal and the Free State; the second dimension was the bringing of the remaining hinterland territories under the jurisdiction of the Crown.

This dimension to the widening of British rule had a defensive, as well as an overtly imperialist, character to it, in that Portugal, Germany and the two Boer Republics were all actively seeking to extend their own areas of sovereignty in Southern Africa. At this time, Angola and Mozambique had, of course, long been Portuguese colonies and were long to remain so; Namibia (South West Africa) was a German Protectorate, as was Tanganyika (Tanzania). But much of the land which was to constitute Bechuanaland (Botswana), Basutoland (Lesotho), Swaziland, the two Rhodesias and Nyasaland (Malawi) was still almost exclusively under indigenous settlement, occupation and rule of various kinds and it was these territories whose status was still to be determined.

By 1885, both Basutoland (Lesotho) and Bechuanaland (Botswana) had become Crown Protectorates.[5] By 1889, British jurisdiction had been extended across the Limpopo River into the Rhodesias, in this case largely through the agency of Rhodes's British South Africa Company, which received a royal charter for this purpose. This major extension was, however, more the result of Rhodes's own ambitions, than of the desires of an already overextended Imperial government. Rhodes's motives were not wholly unconnected with the fact there had been a brief flurry of gold fever north of the Limpopo as early as the 1860s, but which had not been fully worked through before the prospectors were diverted by the spectacular diamond finds at Kimberley. But he was also motivated by the desire to counteract a treaty, signed in 1887 between an agent of the Transvaal's

President Kruger and the Matabele chief, Lobengula, which gave the land-hungry Afrikaners substantial rights of settlement north of the Limpopo. (The Transvaal had already secured *de facto* control over Swaziland in the 1870s, and it was not until after the Anglo-Boer War that Swaziland became a British Protectorate.)

By 1894, after a prolonged struggle to subdue the African inhabitants, and despite vigorous protests from both the Transvaal and Portugal, the Company had acquired effective control of most of Mashonaland and Mata-beleland, between the Limpopo and Zambesi rivers. It then set about carving up and parcelling out tribal land to white settlers (whilst setting aside reserves for the indigenous peoples). As a result, by 1898, the settler population already numbered 13,000. The Company also helped to finance the building of the railway line from the Cape to Rhodesia. Because of the obstacle represented by the existence of the Transvaal Republic, this line had perforce to commence from as far south as Vryburg in the Cape, rather than from the Witwatersrand, and it had to follow a route via Bechuanaland. The definition in the Company's charter of its sphere of influence had omitted any reference to a northern limit. In the hope that the wealth of the Katangan copperbelt extended southwards, the Company proceeded, through the conclusion of some highly dubious treaties, to acquire 'rights' to Northern Rhodesia.[6]

In these early stages, however, despite the extension of the railway from Buluwayo through to Katanga, neither the Company nor the Crown in fact had the same revolutionary impact on society or economy in the northern territory as they had in Southern Rhodesia. This was due to the lack both of immediately exploitable resources and of a significant settler community – in 1924, when Northern Rhodesia finally became a Protector-ate with its own Legislative Council, there were still only 3,600 white inhabitants.

Meanwhile, by the 1880s, Scottish missionaries had laid the foundations for British involvement in Nyasaland. Again, however, had it not been for the threat of Portuguese and, to a lesser extent, German expansionism into the territory from the east and the north respectively, formal involvement would have been less likely at this stage, since the territory held little appeal for the Crown or for the Company. Be that as it may, in 1891, after seven years of diplomatic manoeuvring, Nyasaland was made a British Protectorate.

The economic causes of the Boer War

Following the Great Trek of the late 1830s, the fledgling Republic which the Boers had established in Natal was annexed by the Cape Colony in 1843 and it became a separate Crown Colony in 1856. By the latter date, similar efforts to incorporate the rebellious Boers in the Transvaal and Orange Free State had been abandoned, albeit somewhat reluctantly, by the Imperial government. The minerals revolution, however, naturally rekindled the latter's desire to unify the territories under British rule. East Griqualand – which was also coveted for its new-found wealth both by the Free State and by various indigenous peoples – was annexed by Britain in 1871 and subsequently incorporated into the Cape colony. And even before the discovery of gold, the Transvaal was resubjugated by the British between 1877 and 1880 – a tenure which was as costly as it was brief.

As much as Britain's continuing ambitions in respect of the two Republics were reinforced by the discovery of gold, so they were fiercely resisted by the Boers. As already mentioned, this resistance was particularly evident in the determination of the Transvaal government to retain control over its transport links between the gold fields and the coast. Indeed, as Horwitz has cogently argued, the causes of the Anglo-Boer War of 1899–1902 were to be found not only in the 'imperial factor' of Britain's desire, on strategic and political grounds, to acquire control of the underground wealth of the Witwatersrand, but also in the conflicts between local political and economic interests. It should not be overlooked that the Transvaal and the Free State were not alone in articulating political interests which were independent of British interests. Both the Cape and Natal colonies also had degrees of representative government, and 'the political responses to the market reactions' generated by the minerals revolution gave rise to an 'element of civil war . . . between the Transvaal–Free State and the Cape–Natal [in which] the quarrels were as much over railway and customs revenues of the several governmental units of South Africa as over the strategic imperatives of Downing Street.'[7]

The details of this quarrel are beyond the scope of this work.[8] Suffice to say that the vast costs of laying competing railway systems, over difficult terrain between coastal ports and a single market hundreds of miles into the interior, placed a very high premium both on maximizing the freight revenues and, where those revenues had to be shared, on securing the major share of them. In this respect, the territorial division of interests was complicated by two separate and conflicting railway agreements. Since the railways from the Cape also traversed the Free State, the Cape–Free State Customs Convention of 1889 gave the latter an incentive to encourage Republican traffic to use these routes. However, the Transvaal–Natal Railway Convention of 1894, not only recognized the Transvaal's right to divert a significant share of traffic to the shortest and lowest-cost route through Mozambique, but also ensured competition between the Cape and Natal for the remaining traffic to the Witwatersrand.

In short, while a major consequence of the minerals revolution was to forge the economies of the four different territories into a single economic entity, the coherence of this entity was being undermined by conflicting political interests in appropriating the economic benefits. The fundamental problem, as Horwitz so clearly states it, was that

> when a railway system is state-owned, the market risk and the political risk my be minimized *within the territory of state sovereignty*. If the state-owned system serves a territory *outside* its jurisdiction and subject to *another* state's sovereignty, both market risk and political risk may be maximized. The particular market conditions and capitalization conditions of the railway systems of geographical South Africa . . . exacerbated both market and political risks to the point of being a critical cause of . . . the Anglo-Boer War.[9]

Indeed, these early railway developments in Southern Africa provide a fascinating and highly instructive case-study of both the politics and the economics of transport diplomacy in situations where different political authorities share a common transport system. The separate railway systems of South Africa were, in Horwitz's words, 'the instruments of political autonomy' and, at least to this extent, made a 'negative contribution' to the diversification of economic development.[10] In this sense, they represented early precursors of a problem that was to recur in the wider region many decades later.

Eventually, the combination of these divergent 'local' economic interests together with the competition between British colonialism and Transvaal republicanism led, via a bitterly divisive war, to the defeat of the latter. As Horwitz puts it, 'because the motivations and aims of the political actors in South Africa in the bedevilled situation of the 1890s could not be accommodated to the imperatives of the economy, a single polity could not be established until a war had been fought, lost and won.'[11]

The political framework for development of the regional economy

Thus, once the awkward problem of Boer Republics in the Transvaal and Orange Free State had been disposed of, the hegemony of British colonial rule over the four territories of South Africa itself was re-established. In the meantime, the 'imperial factor' had also secured British jurisdiction, in its various forms, over much of the remainder of the region. Only the two Portuguese colonies – Angola and Mozambique – and German-ruled Tanganyika were not part of the British Empire, and even Tanganyika was added during the First World War. Consequently, a broadly unified and stable political framework now existed for economic development in the wider region.

This stability undoubtedly owed much to the extensive monopoly powers which the British South Africa Company exercised over large areas of the subcontinent. This is not to suggest that there was always an identity of interests between the Company (particularly Rhodes himself), the Colonial authorities and the settler communities. Indeed, in some important respects there was considerable tension between them. In theory, the Company was subject to the authority of the British High Commissioner in Cape Town, and through him, to the Crown, but in practice it exercised considerable freedom of action. However, on occasion the Company overstepped the bounds of this freedom, causing both the Crown and the settlers to seek to clip its wings. In Southern Rhodesia, for example, it was the Company's armed police which Dr Jameson took with him into the Transvaal on his infamous and ill-fated 1895 raid. It was partly for this reason that, by 1898, some of the Company's powers had reverted to the Crown and some had devolved upon the settlers themselves. In Northern Rhodesia, too, British jurisdiction was formally transferred from the Company to the High Commissioner in South Africa at a relatively early stage, and in Nyasaland, the Company's formal role was also severely attenuated.

Whatever the formal position, however, in practical terms the Company effectively remained responsible for much of the administration of the territories north of the Limpopo, especially the two Rhodesias, until the mid–1920s. Moreover, despite the growing tensions between the Company and the Crown and the increasing differentiation of some of their interests, the Company – and especially Rhodes – retained a formidable political influence in the development of the wider region. Rhodes may have disliked Imperial control over the activities of the Company but there was no fundamental difference over questions of broad political and economic interests.

These latter were reflected in the widely-held, if varying, beliefs, hopes and expectations that the four colonies of South Africa, together with – at the minimum – Southern Rhodesia and the three Protectorates of Basutoland, Bechuanaland and Swaziland would, in due course, become a single political – and hence also economic – entity under some form of British rule. In fact, the primacy of local political interests was to compromise these hopes in important – and ironical – ways. In particular, they reckoned without the political ambitions of the Afrikaners who, despite their defeat in the Anglo-Boer War, had no intention of surrendering all their political power and influence to Britain. By 1910, their efforts had achieved the political and economic unification of the four South African territories, with the Transvaal as the dominant political and economic force.

In one sense, therefore, the triumph of colonial rule was short-lived, for the new Union was a self-governing dominion, and its formation brought to an end formal British jurisdiction over South Africa, with external political authority thereafter limited to foreign affairs. It also effectively put paid to hopes of maintaining formal British hegemony over the whole region. In another sense, however, British hegemony remained relatively undiminished. South Africa remained both firmly within the British Empire and subject to considerable British influence. This influence was especially strong over the economy, where, despite the Afrikaners' deep-seated hostility to it, British capital was to retain substantial control for almost another half-century. The strength of this influence also precluded any underlying political differences between Britain and South Africa from threatening the coherence of the framework for the development of the wider regional economy for many years to come.

There was, of course, another scenario which, had it materialized, would have provided the impetus for this coherence to be translated into wider political and economic union of a somewhat different kind. Contrary to many expectations, the formal incorporation of the three Protectorates into South Africa did not occur at the time of Union. None the less, the proposal remained firmly on the political agendas of both Whitehall and Pretoria for several decades to come. In addition, it was widely assumed, both in the region and in London, that Southern Rhodesia would also join the Union. Since, from 1920, South Africa also acquired formal jurisdiction over South West Africa (albeit under a much disputed international mandate), these incorporations would have created a very much larger single political – and hence also economic – entity in the region. In the event, this larger entity failed to emerge. Despite continuing negotiations between London and Pretoria, the three Protectorates remained outside the Union. More importantly, in a 1922 referendum, a majority of Southern Rhodesia's white settlers rejected the proposed incorporation of the territory into South Africa. In 1923, therefore, Southern Rhodesia acquired the status of a self-governing colony.[12]

By this stage, many of the settlers were commercial farmers. Consequently, it could no longer be taken for granted that they would view Southern Rhodesia's economic interests in the same way as the British South Africa Company had done, particularly with regard to relations with South Africa. In rejecting incorporation, the settlers in effect gave notice of their desire to defend their economic interests against total domination by South African interest groups, whether in the form of the Company or of Afrikaners who had settled in the two Rhodesias in not insignificant numbers. Self-government also implied a greater likelihood that the perceived interests of the settlers might begin to diverge from those of Britain. Hence, no single political authority emerged in the region to create, in any formal sense, the framework for a fully fledged common market. In practice, however, a broadly coherent framework did exist for an integrated development process, and such political differences as did emerge remained too small to affect this process in any significant measure.

In sum, therefore, in South Africa itself, the minerals revolution created a coherent economic entity the ultimate prosperity of which, in turn, required accommodation between powerfully divergent political forces. In the wider region, in contrast, there were fewer imperatives for political union. None the less, at this early stage, this lack of political integration was not important enough seriously to inhibit the processes of economic integration. Consequently, the threat which was posed to economic unity and prosperity in Southern Africa by the failure to achieve a single political entity was postponed. It did not, however, disappear.

2 From colonization to economic Interdependence

By the turn of the century, white political authority (of varying forms) was well on the way to being established over all the territories of Southern Africa. Whatever political differences existed between them were still too small to undermine the commonality of their economic interests. This commonality arose partly from geographical necessity, partly from the historical patterns of economic development, and partly from the centripetal economic pull of the Witwatersrand.

The most direct evidence of this commonality of interests was to be found in the development of the regional transport network, and especially of the railways. Indeed, with the solitary exception of the obstruction represented by the Transvaal Republic prior to the Boer War, the growth of the railway system was greatly facilitated by the relative lack of conflicting political and national interests in the development process. Thus, by 1915, with new and more diverse mining deposits continually being uncovered, nearly 11,000 miles of railway track had already been laid throughout Southern Africa. In 1928, the Benguela line, again built by British capital on a concession from the Portuguese government, was completed from the Angolan port of Lobito to the Congo/Northern Rhodesia copperbelt. Meanwhile, the South–West African (Namibian) routes which were constructed originally to serve the Tsumeb copper mines, had been incorporated into the South African network in 1918 as part of the political process whereby the former German colony came under South African jurisdiction. In addition, a major programme of branch-line construction was still being undertaken in South Africa itself. By the end of the 1920s, therefore, all of the major mining and development areas in the region were already linked by transport corridors to the coastal ports on its southern, eastern and western seaboards.

Together, these developments generated a vast increase in the number (and scope) of exchange relationships. Furthermore, they provided a basis for more integrated economic development in the region, albeit with its peculiarly skewed racial and spatial distributional characteristics. Indeed, they carried the potential for the creation of a single market and a unified economy in much of Southern Africa.

In the event, as we have seen, the necessary political conditions for full economic union did not materialize. The extent of subsequent differentiation of national interests, though by no means great, none the less proved large enough to preclude the emergence of a common market. Instead, as the national boundaries of the different territories became more clearly defined and began to acquire greater political significance in the conduct of economic relations, so the system of regional exchange relationships which had been created was gradually transformed into a set of fully fledged interstate economic relations.

The components of economic relations between states

Understanding these relations, and the regional economic structures to which they have given rise, requires a prior appreciation of the formal nature of the different exchange relationships involved. In principle, economic relations between separate states take many conceptually distinct forms. These can be grouped under three main headings, namely trading relations, macroeconomic interactions, and institutional linkages.

Trading relations

The most obvious subset of interstate economic relations comprises trading relations, and the most obvious of these, in turn, are exports and imports of physical goods and commodities. However, trade is by no means limited to these 'visible' or 'merchandise' transactions. Indeed, in some instances, visible trade accounts for only a small proportion of the value of all trading relations. The latter also embrace 'invisible' or 'services' transactions, i.e. trade in non-physical commodities such as freight, banking and insurance. Other components of invisible trade include expenditure by tourists on goods and services purchased while in a foreign country. All invisible transactions count as exports for the country providing the services, and as imports for the country acquiring them.

A further component of international trade is trade in 'factor services', i.e. the services of capital (foreign investment and foreign loans) and of labour ('human capital'). This form of trade has a special characteristic in that, whilst the actual 'factors of production' – the machines, the financial resources, and the labourers – are normally physically transferred to the purchaser's country, ownership of them is retained by the seller: what is being traded is not the capital itself but, in effect, the flow of productive services which the capital – whether of the physical or financial variety – can provide. The same is true of trade in labour services: except in cases of slavery, the labourer sells and transfers only his or her labour services. There is also within this factor services category trade in the rights to technologies and other productive processes (e.g. via licensing arrangements) and trade in intellectual properties (e.g. copyrights). As in the case of invisible trade, all trade in factor services generates export earnings for the country providing the equipment or services or rights concerned, and counts as imports for the country acquiring them.

Another component of international economic relations which has some, but not all, of the characteristics of trading relations consists in unilateral – or, perhaps more accurately, unrequited – transfers of goods or services or factor services. Foreign aid, whether official or non-governmental, and whether in the form of finance, goods or technical assistance, is the prime example of an unrequited transfer, but gifts or transfers of any kind which do not involve sales and purchases fall within this category. Except for unrequited transfers, all these activities have six significant characteristics in common. First, they are all mutual or bilateral trades, i.e. they all involve simultaneous decisions in which one party in one country is a buyer (importer) and another party in another country is a seller (exporter). Second, except in the most exceptional circumstances, they are all voluntary trades: both parties are free to choose, from among a range of alternatives, in which trades to engage; and either party may choose not to effect any given transaction. Third, they are all decentralized transactions: trades do not actually take place between 'countries' but between (largely) autonomous 'economic actors' (or 'agents') who happen to be situated in, or 'belong' to, different countries. These actors are normally 'firms' or other incorporated entities, usually privately owned, and ranging upwards in size from single-person enterprises to the largest multinational corporations. However, particularly where the supply of factor services is concerned, trading relations also take place at the level of individuals or households: any individual can offer to sell his labour services or lend her savings to an employer or borrower in another country. Equally, public sector bodies, such as parastatal corporations and government departments, rather than private entities, can be the economic agents through which trade is effected.

Fourth, all these cross-border transactions involve more than the two ultimate contracting parties of the buyer and the seller alone. In many cases, several intermediaries may be involved, so that the economic ramifications of each act of international exchange extend well beyond the act itself. Even the process of communication between the buyer and the seller involves other economic transactions, if only in the form, for example, of a telephone call or a letter. In the overwhelming majority of trades, physical transport, either of goods or of people, is also involved.

Fifth, except in cases of direct barter and unrequited transfers, each trade generates a corresponding financial transaction in the opposite direction. (Clearly, by definition, barter – or counter-trade as it is also known – is requited by a non-financial transaction.) These financial transactions generally involve a different set of intermediary agents (such as bankers and foreign exchange dealers) from those engaged in the trade itself, thus significantly extending the importance of the fourth characteristic.

Finally, none of these activities can take place in a political, legal or institutional vacuum. As we have already seen, the broad national political context is of critical importance in facilitating or inhibiting the development of interstate exchange relations. But beyond that, effecting and regulating the economic linkages between any two countries requires the presence in both of appropriate physical, economic, social and legal infrastructures and institutions. This, in turn, requires that both countries must devote some resources to investment in these infrastructures and institutions. Some of these investments can be, and usually are, provided through private, decentralized market transactions. In general, such investments will arise from the resources which firms and traders devote to the promotion of their own exchanges. Others, however, can only be provided by governments through the political process. These include the trade, commercial, fiscal, legal and regulatory policies which provide the institutional and policy contexts within which exchanges can be enacted.

Macroeconomic influences

A separate, and qualitatively different, aspect of international economic relations arises from the macroeconomic influences which the fiscal, monetary and commercial policies pursued by one country can have upon economic conditions in other countries via their trade and financial links. These influences, which by definition take place at an aggregative and centralized level, can take many forms. For example, depending upon the degree of capital mobility between them, an interest rate increase in country A can induce a change in monetary policy in country B. Depending upon the exchange rate regime between them, it is possible for country A through its monetary and fiscal policies to influence, often in adverse ways, the rate of inflation or the level of unemployment in B. A rise (or fall) in the international value of A's currency can have major consequences for the level of economic activity in the countries with which it trades, or in countries whose own trade is conducted in significant measure in prices denominated in A's currency. The imposition (or relaxation) by A of a tariff or other trade restriction on imports of particular commodities from B can have significant impacts upon the economic fortunes of the producers of those commodities in B (and in other countries as well).

Except where governments actively seek coordination of their macroeconomic and trade policies, these influences are largely indirect and exogenous. They are often also unintentional. None the less, it is clear that the transmission of macroeconomic policy influences across national boundaries, and especially between trading partners, is both continuous and pervasive. Where one country's economy and trade is large in relation to those of its trading partners, the latter may find their autonomy in respect of macroeconomic management severely inhibited. In the extreme, their very economic prosperity may depend crucially on that of the dominant economy.[1]

Institutionalized linkages

Many countries seek to formalize, to a greater or lesser extent, either their trading relations or their mutual macroeconomic policy influences, or both, in institutional frameworks. These can range from a bilateral trade agreement between two countries in respect of particular commodities to full-scale economic and monetary union between several partners. Regional trading blocs, ranging from loose associations to promote mutual trade to free trade areas and formal customs unions, are particularly prevalent forms of institutions for shaping and managing economic relations between different countries.

Again, it will be apparent that such institutional arrangements can be determined only through the political process and that they require investments, of both a political and economic nature, in proportion to their scope. Obviously, the more comprehensive the intended degree of cooperation and coordination, the more extensive the resources which have to be devoted to them and the more pervasive their impacts. Clearly, too, the existence or otherwise of these institutions largely determines the political, economic and legal contexts within which all economic relations between states are conducted.

Towards an integrated regional economy in Southern Africa

In due course, all these components of international economic relations were to become manifest in Southern Africa as the development of the regional economy proceeded. Initially, of course, where international exchanges were concerned, the colonies were little more than extensions of the economies of the metropolitan powers. They served not only as sources of raw materials and other inputs for, but also as markets for the outputs of, the expanding industries of Europe, especially Britain, and of North America.

However, as the mineral resources began to be exploited and the transport system grew, the region was naturally opened up to more extensive exchange relations. This process quickly began to reflect two characteristics. First, there was a rising level of economic interaction among the territories of the region: visible and invisible trade relations, flows of labour services and the development of common political and economic institutions and infrastructures served increasingly to bind them together. Second, the dominant regional role being played by the South African economy became increasingly evident.

Trade in goods and services

By providing access to world markets, the railways also stimulated the development throughout the region of commercial agriculture – of both the arable and livestock varieties. Before long, agricultural exports joined the minerals being channelled by rail through the various ports for transhipment to Europe and North America. In this sense, therefore, the new transport corridors simply reinforced the familiar pattern of colonial trade. But, where the conveyance of these goods between the ports and the hinterland constituted transit trade through different territories, it also generated, as a necessary by-product, an intra-regional trading component in the form of the provision of invisible services. Obviously, with the advent of Union in 1910, the proportion of cross-border transit trade would have declined substantially, since the bulk of both mineral and agricultural production was concentrated in South Africa itself. However, neither activity was limited to South Africa and the remaining transit trade element was by no means negligible. Traffic to and from the Rhodesias, for example, continued to generate invisible earnings for South Africa, Mozambique, Bechuanaland and (after the completion of the Benguela line) the Congo and Angola; similarly, traffic to and from South Africa, and especially the Transvaal, continued to bring economic benefits to Mozambique.

However, the transport routes soon began to fulfil an additional function, namely to carry rising volumes of merchandise trade within and between the countries of the region: food, cereals and livestock to feed the growing population nodes; coal to generate electricity, to feed iron and steel furnaces and to fuel the railways themselves; and basic consumer goods (such as food products) in search of wider markets for incipient local manufacturing industries.

There is very little data available to permit quantification of the scale of this intra-regional trade in goods and services in the early years. The probability is that, until industrialization began in earnest, the merchandise trade component was small relative to the volume of transit trade of goods to and from overseas. It is more likely that, in so far as the supply requirements of the main population and growth centres were met from within the region, the sources of supply were predominantly local. Moreover, the extent of cross-border trade would again have declined with the unification of South Africa. But, here too, such trade remained important for the other territories. In Southern Rhodesia, for example, when the hopes for significant gold deposits faded, the British South Africa Company was forced to turn to agriculture as its major activity. However, with the settler component of the territory's population rising from 13,000 in 1898 to 24,000 in 1911, it was not until the First World War that the country became effectively self-sufficient in its food requirements.[2] In the interim, at least part of these requirements would have been met from imports from other parts of the region, but especially from South Africa.

Thus, even before the advent of industrialization, a growing number of economic agents throughout Southern Africa were becoming mutually reliant, both for their supplies of goods and services, and for their incomes, upon cross-border trade transactions.

Migrant labour

Meanwhile, intra-regional trade in 'factor services' – especially the services of unskilled labour – had begun to link the developing economies of the region more closely together in a quite different way. As the labour needs of the mines (and subsequently of the farms and factories) became manifest, cross-border migration of labour reached significant scales throughout the region. Despite their rapidly growing numbers, the (mainly white) immigrant workers from abroad were unable to provide more than a fraction of the labour needs of the mines. Indeed, the latter had an almost insatiable demand for labour, and given the high cost of importing skilled workers in sufficient quantities, this demand could be met only by large-scale recruitment of indigenous labour.[3] The form of recruitment which emerged was that of oscillating labour migration – a highly controversial social institution which, for a combination of political and economic reasons, subsequently became firmly entrenched.

Be that as it may, the fact remains that, from almost every corner of Southern Africa (and even further afield), hundreds of thousands of migrant workers were recruited annually to the mines and farms of South Africa; tens of thousands more flocked for similar reasons to Southern Rhodesia from Mozambique, Nyasaland (Malawi) and Northern Rhodesia, and to Northern Rhodesia from Angola, Nyasaland and Southern Rhodesia. In the case of the Transvaal mines alone, over 54,000 black miners were already being employed by the turn of the century. Of these, only 23 per cent came from the Transvaal itself; 60 per cent were from Mozambique; and some 10 per cent were from the Cape Colony. In 1906, the total had risen to 81,000 but recruitment from the Transvaal itself had fallen to a mere 4 per cent of this total. The deficit was made up from virtually all other territories in the region, including 8 per cent from areas north of latitude 22°S (including Angola, the two Rhodesias, Nyasaland, Tanganyika and the northern regions of Mozambique). By the time of Union in 1910, recruitment had risen to 184,000 and over the ensuing thirty years it rose more or less steadily to reach a peak of 368,000 in 1941.[4]

During this period, typically more than half the total came from beyond the borders of South Africa itself. The breakdown of geographic origins of these 'foreign' migrants varied substantially over time, partly because of changes in agreements between the respective governments concerned, partly because 'tropical' workers (from the more northern territories) were at times found to be especially susceptible to pneumonia, and partly because of competition from the growing labour requirements of other parts of the region, such as the copper mines and industries of Northern Rhodesia, the farms, factories and coal mines of Southern Rhodesia and the cotton plantations in Mozambique.[5] As these latter examples suggest, it was not only the mines which attracted the migrant workers to South Africa. By 1951, for example, there were estimated to be no less than 420,000 foreign migrant workers in South Africa, of whom less than one-third were on the mines.[6]

Equally, as the above examples suggest, it was not only South Africa which attracted cross-border migrants. Both Northern and Southern Rhodesia were also major recruiters of migrant labour. In Southern Rhodesia, for example, during the inter-war years no less than 55 to 60 per cent of its African work force were non-indigenous. In 1951, the proportion was still virtually one half: of the total of 488,000 male Africans employed in Southern Rhodesia, 102,000 came from Mozambique, 86,000 from Nyasaland, 49,000 from Northern Rhodesia, and 10,000 from other territories.[7]

The increasing reliance of the region's – but especially South Africa's – mines, farms and factories on these migrant workers was, of course, matched by a reverse reliance by the migrants' home countries both on the employment opportunities thereby created and on the remittances of earnings by the workers. Indeed, for several of the sending countries, these 'exports' of migrant labour quickly became their largest single source of incomes, employment opportunities and export earnings. This, in turn, implied that living standards in these countries were determined to a significant extent by, and fluctuated with, the level of their exports of labour services. With hindsight, permitting this situation to arise might appear to have been an unfortunate, even misguided, policy. The fact remains that, as a result, several countries, but particularly Basutoland, Nyasaland and Mozambique, acquired a strong economic orientation towards South Africa. The latter two, together with Northern Rhodesia, became similarly reliant on Southern Rhodesia's labour needs.

Capital investment

Though much of the region's economic development continued to be financed by capital imported from overseas, locally-owned capital also helped to knit the regional economies more closely together. For example,

South African capital became involved in developing farms, mines, industries and services on a growing scale in every country in the region, apart
from Tanzania. Census data from the early 1960s showed that nearly half
of all foreign-owned companies in Southern Rhodesia were controlled from
South Africa.[8] On a smaller, but in relative terms also significant, scale,
Southern Rhodesian capital was likewise invested in Nyasaland and
Northern Rhodesia.

Other linkages

The increasing density of this network of regional economic relations led
inevitably to the development of further and more sophisticated interlink-
ages. Exports and imports of skilled labour and professional services followed naturally in the footsteps of the trade and investment flows. Indeed,
many skilled and professional people – especially, but not only, from South
Africa – emigrated or relocated to other parts of the region as economic
links developed. Rising living standards (albeit confined largely to the white
minority) and spreading familial links also generated a regional tourist
industry. In turn, the large reverse flows of wages, profits and other payments and earnings which represented the financial counterparts of these
intra-regional exports of goods, services, labour and capital, led to the need
for regional service centres to provide the complex financial, legal and other
business and professional services necessary to sustain and develop these
links. Again, these functions came naturally to be concentrated in the major
South African centres.

The tendency for South Africa to provide the motive force for integration
was reinforced by infrastructural links. For example, the road transport
arm of the South African railways system provided goods and passenger
services in Swaziland; postal and telegraph services in Swaziland, and postal
services in Bechuanaland were administered by the South African Post
Office; the railway through Bechuanaland was operated from South Africa;
South Africa provided considerable technical assistance to all the neighbouring territories, especially in the fields of agriculture, veterinary services
and health services.[9] In the case of education, South Africa's schools and
colleges provided academic and vocational training to large numbers of
residents – blacks as well as whites – from all the neighbouring states. The
unique South African legal system, based on Roman Dutch Law, was
adopted also in Southern Rhodesia and the South African judiciary assisted
in the administration of justice in the three Protectorates.

Common institutional frameworks

These economically integrative processes were further facilitated and promoted by the existence and development of common political and economic
institutions and affiliations among the countries of Southern Africa. The
relevance of the intergovernmental labour agreements regulating the cross-
border recruitment of migrant workers has already been mentioned.
Another point of particular importance was that, except for Angola and
Mozambique, all the countries of the region were part of the British Empire
and hence were part of the sterling monetary area. Though several countries
developed their own currencies, these currencies were assured of full convertibility with the result that cross-border transactions were not subject
to any significant exchange risks.

No less important was the fact that, from as early as 1903, the four South
African colonies had been joined in a Southern African Customs Union
(SACU) with the three British Protectorates of Bechuanaland, Basutoland
and Swaziland.[10] The customs agreement was renegotiated after Union in
1910 and, from 1920, South West Africa was included with South Africa.
In addition, all these countries shared a common currency and a common
monetary policy in that the South African Reserve Bank acted as central
banker to all the SACU members and the South African currency had full
legal tender status throughout the customs union. This, in turn, facilitated
the extension, from South Africa, of modern banking facilities to the more
peripheral countries and reinforced the dominant economic role which
South Africa played in the wider region.

Within this increasingly South African-dominated regional framework,
similar linkages developed on a smaller scale between the countries north
of the Limpopo. Various proposals for formal amalgamation of the two
Rhodesias and Nyasaland dated back as far as 1915, but were continually
bedevilled by problems arising from the differing degrees of self-government, the potential dominance of Southern Rhodesia and, of course, concerns about the direction of 'native policy'. But this did not stop Southern
Rhodesia from assuming a relatively dominant economic role within its
own sphere of influence. Apart from the examples, cited earlier, of the
integrative roles of migrant labour and capital investment, Southern Rhodesian coin became legal tender in all three territories, and Southern Rhodesia
played the leading role in wide-ranging cooperation in the fields of customs
duties, health and veterinary services, agriculture, communications and education.[11]

In 1953, Southern Rhodesia, Northern Rhodesia and Nyasaland were
incorporated into the controversial Central African Federation. Politically,
the Federation proved a disaster. It was widely seen as a mechanism for
entrenching the political power of white 'settlers' and so became the focus
for black nationalist opposition to minority rule. However, Federation did

result in considerable (albeit again controversial) advances in economic integration. In particular, it led to the formal establishment or provision of common services in a wide range of public utilities, such as transport and power – the latter including the giant Kariba hydroelectric project on the Zambesi river.

The limits to economic integration

In short, from the Cape to the southern Congo and from South West Africa to Nyasaland and Mozambique, Southern Africa was being forged into a coherent economic entity, with South Africa exercising a dominant role over the whole region, and Southern Rhodesia becoming a subsidiary centre of influence. Common and mutually reinforcing benefits from cross-border markets for goods and services and for labour and capital, from shared infrastructures, from common monetary and fiscal policy frameworks, and from functional and institutional linkages, were the hallmarks of this progression towards an integrated regional economy.

Of course, the critical role played by the realities of geography in all this simply cannot be overlooked. Six countries in the region – the three Protectorates, both Rhodesias and Nyasaland – were totally landlocked. South Africa, Mozambique and, to a lesser extent, Angola afforded them their only means of access to the coast. (Indeed, as already noted, Mozambique also provided the shortest route to the coast for South Africa's own industrial heartland.) In one sense, all this could be said to have rendered a not insignificant proportion of intra-regional trade 'involuntary'. In another – and very real – sense, however, this trade, and the increased integration which it brought, was the *sine qua non* of economic progress.

Yet, there were important respects in which the process of integration was incomplete. One obvious limitation arose from the historical fact that there was little articulation between those parts of the region which were not located on the major transport routes or were not well-endowed with exploitable resources. While articulation and exchange between the main development nodes and regions grew, many of these less fortunate areas proved to be major casualties, rather than beneficiaries, of the regional development process. As we will see, some policy efforts to correct these imbalances were made within South Africa, but to relatively little effect.

Another reason why the process stopped well short of full economic integration was, as discussed earlier, the lack of an overriding impetus towards political unification. On the one hand, this lack occasioned no serious threats to the dominant economic interests in the region. On the other hand, the incipient differences in national political and economic interests between the major participants gradually became sufficiently large, not merely to inhibit the creation of any such impetus but also to generate forces for independent action. This point is underlined by the fact that the only three major regional railway links to be added after the Great Depression – the Limpopo, Beit Bridge and Tazara lines – were constructed (as will become apparent) in response to very different political and economic interests from those which had spawned the earlier developments.

Within SACU, of course, economic integration did reach an advanced stage, even without political union: apart from virtual free trade and a common approach to tariffs on goods imported into any member country, SACU was as close as could be to a common market, given the general limitations which South Africa's internal policies placed on the mobility of African workers.[12] But even here, South Africa's increasingly stringent laws, both on immigration and on internal mobility of blacks, were destined to reduce the commonality of the market, in addition to creating disruptive political tensions.

Similarly, as the ill-fated Central African Federation was later to demonstrate, the coincidence of both political and economic interests among those countries within Southern Rhodesia's sphere of influence was also ultimately subject to severe limits. Moreover, except for the obvious fact of South Africa's overarching involvement with virtually all the countries of the region, few of these integrative characteristics extended in the same measure to bilateral relations between the remaining regional countries.

Beyond all this, it was becoming clear – particularly after the Second World War – that the division of political and economic interests between the two blocs of countries north and south of the Limpopo was getting sharper. One index of this – as already suggested – was to be found in the construction by the Rhodesian Railways between 1951 and 1955 of a new line direct to Lourenço Marques in Mozambique. The rising post-war demand for commodities rendered the Beira route incapable of coping with the increasing volume of mineral and agricultural exports from both Northern and Southern Rhodesia. Against this background, the new Limpopo line afforded an effective alternative outlet to the Cape routes, which were much longer and hence not always the most cost-effective for freight.

This development in fact was indicative of a deeper-seated reason both for the divergence of interests between some of the regional states and for the limits to their integration. In structural terms, their economies were more competitive than complementary. Their economic development was fundamentally export-led and all their major exports were primary commodities, the majority of which they could not easily sell to each other. There was thus a continual tension between the integrative impulses in the regional economy and the external orientation of most of the regional states to world commodity markets. The stronger the latter orientation, the less uniform the different national interests in the development and structure of the regional economy and the transport network.

The impact of industrialization

In principle, given large enough markets and sufficient structural diversification, industrialization could have been the means for resolving this tension by creating economies that were structurally more complementary. In fact, industrial development did play a crucial role in the process of regional economic integration. But, because the above-mentioned conditions were not satisfied, industrialization also severely complicated the conflict between integrative economic forces and divergent national interests.

In economic terms, the impetus for industrialization in Southern Africa was provided by both demand- and supply-side factors. On the demand side, the input needs of the region's expanding mining and agricultural sectors, together with the incomes arising from the employment opportunities which they generated, created growing markets for manufactured goods. On the supply side, the basis for industrialization was provided by the availability of capital. This came partly from the successful exploitation of the region's mineral and agricultural resources, the profits and export earnings from which permitted the local financing of industrial investment. In addition, investment was facilitated by the significant inflows of foreign capital and technology attracted by the high potential returns.

However, these favourable conditions were not, in themselves, sufficient to overcome the natural economic barriers to industrialization, especially the lack of comparative advantage in the face of competition from imported manufactures. The pace of mining development had been determined entirely by market forces (given the location of the mineral deposits and the timing of their discovery). By contrast, the process of industrialization was influenced far more by policy considerations. It therefore followed almost inevitably that industrial development would be much more nationally oriented from the outset.

This is not to say that exogenous influences were absent. The onset of the First World War, with its consequent shortages of imported goods, undoubtedly stimulated the growth of domestic industries in both South Africa and Southern Rhodesia. But without the appropriate protectionist policy frameworks to reinforce them, these effects were strictly limited. With commitment to free trade still the political orthodoxy in the region, the economic benefits of the war, such as they were, accrued more to the primary export sectors.

Thus, in South Africa, it was not until the advent of the Nationalist–Labour 'Pact' government in 1925 that industrialization became a deliberate policy objective. For this government, the resolution of the 'poor white' problem created by the displacement of large numbers of whites from the depressed rural areas was of overriding political importance. The solution was to be found in the controversial 'civilized labour' policy, by which industries were to be encouraged behind protective tariff barriers for the express purpose of absorbing unemployed whites.[13] The existence of this policy framework meant that during the Second World War, when the availability of imported goods again declined sharply, domestic industries were able to take maximum advantage of the opportunity. Similarly, it was not until 1923, when Southern Rhodesia was granted greater self-governing status, that it acquired the necessary sovereignty over economic decision-making, including the capacity to impose tariffs on imports, to render deliberate industrialization politically feasible.[14]

Not surprisingly, manufacturing industry turned out to be concentrated in location in South Africa and, to a lesser extent, in Southern Rhodesia in a manner which both mirrored and reinforced the spatial development pattern created earlier by the mining industry. There were three main reasons for this. First, given the still limited size of the domestic markets and the geographical concentrations of purchasing power, the new industries tended to locate close to the existing major centres of settlement and demand. Second, this growing concentration of economic activities created 'agglomeration economies' which rendered these centres cumulatively more attractive for the sale of output, for the recruitment of inputs (especially labour), for their reduced cost of access to basic infrastructures, and for their variety and availability of professional and other support services.

The third reason for the reinforcement of concentration in South Africa itself was to be found in the impact of government policies on the location of economic activities. The main vehicle for these policies was railway pricing. Both pre- and post-Union, railway freight rates were widely viewed by the political leadership as serving two potentially conflicting purposes. In part, they afforded a mechanism for redressing the spatial inequalities in the distribution of economic development which had resulted from the minerals revolution.[15] But they were also a prime instrument, perpetually to be manipulated, for the benefit of particular political interests.

The political primacy of the second purpose meant that, in practice, the redress of locational distortions was limited to the stimulation of (white) commercial agriculture in far-flung areas. This was achieved by discriminating heavily, in the freight rating system, in favour of the transport of agricultural commodities over long distances to the main markets. In this way, South Africa was substantially assisted on the path to self-sufficiency in food production.[16] In the case of industrial location, however, the effect of differential freight rates was to favour the development of inland industries at the expense of coastal locations. Though some industrial development did take place around the major South African ports, their physical distance from the Witwatersrand, coupled with the artificially high cost of transporting finished goods, reduced their attractions as locations for industrial development.

Despite their locational concentration, and despite the growth in the size of the markets which they served, these two incipient manufacturing sectors in South Africa and Southern Rhodesia still faced severe difficulties. Many of the industries had been established behind protective tariff barriers which masked their comparative cost disadvantages. For many, too, the latter were aggravated by exceptionally high labour costs. White labour costs were artificially high on account both of a shortage of skills and the benefits of racially discriminatory labour laws; and black labour, though seemingly 'cheap' in money wage terms, was in fact expensive because lack of education and training and the disadvantages of the same discriminatory laws seriously reduced its productivity. As a result, few local industries were in a position to compete effectively in world markets. Moreover, not least because of the concentration of purchasing power in the hands of a minority of the population, their domestic markets were still too small to permit many industries to achieve any potential economies of scale. Consequently, their long-term viability depended to an increasing degree on their reaching markets beyond their national boundaries. Their only hope of expansion, in some instances even survival, thus lay in gaining access to additional markets close to home.

Small wonder, therefore, that the proportion of South Africa's total merchandise exports (excluding gold) which went to the rest of Africa grew rapidly. Recorded data show that, for SACU as a whole, exports to Africa rose from 8 per cent of the total in 1938 to no less than 19 per cent in 1957. Since these figures exclude exports from South Africa to the other SACU members, the effective proportions were even higher.[17] Moreover, South Africa's exports to the rest of the world were overwhelmingly non-manufactured goods, whilst those to Africa were predominantly manufactured goods. Hence, these figures underlined the importance of the regional market for South Africa's manufacturing industries.

Industries in Rhodesia likewise needed larger markets, a factor which contributed in no small measure to the incorporation in 1953 of Southern Rhodesia, Northern Rhodesia and Nyasaland into the Central African Federation. Indeed, it has been argued that the primary rationale for the Federation was 'the creation of a more viable economic unit by merging the essentially complementary economies of the three territories.'[18] The same need had earlier led Southern Rhodesia to conclude a trade agreement with South Africa, to secure preferential access for its clothing manufacturers to the South African market. The importance of the regional market to Rhodesian industry is reflected in the fact that by 1965 – the year prior to UDI – no less than 44 per cent of Southern Rhodesia's total exports of R\$278 million went to neighbouring countries: 26 per cent to Zambia, 9 per cent to South Africa, 6 per cent to Malawi and 3 per cent to Zaire, Botswana and Mozambique. In addition, Rhodesia re-exported goods to the value of R\$31 million to the neighbouring states, almost two-thirds of them to Zambia.

The effect of industrialization was thus to reinforce South Africa's, and especially the Witwatersrand's, position as the centre of gravity for the regional economy, and Southern Rhodesia's position as a subsidiary centre. In the pre-independence era, these two concentrations of economic power and activity, though at times obviously divisive and problematical, still posed no serious threat to overall political and economic stability in the region. On the contrary, they did much to bind the countries of the region together, giving them a common interest in the maintenance and extension of the many bilateral and multilateral economic relationships, infrastructures and institutions from which they all derived considerable benefits.

Against all this, industrialization did little to alleviate the gross inequalities, both spatial and racial, which the earlier development processes had generated. Indeed, in some respects, it aggravated them. Even more importantly, because the region was not – and, in fact, could not become – a single political entity, there were practical limits to the possibilities for the creation of a truly integrated regional economy, embodying a single, common market.

It was in this latter constraint that the seeds of future conflict existed. Indeed, subsequent developments, especially in the post-independence era, were destined to tear apart even the limited underlying unity of political interests and thus to undermine the region's economic stability. In this process, the unequal pattern of development, both within and between the countries of the region had profoundly important consequences.

3 From political independence to economic conflict

Introduction

By the beginning of the 1960s, the accident of the location of mineral deposits, reinforced by both market forces and governmental economic policies, and assisted by a common colonial heritage and relatively non-conflictual political interests, had long since forged a wide range of close economic linkages between the region's constituent national economies. This was particularly true in respect of relations within the two 'economic blocs' centred on South Africa and Southern Rhodesia respectively. Something not far short of formal economic union had been created among the SACU countries south of the Limpopo, and extensive cooperation had also been generated between the territories to its north.

Taking the region as a whole, these interstate relations fell well short of even a common market, let alone full economic integration. None the less, under the unifying influences created by South Africa's dominant position as both a supplier of goods, services and capital, and as a purchaser of labour services and raw materials, Southern Africa was exhibiting considerable degrees of functional economic coherence and interdependence. Subsequently, however, the region's economic and political coherence and stability were to be undermined by two interrelated and seemingly irreconcilable conflicts. One conflict was between the growth of African nationalism and the defence of white minority rule, especially in Southern Rhodesia, in Namibia and in South Africa. The other conflict was between the desire, on the part of the newly independent black-ruled nations, for national self-determination on the one hand, and on the other hand their deeply-felt lack of economic sovereignty in the face of the highly unequal pattern of development, both within and between the countries of the region. The latter conflict emerged only at a relatively late stage under the guise of what became known as the 'dependence' problem. It was, however, severely aggravated by the racial dimensions of the first problem, especially given the close correlation which had emerged over time between white minority rule and economic privilege and prosperity.

Towards political self-determination

The path of the region's descent into conflict and confrontation can be traced first via the major milestones on the road to political independence for the regional states. Political independence in fact came later to most Southern African states than to the rest of Africa, partly because Portuguese colonialism proved more resistant than the British version to the advance of African nationalism, and partly because indigenous white communities in the region had become far more deeply entrenched than elsewhere. For both these reasons, the achievement of self-determination proved to be a particularly divisive and violent process.

In 1961, Tanzania became the first Southern African territory to achieve political independence.[1] Though in many ways peripheral to the region, Tanzania was in fact destined to play a major role in its subsequent affairs, providing political and moral leadership and affording economic and military support to others – especially in Mozambique, Rhodesia and South Africa – seeking to achieve their own liberation from colonial or white minority rule. Then in 1963, the Central African Federation was finally dissolved. Shortly thereafter, both Nyasaland and Northern Rhodesia acceded to independence within the British Commonwealth as Malawi and Zambia respectively.

A key turning-point came in 1965 when Southern Rhodesia unilaterally declared itself independent as Rhodesia, thus triggering a fifteen-year long conflict which was to rend the entire region, militarily, politically and economically. UDI was followed by the imposition by the United Nations of mandatory and increasingly comprehensive international economic sanctions against the illegal regime. Some of the consequences for the political economy of Southern Africa are discussed in greater detail below. Suffice to say for the moment that UDI turned the struggle for majority rule in Rhodesia into a war of major proportions affecting most of the region; that the sanctions profoundly distorted the pre-existing structures of economic relations in Southern Africa; and that the support given to Rhodesia by both South Africa and the Portuguese colonial administrations created great bitterness between white-ruled and black-ruled states in the region.

While the Rhodesian saga was unfolding, other important political changes continued to occur in the region. In the late 1960s, the three British Protectorates of Bechuanaland, Basutoland and Swaziland achieved independence as High Commission Territories within the Commonwealth, the former two adopting the names of Botswana and Lesotho respectively. In so doing, the three 'BLS' countries, as they collectively became known, finally averted the threat of political incorporation into South Africa which had, in fact, been hanging over them ever since Union in 1910.

Much more important, however, was the military coup in Lisbon in 1974 which overthrew the Portuguese government, and led to both Angola and

Mozambique achieving independence in the following year. Although independence brought to an end the long-running guerrilla wars which had been waged by liberation movements from both countries against their respective colonial administrations, it did not – unfortunately – lead to peace in either country. In Angola, the guerrilla war was transformed into a bitter and destructive internal conflict between the two erstwhile anti-colonial allies of the MPLA and UNITA, with the former in government, and the latter in opposition. To this day, the circumstances surrounding this conflict have precluded full international recognition being granted to the government in Luanda. In Mozambique, too, there was only a brief respite before an equally bitter and debilitating conflict emerged between the FRELIMO government and the RENAMO rebels.

The depth and bitterness of the conflicts in these two countries had several sources, not the least of which was that their independence brought to power for the first time in Southern Africa regimes committed to Marxist-Leninist principles (as opposed to the African socialism espoused by a number of the other newly independent states). The political and economic programmes implemented in Angola and Mozambique were doubtless motivated by honourable intentions to rectify the political injustices and to redress the economic inequalities inherited from the colonial past. However, they quickly proved to have devastating consequences for both political liberty and economic prosperity in both countries.

The collapse of Portuguese colonialism thus had decidedly less than satisfactory outcomes for Angola and Mozambique themselves. But the developments in these two countries were also instrumental in bringing about six distinct and major shifts in the balance of strategic and political forces and interests throughout Southern Africa. These shifts were to have significant consequences for political – and hence also for economic – relations in the wider region.

First, they brought a marked increase in Southern Africa's international strategic importance by leading to direct and indirect military intervention by the two superpowers in the region. The Soviet Union, together with its proxy, Cuba, became involved on the side of the MPLA in Angola, whilst US support went to UNITA. The Soviet Union and its Eastern bloc allies also became involved, albeit on a smaller scale, in Mozambique. Second, by facilitating the provision of material and logistic support, especially from Mozambique, to the (again avowedly Marxist) Zimbabwean liberation movements, the Portuguese withdrawal contributed markedly to the prosecution of the guerrilla war against the illegal government in Rhodesia. Having survived, even prospered, during the first ten years of UDI, the escalation of the war, coupled with sharply adverse developments in the international economy, was to bring the Rhodesian rebellion to an end within another five years.

Third, the decolonization of Angola and Mozambique led to the forging of the five-nation strategic, political and economic alliance of the Front Line States (Angola, Botswana, Mozambique, Tanzania and Zambia) against the Rhodesian regime. This alliance was later to become the foundation not only for organized regional opposition to apartheid rule in South Africa but also for regional efforts to transform the hated colonial economic heritage and to 'free' the neighbouring states from their unacceptable 'dependence' upon South Africa. Fourth, it removed two key elements in the white-ruled 'cordon sanitaire' surrounding South Africa itself, so enabling the guerrilla forces of the exiled South African liberation movements, the ANC and PAC, and of the Namibian movement, SWAPO, to step up their operations. Fifth, partly because of the heightened presence of SWAPO guerrillas in Angola, and partly on account of a determination to promote the cause of UNITA in Angola, South Africa itself became militarily involved on a growing scale in Angola – a fact which played a crucial role in reinforcing fears that Pretoria had expansionist ambitions in the region.

Finally, the ending of Portuguese colonial rule played an important role in generating political changes inside South Africa itself by giving an inestimable boost to confidence among black activists that white minority domination was not wholly invulnerable. Coincidentally, this occurred at a time when the decisive internal, domestic pressures for reform of apartheid were first beginning to manifest themselves. However, the coincidence helped to foster the perception that the key to the elimination of apartheid and white rule in South Africa lay predominantly in external pressures. This largely mistaken view encouraged the internationalization, and especially the regionalization, of the internal conflict in South Africa. In particular, it imparted undue significance to the entirely natural desire of the neighbouring states to assist the exiled South African liberation movements, especially in the aftermath of the 1976 Soweto uprising, when thousands of young blacks fled across the borders. This support, together with the political rhetoric which accompanied it, was widely viewed as a determination by the black-ruled states of the region to place themselves in the 'front line' against white rule in South Africa.

All these consequences contributed to a complete reappraisal by South Africa's own policy-makers of the country's role and position in Southern Africa. The results of this reappraisal were to manifest themselves in shifts of truly major proportions in Pretoria's perceptions of, and strategies towards, the region, in strategic, military, political and economic terms. In particular, it led to the theory of a communist-inspired 'total onslaught' against South Africa, and to the perceived need for a concomitant 'total strategy' to counteract it. Out of both of these concepts was born the strategy of regional 'destabilization', in which South Africa sought to exploit its military, political and economic powers in a variety of ways to sustain its hegemony over the rest of the region. By the late 1970s, therefore, the states of Southern Africa were already caught in a conflict which threatened to dwarf even that which was still being waged over Rhodesia.

Given these rising political tensions among the regional states, economic relations between them would in any event have been in danger of being disrupted, not least because the issue of economic relations between South Africa and its neighbours had already moved to the centre of the political debate. In the early 1980s, however, destabilization was to interlock with two further political developments to propel the region ineluctably towards new and unprecedented levels of conflict. The ending of the Rhodesian war brought the birth of Zimbabwe as an independent state in 1979–80. Also in 1980, came the formation, on the initiative of the Front Line States, of the Southern African Development Coordination Conference (SADCC), comprising all nine newly independent states in the region. These new developments were to make explicit the interconnection between the overt racial dimension of the struggle for self-determination in Southern Africa, and the equally evident fact that economic power had long been concentrated in the hands of white people and of white minority governments.

The portents of economic conflict

The consequences of destabilization will be discussed in more detail later. However, they need to be understood in the context of the evolution of economic relations during the progress of the regional states towards political self-determination. There were early indications on two fronts of the potential for both the race and the economic distribution issues to become intertwined in the post-independence era. First, from its inception, the Central African Federation was riven with dissension over the extent to which, and the speed with which, political rights should be accorded to blacks, with white-dominated Southern Rhodesia continually fighting a rearguard action. In addition, there was deep resentment in the other two territories at the perception that the economic benefits of Federation accrued predominantly to white Southern Rhodesian interests. Both these issues soon became the source of deep and long-lasting conflict not only within the Federation but also, following the dissolution of the Federation and the subsequent unilateral declaration of Rhodesian independence, in the whole region.

The second portent of future difficulties was, of course, the accession to power in South Africa in 1948 of the National Party, with its apartheid ideology. The impact of this development on the region's political and economic frameworks in fact was relatively slow to develop, although it was eventually to become overwhelmingly important. Initially, the only obvious issue for the new government in respect of regional relations was to be the management of international relations with newly independent black-ruled states, both in Africa and elsewhere. Could a segregationist South Africa in practice establish diplomatic and other official links with states whose representatives in Pretoria would presumably be black?

During the 1950s, Pretoria did succeed in maintaining trade and other commissioners in some African and other Third World countries. Even so, South Africa was already experiencing the beginnings of international isolation, at least in the political and diplomatic, if not yet in the economic, spheres. Throughout the 1950s, Pretoria found itself in conflict with the United Nations, and its representation in numerous UN bodies, including the Economic Commission for Africa, was terminated or suspended, sometimes as a result of voluntary withdrawal, and sometimes because of involuntary exclusion. In this climate of growing hostility towards South Africa, the newly independent states of Africa played a major role. But, in the absence of such states in Southern Africa itself, the regional impact of these developments remained muted.[2]

The politicization of economic relations

It was not in fact until the 1960s that the crucial question of economic relations between white-ruled and black-ruled states in the region became a matter of serious political contention. By then, the advancing tide of African nationalism, which had already swept aside colonial rule in much of Central, Western and Eastern Africa, had finally begun to engulf Southern Africa as well. In 1960, moreover, world opinion had been outraged by the massacre by the South African police of sixty-nine Africans at Sharpeville. From this time onwards, demands for the imposition of economic, as well as diplomatic, sanctions against South Africa became commonplace in international fora, including both the UN and the newly established Organization of African Unity. Indeed, by 1963, the UN Security Council, including South Africa's traditional Western allies, had already approved a 'voluntary' embargo on arms deals with South Africa.

Meanwhile, in 1961, South Africa had declared itself a Republic, withdrawn from the Commonwealth and severed some of its automatic financial links with the City of London. In different circumstances, the distancing of the region's key economy from the international financial system might have provided the opportunity for even more thoroughgoing economic cooperation, not only in Southern Africa, but extending further north as well. By virtue of their exports of primary products, most African countries exhibited a continuing economic orientation towards the industrialized countries of the world. Even so, given reasonable growth of incomes in these countries (and hence in the size of their markets), and given the political will, the potential for mutual benefit from local economic cooperation was not inconsiderable. Both South Africa and Southern Rhodesia already had relatively well-developed industrial sectors. Both were already supplying, not only many consumer goods, but also some producer goods (machinery, transport equipment, chemicals and other productive inputs), to other African countries. In turn, the numerous raw materials (including agricultural products) produced and exported by the latter countries could have found ready markets in the more developed regional economies. In the event, despite the initial promise of economic growth in the newly independent countries, local economic cooperation actually declined sharply in the early 1960s, and – as will be seen – was subsequently both further curtailed and severely distorted by political and ideological factors.

South Africa's substantial trade with Africa was the first major casualty. The recorded proportion of total exports which went to the rest of Africa fell from 19 per cent in 1959 to only 12 per cent in 1963 and 1964. (Imports from Africa however maintained their 6–8 per cent share through most of this period.) Political hostility towards South Africa, particularly in the guise of boycotts of South African goods, was only partly responsible for the decline in exports. In some instances, political instability in significant parts of post-colonial Africa was another – possibly the major – contributory factor.[3]

On the one hand, as pointed out earlier, these figures almost certainly understate by a significant margin the overall extent of South Africa's commerce with Africa. First, they exclude all South Africa's trade with its SACU partners (including Namibia); second, in the case of trade with the rest of Africa, they also exclude receipts and payments for invisibles and for factor services. Thus, they exclude Africa's considerable earnings from exports of unskilled labour to South Africa and from expenditures by South African tourists, and they exclude Africa's payments for the services of South Africa's capital, skilled labour, transport and other infrastructural and commercial services.

On the other hand, there was no gainsaying the fact that, in overall terms, such commerce had declined. Whatever the reason, moreover, Africa remained the one continent with which South Africa had a merchandise trade surplus. It followed that any decline in this surplus meant that the burden of financing the trade deficit with the rest of the world would fall even more heavily upon the twin pillars of gold exports and foreign capital inflows. With the gold price still fixed internationally and with increasing concerns, especially on political grounds, about the sustainability of foreign capital inflows, the decline in trade with Africa represented a potentially serious problem for the South African economy.

To make matters worse, the post-Sharpeville economic 'miracle' in South Africa, which reinforced the earlier structural shift in output away from mining towards manufacturing, ironically made trade with Africa an even greater imperative. Established behind protective barriers, uncompetitive in international terms, and unable to achieve adequate economies of scale via the domestic market alone, South Africa's industries were increasingly in need of larger markets. This need was further underlined by the fact that the new industries were heavily dependent upon imported machinery and other productive inputs, payment for which could not be sustained without an improved export performance.

South Africa's policy-makers did respond by seeking increased economic links with black-ruled Africa on several occasions. For a while, especially during the latter half of the 1960s, these efforts did not go wholly unrewarded. Despite the initial effectiveness of some boycotts and the growth of the pan-Africanist consensus on isolation of South Africa, the 'outward-looking policy', instituted by Prime Minister Vorster, of detente with independent black Africa did register a number of successes: low-key, but potentially valuable, trade and investment links were established with the Ivory Coast, Gabon and Senegal in West Africa, with Zaire in Central Africa and with the East African island states of Malagasy, Mauritius and the Seychelles. Closer to home, the 1967 trade agreement with Malawi represented something of a diplomatic 'coup'; and, many of South Africa's significant trade and investment links with Zambia survived that country's transition to independence intact. These successes doubtless contributed in some measure to the fact that, by 1971, exports to Africa had recovered their 19 per cent share. (Imports of goods from the rest of Africa, by contrast, fared less well, accounting generally for only about 5 per cent of total imports.)[4]

Again, these figures understate the true extent of economic relations with Africa. This was particularly so in respect of the Southern African Customs Union. The independence of the BLS countries meant that – at least for as long as white rule persisted – there was now no prospect of them entering into formal economic union with South Africa. None the less, all three states opted to remain within SACU and within the (then informal) Rand Monetary Area, so retaining most of the major economic institutional linkages between themselves and South Africa.[5]

Even so, there are two reasons why the recorded increase in exports did not really represent a major breakthrough in raising the level of interaction with black African states. First, at best, without the political legitimacy to sustain them, many of the links which were established could be – and were – only limited and temporary. By the early 1970s, some of the leaders of those African countries which had been willing to engage in commerce with South Africa had already been forced to pay a heavy political price for stepping out of line. As Johnson has observed, this was a case in which trade would have to follow the flag, rather than vice versa as Pretoria so fervently, but vainly, hoped.[6]

Second, most of the recorded increase was confined to trade with the regional neighbours, such as Rhodesia, Zambia, Mozambique and, to a lesser extent, Angola. As will be demonstrated shortly, by far the greatest part of the increase was due to the closer links which were forged between South Africa and Rhodesia following the dissolution of the Central African Federation and especially following Rhodesia's unilateral declaration of independence in 1965. Welcome though this increase was for Pretoria from a balance-of-payments perspective, the fact remained that South Africa was, in effect, merely deepening its trade links with a narrowing range of white-ruled partners in Africa, rather than significantly extending those with black-ruled states. This point was underlined by the failure of its many economic links with the Portuguese colonies to survive the collapse of colonial rule for any length of time. South Africa's mining, commodity, oil-prospecting and other investments in Angola, and its more consumer-oriented trade and investment links with Mozambique, soon withered away. The fact that, in both cases, this may have had as much to do with post-colonial domestic economic disintegration in the countries as with their outright hostility to economic links with South Africa does not negate the validity of the observation that South Africa's economic relations with Africa had both declined and become highly politicized.

South Africa's withdrawal from the Commonwealth thus marked not the beginning of an era of enhanced economic cooperation with black-ruled Africa, but rather a major step towards its impending international political and economic isolation.

Meanwhile, the Central African Federation was another casualty of the decline in local interstate cooperation in the early 1960s. It will be recalled that Federation had resulted in a significant intensification of economic links between the two Rhodesias and Nyasaland. This applied not only to trading relations, but also to institutional linkages which were particularly facilitated by closer political association. For the African nationalists in Nyasaland however, the desire to secede from a Federation which, in their eyes, lacked any political legitimacy, outweighed any considerations of economic advantage; and for those in Northern Rhodesia, who believed that their country in effect was subsidizing the other two territories, even the economic benefits were, at the very least, debatable.[7]

These tensions effectively precluded the economic links between the three territories from being cemented further. That so many links actually survived the break-up of the Federation and the independence of Zambia and Malawi was clearly not due to any active political desire for their perpetuation. Rather it was the combined result of the inescapable realities of geography, the physical indivisibilities of utilities like the Kariba power station, and – as we shall see later – the high costs associated with such economic disengagement attempts. But even these remaining links were destined to come under increasing strain after Rhodesia's UDI and the international sanctions which followed it. Even before then, however, the region had clearly already had a taste of the tendency to call into question, on explicitly political grounds, the value of economic relations between white-ruled and black-ruled states. UDI brought this tendency to the fore.

The impact of UDI and Rhodesian sanctions

The unilateral declaration of independence by Rhodesia in November 1965 outraged international opinion. Not only was the new regime illegal in terms of international law – the territory was still technically subject to British jurisdiction – but by entrenching white minority rule the decision also effectively denied the Rhodesian people as a whole the right of self-determination. Though it was largely the illegitimacy of the regime which exercised the wider international community, in the region it was the racial aspect which, in practice, was most responsible for polarizing opinion, and particularly for determining attitudes towards the implementation of sanctions. Sanctions ultimately had a political objective, but being economic instruments they had economic consequences. Because their scope was wide – at least in theory, they were (eventually) close to being comprehensive, universal and mandatory – their consequences were significant. Sanctions effectively altered most of Rhodesia's – and many of its neighbours' – trading and other international economic relations in several fundamental, enduring and sometimes perverse ways. This was especially true of relations involving Zambia, Malawi, Mozambique and South Africa.

It should first be recalled that, as landlocked states, both Rhodesia and three of its immediate neighbours – Zambia, Malawi and Botswana – could obtain access to the outside world only via Angola, Mozambique and/or South Africa. In practice, they relied predominantly on Mozambique and South Africa, because the Angolan route – the Benguela railway – was always of limited value even when it was functioning: it was expensive; it was operationally inefficient, and its traffic capacity was limited. These geographical imperatives were of supreme importance in determining the impact of sanctions upon the structures of economic relations in Southern Africa.

Prior to UDI, some 80 per cent of Rhodesia's overseas trade passed through the ports of Beira and Lourenço Marques in Mozambique. Apart from oil, which was imported via the pipeline from Beira, most of this traffic comprised low-rated, high-volume and/or low-density goods (such as exports of tobacco, maize, chrome ore and iron ore and imports of wheat) which were expensive to carry over long distances. In addition, the bulk of Zambia's overseas trade, especially its exports of copper, travelled via the Rhodesian railways to and from the same ports. By contrast with most of the other traffic on these routes, copper was a high-rated commodity. Rhodesia was thus able to use the revenues from Zambian through-traffic to offset the high costs of its own transport needs.[8]

Most of the remainder of Rhodesia's and Zambia's overseas trade utilized the South African transport system. Virtually all of this traffic (as well as both countries' bilateral trade with South Africa itself) was carried via Botswana. From 1959, Rhodesian railways had taken over the operation of the Botswana section of the line. Thus, the through-traffic between South Africa and Zambia also generated invisible earnings for Rhodesia. Botswana's own overseas trade was carried either on the South African routes or, via Rhodesia, on the Mozambican system. Apart from overseas trade, Rhodesia also had extensive trading relations with its neighbours: Zambia was in fact its largest single export market, and a not insubstantial source of imports; South Africa was its second largest source of imports (after the UK) and its third largest export market (again after the UK); and trade with Malawi and, to a lesser extent, Botswana was not insignificant.[9]

Sanctions severely disrupted all these transport and trading arrangements. Portugal, like South Africa, refrained from applying any of the internationally imposed sanctions. None the less, sanctions did reduce Rhodesia's total foreign trade volumes significantly, at least in the earlier years. Moreover, the British naval blockade of Beira, through which the greater part of Rhodesia's trade previously passed, forced the rerouting of much of the remaining traffic. Some of this went to Lourenço Marques instead, but because of capacity constraints, much of it had to be routed to the more distant South African ports.

This situation persisted for the best part of ten years. By 1974, however, the Mozambican routes were becoming increasingly disrupted by guerrilla warfare; by 1975, as Mozambique's independence approached, the operational efficiency of its ports and railways had decreased sharply; finally, in 1976, the new Mozambican government closed its border with Rhodesia, and virtually all remaining Rhodesian traffic – now down to less than 30 per cent of the total by volume – had to be diverted to South Africa.[10] Fortunately for the Rhodesians, this diversion was facilitated by the fact that, in 1974, in anticipation of disruption in Mozambique, they had hurriedly built a new spur from Rutenga on the Limpopo railway to join with the South African system at Beit Bridge.

A major consequence of sanctions was thus to generate much closer economic links between Rhodesia and South Africa. Admittedly, this trend actually pre-dated UDI. Following the break-up of the Federation, the two countries had negotiated a new customs and trade agreement in 1964 which accorded duty-free or preferential access for many Rhodesian products to the South African market and vice versa. But these arrangements clearly acquired heightened significance after UDI, when Rhodesia was forced to rely on South Africa, to a greater or lesser extent, for virtually all its foreign trade transactions, including its critical imports of oil. UN estimates suggested that during UDI South Africa accounted for up to one-third of all Rhodesia's exports and nearly one-half of its imports. The increased reliance on South Africa was reflected also in more extensive penetration of all sectors of the Rhodesian economy by South African capital.[11]

Substantial though the disruptions to Rhodesia's external trade links were, those suffered by Zambia were even more traumatic. Prior to its own independence in 1964, one-third of Zambia's imports had come from Rhodesia and most of the remainder from, or via, South Africa. When sanctions were first imposed, there was little that could be done about this, but Zambia committed itself to the total de-linking of its economy from that of Rhodesia. (Because of its vulnerability, Zambia could have been 'excused' from compliance with the sanctions but it elected, on political grounds, to give the maximum support possible.) These efforts resulted in a bitter series of trade and transport wars between the two countries, which were very costly for both and during which Zambia was forced on several occasions to eat humble pie.[12] None the less, the volume of trade did decline dramatically over the years, and when Rhodesia temporarily closed its border with Zambia (except for personal traffic and copper freight) in 1973 on military grounds, Zambia finally elected to cut itself off.

With its foreign trade unable for a number of years thereafter to traverse Rhodesian territory, and thereby to gain access to the South African transport system, Zambia was in dire straits. Some traffic was diverted to the Benguela railway, but this was simply not up to the task and, in any event, independently of the conflict over Rhodesia, it was closed in 1975 by fighting in Angola. Zambia therefore endeavoured, but with only limited success, to truck its imports and exports from and to Dar es Salaam in Tanzania. In fact, it was not until 1976 that Zambia eventually obtained some much-needed relief from the new Tan-Zam or Tazara railway line to Dar constructed in remarkable haste by the Chinese.[13] However, operational difficulties, including severe congestion at the port of Dar es Salaam, meant that the Tazara route was unable to function at anything approaching its nominal capacity.

The obverse side of the coin of Zambia's 'achievement' in severing its economic links with Rhodesia was the need for massive assistance from the international community – assistance which was only partially forthcoming. As a result, Zambia's foreign trade relations, but especially its exports of copper, incurred severe long-term damage. In the light of subsequent developments, it is also particularly ironical that sanctions pushed Zambia – as they had pushed Rhodesia – into closer economic ties with South Africa. Not only was Pretoria one of the main sources of such emergency assistance as was provided – mainly via airlifts of vital supplies – but South Africa replaced Rhodesia as the supplier of many imports.

Zambia was not the only one of Rhodesia's neighbours to suffer substantial economic losses as a result of sanctions. Mozambique was also a major casualty, losing virtually all its invisible earnings from the carriage of both Rhodesian and Zambian trade. These losses were compounded by the declining efficiency of the Mozambican transport system during and after the withdrawal of the Portuguese colonial administration. South Africa, which also made extensive use of the port at Lourenço Marques (now renamed Maputo), sent staff to assist, but still had to shift some of its traffic to South African ports. Malawi was also occasioned some losses because of sanctions. Since Rhodesia and Malawi were not physically contiguous, the border closure with Mozambique had the incidental effect of cutting off much of the trade between the two, even though Malawi took a relatively relaxed stance on sanctions. (Malawi's problems were further complicated by the fact that its own outlets to the sea, via the Mozambican ports of Nacala and Beira, were also effectively severed by the incapacitation of the Mozambican transport system.)

Thus, sanctions clearly had dramatic consequences for interstate economic relations in the region. They severely weakened the close economic links which had been created over an extended period between Rhodesia on the one hand and Zambia, Malawi, Mozambique and Botswana on the other hand. Had black rule come earlier to Rhodesia and with less trauma, most of these links may well have survived. As it is, many of the links – especially between Zambia and Zimbabwe – have never recovered. By contrast, many of the other links which sanctions either helped to create or to reinforce between South Africa and the other states in the region have persisted. Sanctions thus blurred the broad division of cooperative economic interests between the regional states north and south of the Limpopo which had been developing before the Rhodesian problem intervened to distort the structures of intra-regional economic relations to such a marked degree.

But UDI and sanctions had equally dramatic political consequences for regional relations in that they raised both latent and overt political hostilities between white- and black-ruled states to unprecedented levels. The fact that during the UDI period, five regional states – the BLS countries, Angola and Mozambique – achieved political independence merely served to heighten these divisions, not least by generating solidarity among the newly independent countries. As noted earlier, the five independent states (including Tanzania) which bordered on Rhodesia, formed a 'front line' alliance to assist the Zimbabwean liberation movements. In all these circumstances, it might seem surprising that sanctions did not bind Rhodesia and South Africa closer together politically as well as economically. Certainly, the possibility was raised once again of Rhodesia becoming, in effect, the fifth province of South Africa. It is significant, therefore, that this outcome did not materialize.

From the time of self-government, Southern Rhodesia had maintained a careful, if respectful, distance from South Africa within a framework of what might be termed 'competitive cooperation' between the two countries. Exogenous developments had certainly forced them now into closer cooperation, but their interests still remained competitive in too many respects.

In political terms, South Africa naturally had its own reasons for opposing sanctions, but it was also wary of too close an association with a regime which was illegitimate in terms of international law. South Africa would also have had strong reservations about adding another 2½ million blacks to its already complex citizenry (even assuming that such an eventuality would have been politically possible). Even among white Rhodesians, it was doubtful (to say the least) whether they would have been at ease in the Afrikaner-dominated South Africa of the 1960s and 1970s.

Economically, too, there were major obstacles to closer association. Rhodesia was forced by sanctions into a crash programme of import substitution, especially in the manufacture of consumer goods, and finding markets for these goods was crucially important. Even the 1964 trade agreement with South Africa was a source of serious difficulties on both sides on account of the increasing structural similarities between the industrial sectors in the two countries. In many instances, Rhodesian and South African producers were beginning to compete for the same markets. At the macroeconomic level, too, there were difficulties. South Africa exacted its full pound of flesh for bailing Rhodesia out of its trade and transport problems. On the numerous occasions during UDI when the South African transport system became severely congested, especially on the routes to the ports, it was Rhodesian goods which tended to take second place. This was costly for the Rhodesian economy. Moreover, there were significant differences in interests over the external values of the Rhodesian dollar and the South African rand, especially following the several devaluations of the rand in the early 1970s.[14]

On the one hand, therefore, the strategic interest which both countries had in maintaining white minority rule in Southern Africa brought close cooperation in withstanding sanctions and in opposing the international efforts to bring majority rule to Rhodesia. On the other hand, the evident increase in the mutuality of both their economic and their political interests was still insufficient to create the political conditions necessary to achieve unification.

In sum, UDI constituted a unique, extended and difficult phase in the political and economic development of Southern Africa. UDI delayed, and severely complicated, the advance of African nationalism in Rhodesia, though it did not and could not stop the tide; UDI generated great political anger which polarized the entire region, not least because it took a costly and brutal war to remove it; and the sanctions which followed UDI created great upheavals in the structures of intra-regional economic relations and shifted the economic centre of gravity in the region even further towards South Africa.

No less significantly, the UDI episode also underlined the susceptibility of economic relations to the politicization problem. By declaring economic war on Rhodesia, the international community in general, and Rhodesia's black-ruled neighbours in particular, legitimized the practice of overt and large-scale manipulation of economic linkages between trading partners in pursuit of major political objectives. Whether or not the cessation of trade with Rhodesia was feasible or (on any other criterion) desirable, became a question to be subordinated to the political presumption against engaging in such trade.

The formal analytical issues raised by the difficulties of evaluating economic relations between countries with fundamentally different political systems and values will be discussed later. However, for several reasons, the problems which the above-mentioned practice posed for regional economic relations were not resolved when the Rhodesian sanctions were lifted. First, there remained the even greater obstacles of white minority rule in both Namibia and South Africa. The process of politicization of South Africa's international economic links on account of apartheid (which process had actually predated the Rhodesian issue) now required to be prosecuted with even greater vigour; and the fact that South Africa had chosen openly to defy the sanctions against Rhodesia made it even more undesirable, politically speaking, to engage in trade with it.

Second, by this stage, several governments in the region – including the government in newly independent Zimbabwe – had acquired what appeared to be an unquestioning appetite for the employment of economic linkages in pursuit of political objectives. Notwithstanding the lessons afforded by the experience of applying sanctions against Rhodesia, whether a particular economic link, or set of links, was desirable or otherwise was frequently asserted to be a matter to be judged almost exclusively on political criteria.

Third, by this stage too, the twofold belief that political independence had not been accompanied by economic independence, and that responsibility for the denial of the latter rested, both directly and indirectly, with South Africa, had become part of the conventional wisdom concerning economic relations in the region. Hence, the mere fact of economic linkages with South Africa carried with it an element of implied undesirability. Underlying these beliefs was an important two-part presumption concerning the distribution of economic development in the region. This presumption was first, that the overwhelming economic dominance of South Africa in the region was inherently 'unnatural', and second, that the apparent 'dependence' of the neighbouring states upon South Africa was an inescapable corollary of that dominance. It followed that the lack of economic sovereignty could be rectified only by destroying the dominance. The neighbours' ensnarement was understandably aggravated by the unpalatable fact that this power was vested in a country the government of which was committed to the maintenance of white minority rule.

This 'dependence' of the black-ruled states upon white-ruled South Africa rendered even more imperative their need to break free from economic relations with South Africa. Against this background, the creation of

SADCC as an organization dedicated to the achievement of 'economic liberation' could not avoid reinforcing the tensions over political and economic relations in the region. On the other hand, regardless of political differences, the evident increase in economic linkages which UDI and sanctions had occasioned between South Africa and its neighbours seemed to many surely to point to increasingly irrevocable 'interdependence' in the region.

Given the rising political stakes in the region, and the moral and political dimensions to its underlying racial conflicts, it is scarcely surprising that the issue of economic 'dependence', and its associated imperatives, was destined to have particularly unfortunate implications for all the region's economies. At the heart of the problem lay widely divergent beliefs in, and conceptions of, economic 'dependence' and 'interdependence'. It is to the nature of these concepts that we must now turn.

PART TWO
THE POLITICAL ECONOMY OF
DEPENDENCE AND INTERDEPENDENCE

Applying the wrong image and wrong rhetoric to problems often leads to erroneous analysis and bad policy. – Arad *et al.* (1983), p. 13.

4 Economic dependence and interdependence: an introduction

It was noted at the outset that economic dependence and interdependence, though widely employed in discussions of both political and economic relations between nations, in fact command relatively little understanding. This has resulted in considerable confusion in the application of these concepts to specific situations. This confusion is not entirely surprising since, despite the best efforts of vast literatures on the two subjects, both concepts have proved to be conceptually problematical.

That all parties, whether individuals or nations, who engage in economic exchanges with other individuals or nations become, in some sense, reliant or dependent upon these exchanges is self-evident. Dependence, in this sense, is merely a descriptive term. However, this observation does lead to the common-sense conclusion that, if any party were somehow to be cut off from, or deprived of, such exchanges, then that party would lose the concomitant benefits and, hence, presumably would be worse off. Dependence might therefore appear to exist in that, if one party can be instrumental in bringing about this deprivation, then the other party would suffer or be unable to avoid some adverse consequences. There is a clear implication in this argument of an element of one-sidedness to the dependence. It is this presumption of one-sidedness that has been at the heart of the widely-held view that, in the Southern African situation, dependent relations and political and economic conflict are inescapably interlinked.

Yet, in another sense, on the assumption that both parties benefit from their exchange relations with each other, calling this situation one of 'dependence' is subject to a serious logical flaw. If the benefits are mutual, then both parties must lose from their cessation. It would therefore seem to make little sense to ascribe to such a situation the characteristic of (one-sided) dependence. The circumstances would appear to point instead to mutual dependence, or 'interdependence'. It is this mutuality of interests which underlies the view that, if 'politics' could somehow be set aside, cooperative economic relations in Southern Africa would come into their own. These conflicting, but common-sense, observations suggest that if dependence and interdependence are to represent anything more than tautological and descriptive concepts, then they require more analytical content. Consequently, this part of the study will be devoted to dissecting and clarifying different aspects of the two concepts.

Two preliminary remarks are in order. First, since dependence and interdependence self-evidently have both political and economic connotations, wherever possible the analysis will seek to distinguish and to clarify the economic and the political aspects of dependent or interdependent relations. Second, it should be made clear from the outset that there are no straightforward answers to many of the questions to be posed. As Michaely has pointed out in respect of the concept of dependence (and his remarks apply equally well to interdependence)

Being definitions, none of the interpretations given to the concept . . . is either logically right or wrong. Some are clearly stated, while others may be confused and vague. Some are of a more operational nature, while others may be devoid of operational usefulness (the more so, one suspects, the more inclusive and ambitious the interpretation).[1]

However, the lack of straightforward answers to complex questions does not absolve one from the need for a systematic approach to discussion of the relevant issues. Indeed, the above observation suggests that such an approach carries a substantial premium. Systematic analysis will thus be a key objective of the exercise.

5 The theory of global 'dependence'

A considerable body of post-war literature depicts many aspects of inter-national economic relations between the industrialized countries of the world on the one hand and the developing (Third World) countries on the other, as embodying or reflecting economic 'dependence'.[1]

In its original form, this notion of 'dependence' emanated from the arguments of some economists to the effect that structural differences between the economies of the industrialized and the developing countries qualified the traditional presumption in favour of free trade. Drawing par-ticularly on studies of Latin American economies, they argued that the effective operation of the price mechanism (which is an essential element in the free trade argument) was hindered by structural rigidities in developing economies. Free trade with, and foreign investment from, the industrialized countries at the 'centre' of the world economy were not therefore neces-sarily desirable – indeed, could even be potentially deleterious – for the countries at the 'periphery'. The lesson drawn was that deliberate state policies, including fostering local industrialization by means of protection, should be employed to transform developing economies. Only by this means could developing country governments acquire the autonomy neces-sary to enable them to achieve the structural change and economic diversifi-cation which would free them from the constraints on their development.

These ideas were criticized by radical, neo-Marxist theorists on the grounds that they failed to recognize the social processes and class relations which governed the imperialist relationships between the capitalist 'centre' and the 'dependent periphery'. The literature which they subsequently generated sought to develop a view of dependence not merely as a descrip-tive term, but rather as an analytical construct which both promotes holistic understanding of the character of international economic relations and which carries with it important implications for policy towards such relations.

The most widely accepted definition of dependence in this literature is that provided by Dos Santos: dependence is 'a situation in which the economy of certain countries is conditioned by the development and expan-sion of another economy'.[2] Furthermore, there is a general presumption that the conditioning process is anything but benign. The development of countries at the 'centre' of the international political economy is believed to take place at the expense of the 'peripheral' countries. Albeit expressed in varying forms, the thesis is that the periphery is not simply 'exploited' by the centre, nor merely hindered in its development aspirations, but that it is in fact further – and inescapably – impoverished. In this view, development of the centre – meaning, in practice, the prosperity of international capitalism – necessarily requires 'underdevelopment' of the periphery.

At the heart of the argument lies monopoly capital which, in Marxian analysis is driven inexorably to find new and external sources of demand for its outputs and profitable outlets for investment of the monopoly profits which it continually accumulates. This need drove it to expand beyond the confines of the centre and to incorporate and exploit the periphery. Southern Africa, of course, was part of the periphery, and colonialism and imperialism had been the instruments of its exploitation. From the outset – but especially, of course, from the time of the minerals revolution – monopoly capital, emanating from the imperial centres of Europe, had been used to exploit and impoverish the region (as also the rest of the colonized world). Most specifically, international capital, operating through local subsidiaries of transnational (or multinational) corporations, extracted the mineral wealth of South and Southern Africa and, in so doing, expropriated the profits (or 'surplus') which, by rights, should have accrued to the peoples of the region. These profits were repatriated to the centre by both legitimate and illegitimate means.[3]

But these profits merely aggravated the structural problems confronting monopoly capital, forcing it to seek yet more investment opportunities and more markets for its outputs. Hence it extended the search for minerals in Southern Africa and supplied the equipment and consumer goods which the new mines and mining communities required. It was thus (according to this thesis) no accident that British colonial authority was extended over the region and that Britain went to war with the Boer Republics in an endeavour to secure control over the mineral wealth. Moreover, through manipulation of markets and of political influence in Southern Africa itself, and through the creation of institutional mechanisms (such as the migrant labour system), international monopoly capital held down the cost of the local labour it needed to extract the minerals, thereby further raising profits, which it again drained from the local economies.

Though originally applied to the world economy as a whole – excepting, of course, the (then) planned socialist economies of Eastern Europe – this dependence hypothesis was subsequently extended to apply at regional levels as well. From its regional outposts, such as Brazil or South Africa, international capitalism – somewhat paradoxically – set about 'replicating' these centre–periphery relations within its local spheres of influence. This was achieved partly through its own direct actions in establishing further subsidiary enterprises in the peripheries of these regions.

At the same time, by cooperating initially with international capital, but by seizing any opportunities to assert a modicum of independence from it, 'national' or 'local' capitalist classes also succeeded in establishing themselves. These local capitalists set out, in turn, to create regional and local dependent relations. Prosperity for the regional centre was again detrimental to the prosperity of its own periphery. Thus, by virtue of their dependence upon capitalist centres like the Witwatersrand, both the (black) rural areas of South Africa and the other countries of the region were trapped in a vicious cycle in which greater capitalist enrichment in the centre and increased impoverishment and economic decline in the periphery were merely two sides of the same coin.[4]

This relationship was neither static nor was it conducted at arm's length. It was instead a dynamic and interactive process. By drawing migrant labour from (say) Mozambique and Lesotho, and by expropriating – and, especially, by repatriating – profits ('surplus') on capital invested in (say) Zambian mines or Zimbabwean insurance companies, capitalism in the regional centre, South Africa, was extending its tentacles into the periphery and denuding it of its productive resources. The more these resources were siphoned off to feed the growth of the centre, the poorer the peripheral areas became, and the greater the reduction in their prospects for ever achieving growth on their own account.

These local capitalisms had an ambiguous relationship with international capitalism. On the one hand, they were clearly competitive: local capital was making profits which might otherwise have accrued to international capital. On the other hand, the survival of international capital depended on exploitation of the periphery being pushed ever further and further afield. In so far as national capital both promoted this process and, simultaneously, through its own prosperity, extended the base to be exploited by international capital, they were complementary.

Nor did the process stop at the broad regional level. Within the Southern African periphery, for example, a Southern Rhodesian capitalist class also succeeded in establishing itself. Though still subject in considerable measure to control and exploitation by international capital and, subsequently, by South African capital, it created its own set of centre–periphery relations which extended into its (black) rural periphery and into the neighbouring territories, especially Mozambique, Nyasaland and Northern Rhodesia.

The dependence hypothesis thus postulated the creation of a world-wide hierarchy of centre–periphery relations. Within this hierarchy, different 'fractions' of capital, sometimes complementary and sometimes competitive, at the respective centres sought continuously to sustain their capacity for exploitation of their respective peripheries through the elaboration of 'dependent' economic relations.

But, as already implied, the hypothesis sees this 'dependence' as being not only economic. It is also political in character. Capitalist classes and forces operate through the political process in an attempt to ensure that governmental policies do not compromise capitalist interests. One major thrust of the literature has therefore been to argue that 'dependent' economic relations also severely compromise the political freedom of dependent states. At the minimum, these limitations are considered to redound to the disadvantage of the dependent states. Their freedom of choice over both political and economic policy options is inhibited by the need to avoid giving offence to the centre country or putting at risk the economic relationships upon which they 'depend'. At worst, centre country governments (and the capitalist interests which they represent) effectively determine the policy choices which the dependent states make. These limitations are thus no less than the intended outcome of the dependent relations and they provide the rationale for maintaining the dependent states in their condition of dependence. In sum, notwithstanding its origins, for many, 'dependence' has merely come to signify a shorthand expression for the application of the entire paradigm of radical, neo-Marxist and neo-imperialist analyses to the study of the international political economy.

According to this paradigm, the main consequence of dependence for developing countries is that it imposes upon them a mode of development which is wholly inappropriate for their needs. Economic advancement is restricted to the capitalist elites in each country and national economies are structurally distorted by the centre–periphery relationships. The key policy implication is that developing country governments must seize control of the development process and thereby ensure that the 'surplus', instead of being expropriated by both international and national capitalist classes, is utilized for the benefit of the masses. Since foreign capital, in the form of transnational corporations, would compromise these efforts, it is to be discouraged; and since the existing structures of international trade have deleterious consequences for developing economies, foreign trade must be carefully managed and new – and more appropriate – structures developed.[5]

The seeming plausibility of this total and all-embracing explanation for the structure of the international political economy, and for the lack of economic progress in developing countries, afforded the 'dependence' school considerable intellectual and political appeal, especially in the 1960s and 1970s. Its philosophy informed and underpinned discussions within several major international economic and political institutions, including UNCTAD and the OAU. It was also instrumental in fuelling demands for a 'new international economic order'. The concept of dependence as a one-way street towards impoverishment for developing countries found particularly ready acceptance in Southern Africa. The prominent role played by international capital in the development of the regional economy was undeniable, as was the existence of gross inequalities of income and wealth. But it was the racial dimension to the region's ills, and particularly the association of these inequalities with white minority rule, that gave added impetus to the attraction of these radical, structuralist explanations for their origins.

In South Africa itself, application of neo-Marxist analyses led to radical arguments that capitalism and apartheid were mutually reinforcing phenomena, and that elimination of the former was impossible without elimination of the latter. Likewise, in the wider region, capitalism – including now the outreaches of South Africa's own foreign trade and investment – came to be regarded by many as the primary source of the relative lack of economic development in the neighbouring states.[6]

At the minimum, these beliefs helped to generate an anti-capitalist ethos among several of the region's post-independence governments. They encouraged widespread suspicion of foreign private capital investment, including South African investment, in the region. They led to a predis-position against market-based criteria for resource allocation decisions. Beyond that, they generated an obsession with 'self-reliant' and 'independent' economic development. All this led, in turn, to adoption of, or experimentation with, Marxist-Leninist and related economic doctrines, concerned primarily with the imperatives of controlling the development process at home and restructuring the international economic order abroad. Most importantly, however, they spawned the belief that economic development in the region, dominated as it was by South Africa, reflected 'dependence' of a kind that was 'one-sided', 'unnatural' and 'obstructive of economic liberation' for the neighbouring states. One of the clearest expositions of this is to be found in the Lusaka Declaration, the founding statement of principles for the Southern African Development Coordination Conference (SADCC) formed by South Africa's neighbours in 1980. Under the heading 'Dependence in Context', the Declaration states that

Southern Africa is dependent on the Republic of South Africa as a focus of transport and communications, an exporter of goods and services and as an importer of goods and cheap labour. This dependence is not a natural phenomenon nor is it simply the result of a free market economy. The ... [SADCC States] were, in varying degrees, deliberately incorporated – by metropolitan powers, colonial rulers and large corporations – into the colonial and sub-colonial structures centring in general on the Republic of South Africa. The development of national economies as balanced units, let alone the welfare of the people of Southern Africa, played no part in the economic integration strategy. Not surprisingly, therefore, Southern Africa is fragmented, grossly exploited and subject to manipulation by outsiders. ... Future development must aim at the reduction of dependence not only on the Republic of South Africa, but also on any single external State or group of States. ... Our urgent task now is to include economic liberation in our programmes and priorities. ... It is necessary to liberate our economies from their dependence. ... [7]

Indeed, this 'dependence' of the neighbouring countries on South Africa became not only a matter of conventional academic wisdom but also, in effect, both an article of faith and a litmus test of the political bona fides of any analysis of the political economy of the region. Its entrenched ideological position is well-illustrated by Arne Tostensen's comment that 'the dependence of the Southern African states on their giant neighbour ...

South Africa . . . has become an axiom in practically any discussion of the political economy . . . of the region.'[8]

The consequences of all this for the region will be discussed later. (Suffice to say for the moment that they were profound.) Of more immediate interest is the validity of the hypothesis upon which such unquestioning reliance was placed. In this respect, the position is somewhat disturbing. For, despite the volume of attention accorded to it, pinning down the nature of this form of 'dependence' and explaining the relationship between its economic and its political components have proved elusive tasks. There have been three main reasons for this.

First, those who have employed the concept have given it a very wide range of definitions and interpretations. Sometimes it has been seen as specific to particular contexts or circumstances; at other times it has been interpreted so widely as to be almost tautological: in one famous phrase, dependence appears sometimes to reduce to the statement that 'less developed countries are poor because they are dependent, and any character- istics that they display signify dependence.'[9] As Ian Little has noted, in discussions of dependence it is common for 'all key words . . . [to be] placed in quotation marks because their meanings are unclear'.[10]

Second, the strong ideological associations which dependence acquired with the neo-Marxist and neo-imperialist paradigms have sometimes been more of a hindrance than a help in analyses of international economic relations. On the one hand, there is the obvious and undeniable fact that the industrialized countries 'have considerable economic and political lever- age' over the developing countries. On the other hand, the major contri- bution of 'dependence' to the understanding of this problem has all too often appeared to be limited to 'pages of rhetoric, full of pejorative terms . . . but [lacking] precise definitions'.[11] Moreover, both the arguments and the terms employed in them – monopoly capitalism, exploitation, surplus (profit), etc. – are (deliberately) rendered value-laden, with the result that ideological assertions squeeze out systematic analysis.[12]

Third, equally unhelpful has been the assertion of 'dependence' as a condition which denies that 'LDC governments possess any leverages at all, or have any influence whatsoever over their fates'.[13] Apart from being a counsel of despair, this assertion was not only not substantiated, but in face was at odds with the evident capacity of developing countries all over the world to display widely varying degrees of political and economic self- determination. Indeed, a curious feature of the analysis of 'dependence' (as opposed to its policy implications), is that it does not readily appear to accommodate a role for the state as a decision-making unit.[14] Instead, the emphasis is on the domestic and international relationships between class forces, and particularly between the class interests of different and contend- ing 'fractions of capital'. These class forces assume (or are assigned) different roles and statuses within the international political economy, and the role of national governments in determining the nature and structure of their countries' international economic relations becomes secondary to the role of this class-determined international economic order.

These are general weaknesses of the 'dependence' paradigm. However, they are particularly pertinent to Southern Africa. Even the most casual glance at the voluminous literature on Southern African 'dependence' will confirm that the first two criticisms are self-evidently valid; and the third weakness makes the application of the paradigm to the region especially ironical: as will be shown later, in Southern Africa, national autonomy is highly prized and national interests in international exchange relations are frequently and strongly articulated by and through national governments.

The 'dependence' approach undoubtedly offered valuable and important analytical insights into the ways that the social, economic and political interests of different classes and interest groups interact to determine their relative positions in society and how they use their status and their power to advance those interests. However, its weaknesses contributed to a lack of clarity both on the operational validity of the 'dependence' concept, and on its policy implications (which were seldom given explicit content). This, in turn, served to undermine the general currency of 'dependence' theory in the study of international economic relations. As Little puts it, 'The main doctrines of the dependency school have found little acceptance. Few outside a small magic circle would agree that desirable development is impossible if there is much contact with foreign capitalism. Few leaders of less developed countries could admit to the role in which most of them are cast.'[15]

Yet, the notion of 'dependence' as a characteristic which constrains 'dependent' countries in some undesirable – if neither well-defined nor well-understood – manner still carries a powerful intuitive appeal. Furthermore, to judge by the continuing references to it, it is still popularly assumed to have some analytical and policy relevance in the international political economy in general and in Southern Africa in particular. For this reason alone, the concept demands further examination, especially to clarify the economic aspects of 'dependent' relations, which (as the wording of the Lusaka Declaration, quoted earlier, demonstrates) are the primary sources of concern.

This examination is taken up in the next two chapters. The first chapter deals with the measurement of the extent of economic dependence: What are the appropriate yardsticks for measuring dependence in principle and what are the difficulties of obtaining such measures in practice? The second chapter considers the adverse economic consequences – the costs – which would ensue for the dependent party from loss, or interruption, of its exchange relations: What is the nature of the relevant costs and how extensive are they?

6 Measuring economic dependence

Discussions of economic dependence clearly require some yardstick(s) for measuring the extent of dependence. Since dependence is likely to be costly (in some sense), the size of the costs might be thought to constitute one yardstick. However, the costs of dependence are themselves likely to be determined, at least in part, by its extent. Measuring the degree of dependence would therefore appear to be logically prior to assessing its costs.

The most comprehensive attempt to clarify the economic issues involved in determining the overall dependence of a country on its economic relations with other countries is to be found in the work of Michaely.[1] Though limiting himself largely to the question of foreign trade in commodities, Michaely has amply demonstrated the complexities of both the theoretical and the empirical aspects of the dependence concept – complexities which are usually overlooked in discussions of dependence, especially in contexts like that of Southern Africa.

It is not possible here to do much more than provide a summary of some of the main issues considered by Michaely and of the conclusions which he reaches. Unfortunately, lack of data also precludes detailed application of the measures which Michaely develops to the economies of Southern Africa. Wherever possible, however, the relevance of the theoretical issues for any discussion of dependence in the region will be illustrated. Michaely interprets dependence on trade (or any other aspect of economic exchange) as implying

vulnerability . . . to its complete disappearance or to disturbances in it. . . . The more severe the vulnerability, the heavier the dependence. . . . Vulnerability is a function of two components. One is the *extent of the damage* that would occur should the disruption . . . take place; the other is the *likelihood* . . . of the disruption actually occurring. . . . The larger either of the two components is – given the other – the larger is the vulnerability and the higher the degree of dependence.[2]

As will become apparent, neither the extent of the damage nor the risk that trade will be disturbed are simple concepts. For both concepts, the nature, structure and composition of the relevant trading relations are of crucial theoretical and empirical importance, especially in so far as they relate to the ease with which the consequences of interruptions to trade can be mitigated by substitute activities. Moreover, finding appropriate empirical measures for the two concepts is a task fraught with obstacles. The general definitional, measurement and compositional aspects of the scale of the losses will be dealt with first, leaving the probabilistic aspects of the problem until later.

In economic terms, the first component of one party's dependence or vulnerability – the extent of the damage – must be measured by the overall extent of that party's 'openness' to economic exchanges with other parties. This is true even for individual economic agents. A Robinson Crusoe who lives a wholly subsistence existence, producing only for his own consumption, can experience no trade dependence. But the moment specialization begins to emerge and individuals begin to rely on exchanges with other economic actors to satisfy some of their needs, by definition they become trade dependent. In other words, all exchange renders its participants hostage both to the fortunes and to the actions of their trading partners. Clearly, the greater the degree of openness to trade, the greater (in some sense) will be the dependence on trade.

But what constitutes the degree of openness to trade? In formal, economic-theoretic terms, openness should be measured by the size of the 'gains from trade' relative to the total gains from all economic activities. The ideal measure of these gains (whether at the level of a Namibian labourer selling his labour services to the local farmer, or of Botswana engaging in international trade with Zimbabwe), would be the (proportionate) increase in total 'economic welfare' due to participation in trade, relative to the level of welfare without trade. The degree of dependence would then be measured equivalently by the extent of the loss in total 'welfare' which would ensue from the complete cessation or denial of trade.[3]

Individual trading relations and dependence

Though it might, at first glance, seem somewhat incongruous, the example of the gains from trade for an individual economic actor can usefully be used to anticipate some of the issues which are pertinent to the analysis of economic dependence at the country level.

Individuals who are not Robinson Crusoes do not normally engage in only one single act of exchange but in a range (or 'portfolio') of exchanges. A key purpose of this diversification of trades is to seek, even if only implicitly, to guard against the risk of one or more acts of exchange failing to materialize (for whatever reason). In other words, a diversified portfolio is an insurance against the 'dependence' which might ensue from putting all one's eggs in one basket.

On the other hand, there are conceivable circumstances in which this form of insurance might become impossible. Consider, for example, a patient who contracts a life-threatening disease and whose life depends upon continued supplies of a particular drug. Clearly, this would represent a situation of potential 'critical' dependence. Should the supplies somehow be permanently cut-off or exhausted, the dependence would become real. Prior stockpiling of supplies may have provided some temporary defence, but in the absence of any substitute, the dependence would be total and the patient would die. To put this point in more technical parlance, dependence in this sense becomes a function of the elasticity of supply of the good in question. The lower the elasticity of supply, the higher will be the welfare loss and hence the higher the degree of dependence.[4]

In the above example, the welfare loss is total because the supply elasticity is (ultimately) zero. A similar result can arise when the inelasticity lies on the demand (consumption) side, rather than on the production or supply side. Suppose that an alternative drug is available, which would be life-preserving, but which induces such nausea that the patient refuses to take it. In this extreme case, the reduction in welfare would still be the same, namely the death of the patient. In the final analysis, the dependence is due in this instance to a total inflexibility in the patient's preferences. In both the above instances, the yardstick for measuring the extent of the dependence is the patient's own subjective valuation of his/her welfare. Death in either of these circumstances can therefore reasonably be regarded as equally welfare-reducing.

This hypothetical example, extreme though it is, illustrates three important features of economic dependence. First, it confirms that the relationship between dependence and the gains from trade is not one-dimensional. Finding a single measure of 'openness' is therefore likely to be difficult. Second, it shows that some exchange relations are more readily replaceable than others, and that this has a direct bearing on the extent of the damage which would ensue should the relationship be disturbed or interrupted. Thus the composition of the exchange relations must also be an important qualifying factor in interpreting aggregate measures of dependence.[5] Third, it demonstrates that there is a crucial distinction between the potential for dependence and its realization. There is no (evident) damage if the relationship is not disturbed. However, concern about the possibility of disturbance induces changes of behaviour (e.g. keeping a stock of the drug in excess of immediate needs). As will be seen, these results all generalize to exchange relations involving groups of individuals. The most obvious (though not the only) unit for grouping individuals is, of course, the 'nation'. Somewhat misleadingly, however, the standard unit of analysis in international economic relations has become, not the nation, but the geographic entity of 'the country' or 'the national economy' – misleading because it encourages the tendency to conceive of the exchanges as being conducted by the composite unit itself, rather than by the individual actors of which it is composed.

Openness, trade ratios and the gains from trade

The ideal measure of openness, as already noted, would be the changes in 'economic welfare' arising from the gains from trade. But gains and losses in 'welfare', whether for individuals or countries, are not directly measurable in practice. Proxy measures for openness are therefore required instead. At the country level, the most commonly used proxies involve measures of the size (expressed in terms of monetary values) of trade relative to some measure of total income. The trade ratio most commonly employed is that of the value of exports plus imports relative to GNP (or GDP). Other things equal, the higher this ratio, the greater the measured degree of trade dependence.[6]

Data presented by Michaely for forty-one countries, ranging from some of the poorest to the richest and from some of the smallest to the largest, show that, empirically, measures of the ratio of their total trade (exports plus imports) to GDP in 1960 and 1978 ranged from as low as 10 per cent to as high as 212 per cent. This would appear to suggest vast differences between countries in the degree of openness and, hence, in dependence upon trade, although more than half of Michaely's sample had trade ratios between 30 per cent to 80 per cent.[7] Trade ratios in Southern Africa generally fall within this latter range. In 1987, Mozambique had the lowest ratio (39 per cent of GDP) and Zambia the highest (80 per cent). Malawi, Tanzania, Zimbabwe and South Africa (excluding gold) were all within the 46 to 49 per cent range.[8] By this measure, therefore, trade dependence in the region's economies does not appear to be abnormally high.

Interpreting trade ratios

That large cross-country differences should exist in the ratio of traded goods to total output is scarcely surprising: both the propensity to import goods from abroad and the ability to sell goods in foreign markets can be expected to vary significantly from country to country.

However, as Michaely is at pains to point out, the operational validity of these trade ratios is frequently severely limited. For any given country, the degree of openness suggested by the trade ratios needs to be qualified – in some instances, severely qualified – by information on a wide range of other variables. For this reason, too, cross-country comparisons also need to be treated with the utmost caution. The same caveat applies to attempts to compare degrees of trade dependence in any particular country at different points in time.

Systematic elucidation of all these caveats is beyond the scope of this study. Brief summaries of the issues will therefore have to suffice. Two qualifications relate directly to the validity of the information concerning the degree of openness which is conveyed by the trade ratios themselves. Four further qualifications relate to the composition of trade and the ease with which interrupted trade can be replaced by other – especially domestic – activities.

Adjusting for imports of intermediate inputs

The first qualification derives from the fact that, in all countries, some imported goods (e.g. raw materials) are 'intermediate' goods, i.e. they are used as inputs in local production, rather than for 'final' domestic consumption. Since imported intermediate inputs can be used in the production of goods which are to be exported, the degree of openness suggested by the simple trade ratios will be overstated. The value of exports (the numerator in the ratio) will include the value of any imported intermediate inputs used in their production, whereas total income (the denominator) will – by definition – reflect only the value added by domestic resources. Thus, if a country's exports have a high import content, the simple total trade ratio (exports plus imports relative to GDP) will overstate the true degree of openness.[9]

In principle, therefore, the simple trade ratios need to be adjusted to take account of this. In practice, lack of data frequently makes it impossible to get accurate figures. Estimates made by Michaely for fifteen countries suggest that the distortion is likely to be especially significant when the unadjusted figures show relatively high total trade ratios (e.g. 50 per cent and higher).[10] Since these estimates relate predominantly to developed, industrialized countries, it is difficult to draw conclusions for the openness of less-developed countries. There are, however, a priori reasons to expect that the overstatement inherent in the trade ratios will be generally less severe in semi-industrialized developing countries, and least severe in low-income primary-exporting countries with relatively little manufacturing activity.[11]

In Southern Africa, these considerations would suggest that South Africa, and to a lesser extent, Zimbabwe would be somewhat less trade-dependent than suggested by their simple trade ratios on account of their manufacturing sectors. The same would probably also apply to Zambia in so far as the copper industry is reliant on imported capital equipment and other productive inputs.

The problem of price changes

The second qualification arises in relation to attempts to measure changes in the degree of openness (and hence of trade dependence) by comparing trade ratios at different points in time. Two preliminary comments are apposite here. First, in any country, openness to trade will not be a static phenomenon: it is likely to vary continuously from one period to another. As both domestic and international economic conditions change, the ratio of the volumes of goods which any given country buys and sells abroad to total income will change continuously.

Second, these variations, which can be substantial, cannot be measured in practice without reference to prices. Because bags of maize and barrels of oil cannot be added together, trade ratios are measured not in volume terms, but in value terms, i.e. by evaluating the physical volumes of exports, imports and domestic production at their market prices.

This gives rise, in turn, to another problem. If, between period 1 and period 2, the prices of these goods change, then the consequent change in the trade ratio can be measured either in terms of current prices (i.e. the prices actually ruling in each period), or of constant prices (i.e. the prices of one period only). Whichever set of prices is used – and there are no theoretical grounds for preferring one to another – will lead to different measures of the change in openness over the period in question.[12] Indeed, the two methods can lead not only to different conclusions about the extent of change in trade dependence, but even about the direction of change.[13] Thus, both for comparisons within given countries at different points in time, and for comparisons between different countries over time, there are potentially severe pitfalls in relying on the use of trade ratios.[14]

In practical terms, whether the two methods – using current prices or constant prices – will in fact lead to significantly different conclusions about changes in a country's trade dependence, will depend upon the magnitude of the price movements involved. This problem is likely to be particularly acute in the case of countries – like those in Southern Africa – where the prices of the goods which they buy and sell internationally – but especially the prices of their primary exports – are subject to considerable fluctuations from year to year. In short, comparisons between the trade ratios for a particular Southern African country at two different points in time, whether calculated on the basis of current or of constant prices, will reveal relatively little at face value about the true extent of changes in the degree of openness and, hence, in the degree of trade dependence.

The relevance of the commodity composition of trade flows

The use and interpretation of trade ratios as measures of dependence is further complicated by questions concerning the structure and composition of a country's trading relations. Only through disaggregation of both imports and exports can an accurate assessment be made of the overall degree of openness.

Ease of replacement of imports

There are several structural aspects which impinge upon the ease with which imported goods can be replaced with domestically produced goods, whether in production or in consumption. This is the generalized country-level analogue of the earlier life-saving medicine example. Put most briefly, the true extent of dependence again depends significantly on the elasticities of supply and demand for importable goods, but the determinants of these elasticities are, to say the least, complex.

An example will serve to illustrate the point. Suppose that Botswana and Namibia were equally 'open' in terms of their total trade ratios. Now consider one particular category of imports, namely fish. Suppose both countries are suddenly precluded from importing fish. Since Namibia has a major fishing industry and Botswana does not, fish supply is less elastic in Botswana than in Namibia. Because Botswana is less easily able than Namibia to replace imported fish with home-produced fish, Botswana would seem to be more dependent than Namibia in respect of fish imports.

But the argument clearly cannot rest there. First, Namibian consumer preferences may be more inelastic when it comes to fish: Botswanans may be happier than Namibians to eat beef instead of fish. To this extent, Botswana may appear less dependent on fish imports than Namibia. Second, the ratio of fish imports to total fish availability (imports plus local production) in the two countries may differ. If the proportion of total fish consumption which is met from imports is higher in Botswana than in Namibia, on this criterion Botswana would again be more dependent. And third, the ratio of fish imports to total imports in the two countries may differ significantly. If this ratio is higher in Namibia, then Namibia would seem to be more dependent on fish imports.

Thus, whether Botswana or Namibia is more dependent upon fish imports, in the sense of the lack of ease with which domestic production can substitute for the unexpected loss of a foreign source of supply cannot be measured by any simple ratios. Furthermore, similar considerations will apply to all other imported commodities. Nor is it easy to conceive of any measures which will neatly encapsulate all these different influences, some of which have offsetting, and others reinforcing, effects on the degree of dependence. In principle, some of these disaggregated effects can be captured by means of weighted averages. For example, Michaely has formulated a weighted index to calculate a country's aggregate dependence due to the ratio of imports to total availability across all goods. But leaving aside the almost inevitable lack of appropriate data, which usually means that even these indices have to be proxied by other measures, this still deals with only one aspect of the problem.[15]

The relative importance of intermediate goods in imports

Further dimensions to the problem arise from the expectation that imports of intermediate goods will be more difficult to replace than imports of 'final' goods, such as consumer goods. One reason noted by Michaely is that much trade in final goods is due to 'product differentiation'. For example, both Zimbabwe and South Africa sell each other similar kinds of clothing. Consequently, unless there are extreme rigidities in consumers' preferences, the loss of particular brands or variants of such goods should be relatively easily made good by alternative, domestically-produced goods. By contrast, imports of intermediate goods often arise because of supply-side inelasticities: the lack of the capacity and of the requisite domestic resources to manufacture such goods requires that they be imported, and their replacement by domestic substitutes is thus more problematic. Thus, in the above example, if Botswana imported fish mainly to manufacture animal feeds for its beef production rather than for 'final' consumption, its dependence would be correspondingly greater.[16]

As an extension of the latter point, many production processes require inputs in roughly fixed proportions. Consequently, the loss of supplies of particular intermediate goods – especially those for which there is no (or only limited) local production capacity – can lead to rapid and considerable disruption to domestic productive activity. The more stages of production into which a given input enters – fuel is an obvious example – the more dependent the economy will appear. Unfortunately, however, it is again easier to note the existence of this effect in principle than to obtain the required data to measure it empirically.[17]

The relative importance of exports by industrial group

Compositional issues are also important on the export side. If the export market for a particular industry is cut off, the ease or otherwise of the adjustment process for the exporting country will depend partly on the share of exports in that industry's total sales.[18] Other things equal, the higher the share of exports in total sales, the more difficult it will be to replace the lost exports with domestic sales. For example, virtually all of Zambia's copper output and virtually all of Zimbabwe's tobacco crop is exported. On this criterion therefore, the two countries could be adjudged equally highly dependent. In the event, in the face of the sanctions which followed UDI, Rhodesia's tobacco growers did find a domestic buyer in the form of the Rhodesian government, thereby substantially mitigating the dependence, whereas Zambia was less fortunate.

But any measure of dependence based on export shares would clearly also need to take account of the extent to which the country's exports are concentrated or dispersed among industry groups. For this, a weighted index of the ratio of exports to total output is required. The more concentrated exports are in a few key industry groups, the higher would be the value of this index, and hence the higher the degree of dependence. Moreover, it can be anticipated that dependence, as measured by this kind of index, will be most severe in low income countries, such as those in Southern Africa. As Michaely puts it, 'less-developed economies tend to specialize, by and large, in a very limited range of export goods, in each of which their own home market would normally be small relative to the size of exports.'[19]

A related issue, even more difficult to measure, is the specificity of the resources employed by the industry in question. Other things equal, the more specific the resources to that line of production, the harder it will be to reallocate them to production of other goods, and the greater will be the net reduction in output and employment.[20] The Zambian copper and Rhodesian tobacco examples are again instructive. The resources used in copper mining, especially the capital equipment, have few alternative employment possibilities. By contrast, the land and capital equipment, as well as the labour, employed in tobacco farming could be (and were) reallocated to other forms of agricultural production, albeit with a time lag.

Instability in commodity composition

A further issue which is likely to have particular relevance for developing countries again relates to efforts to determine trends in trade dependence over time. As with the price fluctuation problem discussed earlier, the commodity composition of the exports and imports of developing countries is also subject to substantial changes over relatively short periods of time. These compositional changes are, of course, partly a reflection of the impact of the price changes themselves. But they can also be due – in the case of exports, for example – to climate-related fluctuations in harvests of agricultural commodities or to supply difficulties in minerals production. In the case of imports, they can again be partly climate-determined (especially as regards the scale of food imports), but they can also be due to policy changes, such as currency devaluations or import restrictions – the latter being most relevant when there are shortages of foreign exchange. Considerations of this nature are clearly pertinent in any discussion of dependence in Southern Africa.

In sum, three general conclusions stand out from the foregoing discussion. First, it is clear that the degree of dependence facing any particular country is crucially affected by the structure and composition of its external trade relations. This applies both to the question of measuring dependence and to the implications which dependence could have for efforts to mitigate the effects of interruptions by replacing the relevant trade relations with other activities, particularly within the domestic economy. For these reasons alone, there is need for the utmost care in extrapolating from a simple overall trade ratio for a given country to conclusions about the degree of its trade dependence.

Second, empirically, there are severe difficulties with regard to measuring these various effects, because the data requirements are demanding. Third, in the case of developing countries, a number of the issues discussed lead to the general presumption that dependence, as measured by simple trade ratios, is likely to be understated. Against this, however, the extremes of both price and volume fluctuations which frequently characterize the trading relations of developing countries, provide grounds for considerable distrust of the accuracy with which even relatively sophisticated measures can reflect the degree of dependence of individual countries at particular points in time.

The likelihood of trade disruption

The discussion so far has emphasized the issues and the difficulties involved in measuring the size of the economic welfare losses which would in fact ensue were trade links to be disturbed or, in the extreme, completely severed. But, as Michaely's definition of dependence makes clear, it is also necessary to consider the probability or likelihood that the costs associated with dependence will actually be incurred. An assessment of this risk component of dependence is of the utmost importance, since country X could appear highly dependent on the openness criterion, yet, given a low risk of disturbance, may well be less dependent than country Y, for which trade is much less important relative to total income, but is subject to high levels of uncertainty.[21]

It will be clear that the major determinant of this risk must be the possibility that, for political or strategic reasons, deliberate disruption or severance of trading relations will occur. However, Michaely demonstrates that there are also purely economic determinants of the likelihood that the damage will in fact be incurred. As with openness, it is the compositional characteristics of trade which are most relevant. In other words, there are some elements in the structures of exchange relations which may predispose some participants to be more at risk from trade interruptions – and hence more dependent – than others.

These economic determinants are discussed at length by Michaely.[22] For present purposes, however, it will suffice merely to note the key factors in general terms. For any country, the main characteristics which would contribute to greater risk of trade disruption include a lack of diversity in the commodity composition of its trade; a high share of the world markets for its exports and for its imports; a lack of competitiveness in the structure of its export and import markets; and a lack of diversity in the geographic composition of its trading partners.

In short, neither of the two distinct economic components of the measure of a country's economic dependence – the degree of openness and the likelihood of disturbances – are independent of the nature and composition of the country's trading relations themselves. It follows that, even without taking account of any non-economic determinants of dependence, sweeping generalizations about the extent of a country's dependence are likely to be highly misleading.

7 The costs of economic dependence

Economic exchange confers net gains on all the participants. It follows that any interruption of exchange correspondingly must involve all relevant participants in the loss of those gains. From this perspective, dependence in exchange relations is a matter of concern only in so far as it imposes, or threatens to impose, costs on the dependent party. As Arad *et al.* have put it, 'Reciprocal effects among countries or among actors in different countries . . . must be distinguished from inter-connectedness. . . . Where interactions do not imply significant costly effects, there is simply inter-connectedness.'[1]

The 'costly effects' to which any trade and other exchange dependence might give rise fall into a number of different categories. Here it is helpful to distinguish first, between private and social costs, and second, between actual and potential costs. In discussing these costs, it will sometimes be analytically more convenient to restrict the examination in the first instance to the view from one side of the exchange relation only, even though (as will be apparent) the issues involved are pertinent for the parties on both sides of the relevant transactions.

Several steps in the ensuing analysis can be illustrated by reference to two typical economic transactions in Southern Africa, which are widely considered to provide the foundations for economic 'dependence' in the region. They involve four wholly fictional (but again representative) economic actors. The one transaction is between a Malawian migrant worker, Mr Zomba, and his Zimbabwean employer, Mr Kariba; the other is between a Zambian copperbelt engineering firm, Zamco, and its South African supplier of machine tools, Safco.

The private costs of dependence

In any act of economic exchange (whether international or otherwise) certain unavoidable 'opportunity costs' are incurred by all the individual economic agents who participate in the transaction. By devoting resources to the transaction, each participant precludes those resources from being applied elsewhere. The opportunity cost is therefore the benefit, which each participant forgoes, from the best available alternative course of action.

By accepting work from Mr Kariba, for example, Mr Zomba passes up all the gains which he could obtain from any other job choices available to him. In general, this opportunity cost will be positive, unless Mr Zomba would otherwise be wholly unemployed, in which case there would be zero opportunity cost. Equally, by acquiring the benefits inherent in the machine which it purchases from Safco, Zamco forgoes the possibility of using the same funds to purchase (say) a German machine.

Opportunity costs are therefore simply measures of the value to the economic actor concerned of the resources being devoted to the transaction. Unless the fact of dependence somehow destroys the productive capacity of these resources, their opportunity costs cannot legitimately be counted as contributing to the 'costliness' of (say) Mr Zomba's dependence upon any transaction with his trading partner, Mr Kariba. However, any loss of income which Zomba might suffer clearly does constitute part of the costs of dependence.[2]

Instead, the relevant costs of dependence are those which would arise for Mr Zomba (or for Zamco) if their transactions were to be disturbed for reasons not of their own choosing. Such disturbances could be the result of deliberate – and unilateral – termination of the transaction by one party. For example, Kariba may dismiss Zomba. In this case, Kariba might be regarded as 'exploiting' Zomba's 'dependence', and the resultant cost to Mr Zomba is what Arad et al. have called the 'cost of dissociation', namely 'that cost which A [in this case Zomba] incurs if B [Kariba] decides to sever economic relations [with Zomba]'.[3] Alternatively, the disturbance could arise simply from exogenous changes in market conditions affecting either or both parties to the transaction. Bankruptcy may prevent Safco from supplying the machine to Zamco; or the Zambian government may deny Zamco the foreign exchange to complete the purchase. Despite the absence of the deliberate intent implied by the above definition, Zamco clearly also incurs dissociation costs. Indeed, Zomba and Zamco would incur dissociation costs no matter what the source of the disturbance. Of course, the costs would be much less severe if the disturbance were merely temporary – a labour strike at Safco, or Mr Kariba recants his decision – and the relationships were not actually severed.

There are, in turn, two components to Zomba's and Zamco's dissociation costs. One is the loss of the current benefit derived from the existence of the transaction: wages and the output from the machine. Part of this loss may be potentially recoverable through substitution of an alternative transaction with a third party. Zomba may find another job and Zamco another supplier. But the element of current cost will still be non-zero.[4] This would apply even if the dissociation were temporary. The second component arises when the dissociation is both total and permanent. This leads to a 'sunk' cost, which refers to the 'economic resources [which] are permanently lost'.[5] Even at the simplest of levels, economic transactions cannot take place without some investment of resources by the individual economic agents concerned. Mr Zomba will have made several such investments, including his travel costs from Malawi to Zimbabwe, his search and information costs in finding the job with Mr Kariba, and probably also the costs of obtaining a work permit or meeting other bureaucratic requirements in Zimbabwe. If he can no longer work in Zimbabwe, he loses all these investments: these are his sunk costs.

Similarly, Zamco will have devoted resources to establishing its relationship with Safco; it will have trained its workers to operate Safco's equipment, bought in stocks of materials to be used in conjunction with Safco machines, and spent time and money on obtaining trade permits and acquainting itself with the laws and regulations regarding trade with a South African firm. Sunk costs thus comprise all those specialized investments allocated to the severed trade. In so far as these resources were specific to that trade and therefore have no alternative uses, they are not recoverable. Even where they are transferable to alternative uses, but only after modification and/or some lapse of time – e.g. Zamco's workers adapt their skills to a replacement German machine – there is still some permanent loss involved.

It must follow from all this that the costs of dissociation to the 'dependent' parties will rise with the value of the benefits which they derive from the relationship. It also follows (from the second component) that their costs of dissociation are likely to be higher (a) the less the diversity of their trade relations with other parties (i.e. the fewer the alternative uses to which Zamco and Mr Zomba can put the resources already invested in the relationship), and (b) the greater the value of those resources.

Insurance against dissociation

An obvious question which arises is whether these losses from dissociation can be avoided through insurance. One method open to Zamco for insuring against the losses arising from temporary interruptions to supplies of spare parts for its Safco machine is the normal everyday business practice of holding inventories. In effect, the opportunity costs involved in stockpiling – such as the interest which Zamco forgoes in paying for the spares before they are required and the cost of the facilities needed for storing them – constitute the insurance premium. Beyond that, it may indeed be possible formally to insure against some of the risks inherent in the potential for dissociation: insurance policies may cover delivery delays or Zamco's contract with Safco may entitle it to compensation. In the event of dissociation, this would limit Zamco's own costs to the insurance premium and contract costs and would displace the remaining costs onto other economic agents, such as the insurance company.

Insurance could not, however, obviate the costs being incurred by someone. It can only redistribute them, in this instance entirely via (voluntary) market-based transactions. Moreover, it is clear that only a small proportion of all the risks of dissociation can be insured against via the market. On the other hand, to the extent that Zamco chooses to avoid buying its machines only from Safco, then it is implicitly insuring internally against the costs of any disturbance of the link with Safco. On the assumption that Safco is the optimum supplier, then the cost to Zamco is the smaller (net) benefit which it derives from buying other machines rather than relying solely on Safco. (It will be self-evident that Mr Zomba has very few opportunities for insurance of this kind.)

Apart from these strictly limited elements of insurance, however, it must be emphasized that the costs of dissociation are normally only potential, not actual, costs: they will not actually be incurred by Zamco unless its relationship with Safco is disturbed or severed. The nature of Zamco's (or Mr Zomba's) 'dependence' will therefore be qualitatively different, and the extent of dependence will be quantitatively different, according to the degree of certainty or uncertainty surrounding the perpetuation of the relationship. If they believe that their respective exchange relationships will continue, there would seem to be a lesser element of dependence – and hence a lower (potential) cost – than if they lack confidence in the permanence of the relationships. Thus, the degree, and the cost, of Zomba's and Zamco's dependence on Kariba and Safco must be measured also in relation to the probability that the links will be disturbed or severed.[6]

The probability of dissociation

This issue of the probability of disturbance is as crucial for determining the costs, as it is for determining the degree, of dependence. Once again the problem of dissociation will be determined by a number of variables, some of which are 'objective' (structural) economic variables, and others of which are behavioural or political variables. For example, the probability of disturbance will depend in part on the structure and composition of a 'dependent' party's trading relations. The diversity and substitutability of the machines which Zamco uses, the diversity of its sources of these machines, and the economic structures of the markets for the machines will all have differing implications for the probability of dissociation. In other words, each trading relationship will carry with it a different level of risk of disturbance – differences which are, at least to some extent, objectively measurable. Even for Mr Zomba, the risk of dismissal by Mr Kariba will vary according to the state of the labour market, being lower in times of labour shortage and higher in times of labour abundance.

But the probabilities will also depend upon considerations which are inherently unmeasurable. For example, both Mr Zomba's and Zamco's own attitudes to perpetuation of their respective relationships may be of importance to the issue of 'dependence'. If Mr Zomba were to insult Mr

Kariba, or if Zamco were to be slow in paying Safco for its machine, then the extent to which each is dependent upon the other party to the exchange is not independent of their own behaviour; and the costs of their dependence are likewise not wholly exogenous to the relationships. Clearly, it is the significant subjective element to this aspect – both Zomba's behaviour and Zomba's assessment of the risks will depend upon his perception of Kariba's intentions – which renders the probabilities less readily measurable (though no less relevant for that fact).

More generally, of course, the probability of dissociation will be affected, often crucially, by a wide range of 'political' variables, which will be beyond the dependent party's control or influence. For example, the Zimbabwean government may decide to repatriate Malawian workers, or the South African authorities may refuse to issue Safco with an export licence for its machine.

The social costs of dependence

Whilst the private costs of dependence on foreign trade relate only to the costs borne by individual economic agents, such as Zamco and Mr Zomba, the social costs refer to those incurred by the countries (or nations or societies) as a whole to which these agents belong. The social costs of trade dependence for Malawi (say), whether on one particular country (e.g. Zimbabwe) or on the rest of the world, can be measured, in principle, by the difference between national income before and after dissociation has taken place.[7]

Broadly speaking, there will be two components to these costs. The first is the reduction in national income due to the interference with trade: the gains from trade will be smaller, hence national income will be smaller. The second component is again the sunk costs, which are the losses arising from the redundancy of the infrastructural and institutional investments and the specialized resources which have been devoted to facilitating economic relations with the erstwhile trading partner. But these costs would not consist simply of the aggregated private dissociation costs of all the individual participants – like Mr Zomba – who make up Malawi's relevant trade relations. The total loss of Malawi's national income from severance of all its economic relations with one or more countries would include some additional losses not accounted for by the sum of private costs.

Most of these extra losses would likely arise as a consequence of the non-economic (political, strategic, etc.) aspects of dependence, which have been mentioned above, but they will still be measurable in terms of economic resource costs. However, unlike the private costs of dissociation, which – except for a small insurance element – are predominantly potential costs, the social costs of dissociation have much larger 'real' or actual components.

Some of these extra costs are again in the nature of 'insurances'. If, say, Zambia were to consider itself economically dependent upon South Africa, then Zambia will probably take steps to protect itself against the threat of disturbance or severance of its economic links with South Africa. In general, these steps will consist in investments which, in the absence of uncertainty about these links, would not otherwise be undertaken.

Four broad comments can be made about insurances of this kind. First, the costs to Zambia – the size of the 'insurance premium' – consist in the lower returns on these extra investments compared with the returns which would have been obtained had the resources been put to their 'first best' use. Second, except in cases where the original investments in trade links with South Africa were seriously inefficient, or where the new investments exploit previously unrecognized 'infant industry' advantages, the conse-quent costs of these defensive measures could well be large. Third, though it is possible for the government of Zambia to pass part of the cost burden back onto individual economic agents (such as Zamco), this does not obviate the social cost; it merely redistributes it. In this instance, the redistribution is achieved through largely involuntary and non-market mechanisms, such as legislated requirements and the fiscal (tax) system. Fourth, the need to incur such costs is likely to be greater the higher the perceived risk that relations will be disturbed.

Again, therefore, the observations made earlier about the crucial role of the probability of dissociation between the individual economic actors, Zamco and Safco, apply *pari passu* to Zambia and South Africa. There will thus again be both structural and behavioural determinants of the risk, some of which will be objectively measurable and others not. Moreover, the risk can again be affected by Zambia's own behaviour within the relationship, rather than being determined solely by factors beyond Zambia's control. If Zambia were to impose restrictions on economic relations with South Africa, the risk that South Africa would 'exploit' Zambia's 'dependence' through dissociation would presumably alter.

Extreme examples of the social costs of insurances of this kind can indeed be found in the Southern African situation. One example is afforded by South Africa's considerable – and continuing – investments in oil-from-coal and oil-from-gas industries as an insurance against the possibility of oil sanctions. Though no authoritative estimates exist of the social cost (as defined above) of these investments, they can scarcely have been negligible, especially in view of the fact that the policy has already had to persist for more than thirty years. Another example can be found in the strenuous efforts made over the past decade by South Africa's neighbours to acquire or restore alternative transport routes to the coast. These investments rep-resented (at least in part) an attempt to insure against the possibility that Pretoria would deny them access to the trade routes through South Africa itself. However, less striking examples of such 'strategic' social investments can be found in virtually all countries. For example, the common desire to have one's own national airline or energy supply or steel plant is at least partially based on concern about 'dependence', i.e. about the possibility of dissociation. Many governments also finance – to a greater or lesser extent – the holding of national stockpiles of 'strategic' commodities, though this can again be, at best, only a temporary buffer against dissociation.

In addition to these actual social costs, there are again potential costs which would be incurred only if dissociation took place. These would include the costs of any steps not taken by private economic agents to make good the losses arising from dissociation but which the government considers to be necessary. They would also include the provision of any additional resources from the public purse to subsidize the costs to individual economic agents of switching to alternative sources of supply or of seeking out alternative markets. And they would include any efficiency losses arising from additional public expenditure to offset any adverse macroeconomic effects of dissociation, such as increased unemployment.

There are again extreme examples of such dissociation costs to be found in Southern Africa. The building of the Tazara railway line from Dar es Salaam to Zambia during the Rhodesian sanctions period was a major cost arising directly out of the dissociation from trade with Rhodesia. In addition, part of the cost burden of seeking to restore the damaged transport routes through Mozambique and Angola has been a response to dissociation caused by war. (In both of these examples, it should be noted that the social costs have been borne not only by the inhabitants of the countries concerned, but also – often in very large measure – by the taxpayers of the donor countries who financed the investments.)

To sum up, sticking strictly to the economic aspects of the problem, the costs imposed by the fact that a country is 'dependent' upon its foreign trade are borne both directly by the individual participants in the trade and indirectly by a wide range of other parties and interests both within the country and outside it. Furthermore, the actual extent of the costs depends crucially upon whether or not the 'dependence' in fact becomes binding. This, in turn, is a function of the probability that trade will in fact be disturbed.

8 The analysis of economic interdependence

Up to now, the discussion has focused on the nature and determinants of economic dependence, viewed largely from one side of an exchange relationship. Except in so far as the probability of dissociation depends in part upon the behaviour of a trading partner, the implications of the reciprocal nature of dependent relationships have so far been set aside. These implications must now be considered.

The general literature on economic interdependence happily lacks the fundamental ideological divisions which so bedevil discussions of economic dependence. Even so, there is again a decided lack of clarity on the real meaning of the concept, and particularly on the policy implications which flow from it. Few would dispute the interpretation of interdependence between nation-states as implying reciprocal or mutual dependence upon each other. However, this still begs understanding of the precise meanings of both 'mutual' and 'dependence', and it provides no direct pointers to the economic and political consequences which might flow from a situation of mutual dependence.

The early 'classical' view was that interdependence, thus interpreted, leads naturally to a convergence of interests between trading partners. Mutual reliance upon exchange relations and mutual enjoyment of the benefits derived therefrom were assumed to reduce the likelihood of conflict.[1] This view has been widely criticized as Utopian in that it denies the possibility that, underlying the partners' willingness to promote their exchange relations, there may be conflicting interests. Indeed, it would be irrational to assert that the pursuit of interdependence is incompatible with the pursuit of vested national self-interest. Moreover, there is no reason to suppose that one country's national self-interest should not diverge from, or conflict with, the interests of its trading partners. However, this potential for conflict has not prevented a significant increase in interdependence from taking place in the post-war era. On the contrary, interdependence has become both much more global in scope and much more complex in character.[2]

On the other hand, more 'modernist' arguments that the world is becoming a 'global village' in which national boundaries will become increasingly irrelevant show few signs of early realization. Countries may well be willing to countenance closer and more complex relations with each other, but even before the recent resurgence of nationalist aspirations in Eastern Europe there was little convincing evidence that nationalism yet appeared ready to allow the role of the nation-state in international economic relations to wither away. In short, as Keohane and Nye (1977) have emphasized, interdependence between nations does not imply absence of conflict between them.[3] It does, however, point to the need for new and different mechanisms for managing international relations. This is obviously relevant where political and economic pressures are pushing in opposing directions, and especially relevant where 'the self-determination of small nations [is] incompatible with unbridled economic power and complete economic interdependence'.[4]

An increase in the scope or volume of bilateral exchange relations necessarily has two consequences for both partners: it increases the gains from trade; and it increases the level of interdependence with the other partner.[5] The former effect is unambiguously positive; the latter effect may be either positive or negative, in that more interdependence may be viewed as either a good or a bad thing. It follows that each individual state has to determine for itself the extent to which it is willing to trade off its political autonomy and sovereignty for greater economic interdependence.

From the perspective of economic theory, stating the problem in this form suggests that its solution must embody two key components: the determination by each country of the 'optimal' level of exchange relations with its trading partners; and the determination of the 'terms of trade' between the trading partners, i.e. the relative prices at which their mutual economic transactions take place.

Economic analysis can cope passably well with the first problem, at least in principle. In so far as increasing interdependence involves both increasing benefits and increasing costs (including the surrender of sovereignty), it may be assumed that it is subject (ultimately) to diminishing, possibly even negative, returns. The optimal level of interdependence would thus be, by definition, the point at which the marginal benefits and marginal costs of an increase in trading relations exactly offset each other.

Standard economic analysis clearly also has something to say about the determination of the terms of trade. The price ratios which will emerge will depend crucially on the relative 'market power' – the bargaining strengths – of the trading partners. The partner with the greater market power will have the greater capacity to influence or manipulate the terms of trade in its favour. This partner will be able to 'extract' higher selling prices, and to 'concede' lower buying prices, for itself in the transactions.[6]

But there is a problem here for economic theory. The distribution of the gains from trade depends upon the terms of trade; and the terms of trade depend upon the balance of market power. Taken together, these two facts render distributional conflict highly likely, if not inevitable. But the very existence – or even the potential – for distributional conflict brings to the fore a more fundamental problem, namely the political aspects of economic power. For as long as economic power is applied only to the determination of the terms of trade the problem remains fundamentally an economic issue. But the crucial question which arises is whether, especially in situations of highly asymmetrical economic power, the capacity exists for the stronger trading partner to extract political concessions, quite unrelated to the gains from trade, from the weaker partner. In short, can the latter be 'forced' by economic power to take unwanted policy decisions or to behave in other ways contrary to its perceived real interests? For the answers to these questions it is necessary to draw also on the literatures on economic statecraft and bargaining theory.

The determination of the optimal level of interdependence will be dealt with in this chapter; discussion of the problems of economic power and political leverage is deferred to the next chapter.

Optimizing economic interdependence

As noted earlier, for any two international trading partners, there is generally a positive relationship for each country between the level of bilateral trade and the gains from trade. At the same time, each increase in the level of dependence generates not only extra gains but also additional costs. The latter are represented partly by increased costs of dissociation and partly by a further loss of sovereignty or autonomy. Since the costs of dissociation are – at least in principle – measurable, they can be taken as a first approximation for each country's degree of dependence upon the other. Indeed, Arad et al. have provided a taxonomy of states of dependence and interdependence in bilateral relations using the relative extent of dissociation costs to determine the criteria.[7]

Specifically, interdependence between two countries may be defined as a situation in which 'the cost of dissociation of both, regardless of who decides to dissociate, is balanced in the sense that dissociation for one country is more or less as painful as it is for the other.'[8] It may reasonably be surmised, therefore, that if both countries' dissociation costs rise by the same amount, then the extent of mutual dependence or interdependence between them increases accordingly. Conceivably, the extent of mutual trade may ultimately become so large that neither country would be willing to bear the costs of dissociation. In these circumstances, interdependence would become (in the terminology used by Arad et al.) 'irrevocable' because 'dissociation becomes unthinkable'.[9]

In practice, for each level of country A's dissociation costs, there is likely to be a range of country B's costs within which interdependence (as defined above) will continue to hold (and vice versa). The extent of this range will depend on each country's perceptions of the general risks associated with trade dependency. Among the relevant factors determining this range could be concerns about the relative (economic) size of the two countries and evaluations with regard to the loss of sovereignty. On the former point, if the two economies are of unequal sizes, 'the smaller country is likely to insist on higher absolute costs being incurred by the larger one before regarding itself as being interdependent with it.'[10] Equally, a country which places greater value on its autonomy and sovereignty may require that the other country's dissociation costs be higher than its own by some proportion before considering itself interdependent. It follows from the above that, outside of these ranges, either A or B will consider itself dependent upon (rather than interdependent with) its trading partner. Thus, if A's dissociation costs are too high relative to B's, then A will be dependent upon B (and vice versa). Again, it is conceivable that if, given B's dissociation costs, A's costs exceed some threshold, then A may become 'irrevocably' dependent upon B (and again vice versa).

As Arad *et al.* are at pains to acknowledge, this stylized taxonomy of states of strictly bilateral dependence and interdependence may have somewhat limited practical applicability in a world characterized by predominantly multilateral economic relationships. None the less, it is of value for the understanding it affords of the nature of bilateral economic relations between two countries.

By way of illustration, it may be surmised that, prior to UDI, Zambia and Rhodesia were interdependent: given the range and scope of their mutual economic linkages, their costs of dissociation were, if not equal, at least within a range that made the process of dissociation an extremely painful one for both countries. Certainly, they were not 'irrevocably interdependent' since neither found dissociation 'unthinkable'.[11]

Botswana's relationship with South Africa, on the other hand, would presumably be classed as one of dependence, since its dissociation costs would likely be substantially higher than South Africa's. However, by any criterion, Lesotho would have to be classified as 'irrevocably dependent' upon South Africa, because its dissociation costs would indeed be so high as to be 'unthinkable'.

The above taxonomy also provides pointers for policy towards the achievement of the desired extent of dependence or interdependence in bilateral relationships. For example, if A were dependent upon B but wished to achieve instead a state of interdependence with B, then A would need either to reduce its own dissociation costs relative to those faced by B or it would have to induce an increase in B's costs relative to its own. Similarly, if A and B are interdependent but remain uneasy about their capacity to inflict costs on each other through dissociation, then they could achieve greater security through mutual agreement to raise their dissociation costs above their respective thresholds of irrevocability. The need for such an agreement to be jointly made and implemented is reflected in the fact that if A (say) were to permit an increase in its dissociation costs without there being a concomitant rise in B's costs then A would risk making itself dependent upon (rather than interdependent with) its partner. In the limit, if A's costs were to rise by a sufficiently large margin, A could even end up being irrevocably dependent upon B, despite having started from a point of interdependence.

These possibilities highlight again the ambivalence which is an inherent characteristic of attitudes towards interdependent economic relations. This point is further underlined by the fact that, as Arad *et al.* put it, there is a 'potential conflict . . . between the "public" and the "private" interest' in interdependence.[12] Since international economic relations are, in general, the result of transactions at the level of individual economic actors, the aggregate level of such transactions may appear inappropriate from a 'national interest' point of view, even though all the individual transactions themselves bring mutual benefits. Thus the determination of the optimum level of bilateral transactions between A and B cannot simply be left to market forces. It requires the active provision by their respective governments of the requisite institutional, infrastructural and policy frameworks for facilitating and cementing the appropriate level of transactions, and it requires also the appropriate degree of governmental supervision and regulation of the relationships.[13]

These issues are particularly pertinent in situations where there is considerable scope for increasing the scale of transactions between two trading partners but where there is suspicion – mutual or unilateral – of the other side's intentions or motives. Where two countries have recently endured a period of tension in their relationship, whether due merely to political differences or, more significantly, to ideological hostility or even military conflict, their fears and suspicions of each other are likely to undermine their chances of realizing the potential benefits from establishing, or from increasing the existing levels of, bilateral economic relations.

Indeed, in these circumstances there may well be a temptation for the two governments to build a relationship, not of 'positive' interdependence based on a 'balance of prosperity', but rather of 'negative' interdependence based on a 'balance of terror'.[14] A balance of terror arises from deliberate efforts to deter aggression or domination by the other party and hence to ensure that one's own capacity to inflict damage on the other side is at least as great as the latter's capacity to do likewise to oneself. It represents a negative form of interdependence because it causes both sides to build a mutually reinforcing capacity to inflict damage on each other, mainly by diverting more and more resources to deterrent-enhancing activities, such as armaments and other defence expenditures.[15]

A balance of terror thus stands in stark contrast to a balance of prosperity. Although a balance of prosperity also involves the creation of a mutual capacity to inflict damage (by virtue of the increasing dissociation costs which accompany it), this capacity has to be weighed against the mutual economic benefits generated by the rising gains from trade. A balance of terror creates a mutual capacity for inflicting damage but without simultaneously creating mutual benefits.

However, negative interdependence may well have a greater appeal to policy-makers than positive interdependence because it allows for more autonomous decision-making. By contrast, creating a balance of prosperity requires mutually consistent policies which are inherently more difficult to achieve and which necessarily involve a reduction in some aspects of sovereignty. Hence, the central policy conclusion is that, because economic interdependence between countries carries risks and costs as well as benefits, it is a state which also requires actively to be managed.

For all their limitations, these concepts of positive and negative interdependence provide a useful framework for consideration of a wide range of problems in the management of international economic relations and particularly in the determination of the optimum levels of surrender of autonomy in return for the benefits of interdependence. The notions of building a balance of prosperity and of achieving irrevocable interdependence could well be applied to the current debate about the appropriate economic relationship between Britain and the European Community. However, having been developed initially in the context of the Egyptian-Israeli peace treaty, the framework offers particular potential for useful insights into the problems of economic relations between countries emerging from long-standing states of conflict and hostility. The concepts have obvious relevance, for example, for international economic relations between East and West, and particularly for efforts to build new relationships as the hostility of the Cold War era dissipates; equally, they will be relevant to the efforts of the formerly centrally planned economies of Eastern Europe to fashion a new structure for economic relations among themselves. But they surely also have potential relevance for other conflict-ridden regions of the world, such as Southern Africa.

In this respect, as Arad et al. point out, the potential for gains from trade between neighbouring (i.e. physically contiguous) ex-belligerents is especially large for two reasons. First, there is the possibility of realizing economies of scale, particularly for manufacturing activities which are constrained by small domestic markets. Second, international trade in many commodities is characterized by non-negligible transport costs, and trade between neighbouring countries frequently can benefit from the possibilities for significant reductions in these costs. This is borne out by the fact that high levels of 'border trade' frequently exist even between hostile neighbours.

But beyond these two considerations lies a more general point: 'Since international economic transactions bring such obvious gains to the parties involved, they might also be used as an instrument in strengthening peace and, too, as an additional inducement to peacemaking [between neighbouring ex-belligerents].'[16] This possibility of using economic instruments to stabilize and safeguard peace is reinforced by consideration of Boulding's view that exchange relations, whether at the interpersonal or the international level, can be conceived of as comprising a hierarchy of three systems: the integrative, the exchange and the threat systems. Progress is measured by a reduction in the scope of the threat system (which involves trade in 'bads'), by an extension in the scope of the exchange system (which involves trade in 'goods'), and ultimately by a shift to the integrative system, in which the parties to exchange become more closely bound together through their mutual interests.[17] There should, of course, be no illusions about the obstacles to the achievement of such idealized outcomes as a 'balance of prosperity' and an 'integrative' system of international economic relations, especially between countries whose relations have been or still are characterized by suspicion, hostility and conflict. Furthermore, it has to be recognized that economic linkages are no guarantee of stability and peace among trading partners: on the contrary, they can be the source of, rather than the antidote to, conflict and instability.

None the less, the point that, because of the mutual benefits which they confer, economic transactions have the capacity to play a stabilizing role in such relations is a valid one. Clearly, both governmental and non-governmental attitudes towards economic relations between recently hostile countries, especially neighbours, will be crucial in tilting the balance one way or the other.[18] As Arad *et al.* put it, the governments concerned must 'actually seek to contain their political rivalry and develop bilateral economic relations based on an acceptable compromise between the gains available from transactions with the past enemy and the negative impact of the conflicts over their distribution and of dependence, which are both inevitable by-products of international economic transactions'.[19]

In this respect, joint infrastructural developments offer particularly fruitful possibilities for mutual welfare gain. Again, however, it will be essential to beware of the destabilizing potential of distributional conflicts, over which acceptable compromises will have to be negotiated.[20] However, before turning to the application of this analytical framework to Southern Africa, it is necessary first to address the questions of economic power and political leverage.

9 Economic interdependence, economic power and political leverage

The mutually beneficial consequences of economic exchange do not, as noted earlier, preclude the emergence of conflict between the participants in the exchange. The primary issue over which conflict arises is the distribution of the gains from trade, and the reason for conflict is the lack of any 'natural' rules or mechanisms for determining the 'correct' division of the spoils. The distribution which actually obtains in practice is primarily the outcome of a bargaining process and, hence, depends on the participants' relative bargaining powers. It is only in the limiting case, when each participant's trade is too small, relative to the total volume of trade, to exert any bargaining power, that the scope for distributional conflict is completely removed. In all other cases, the equilibrium terms of trade will depend, in the final analysis, on the distribution of market power.[1]

In trade between countries, there are two components to market power. The capacity to influence the terms of trade resides in the first instance with the individual economic agents who undertake the trade. However, governments also exercise market power through the medium of their commercial policies. These policies are most commonly reflected in the levels of protection which governments afford to their domestic producers of tradable goods, but they also extend to the whole range of regulatory and institutional arrangements which underpin any bilateral set of trading relations. They also include the capacity to curtail the scope and scale of trade in both directions, ultimately even to totally proscribe economic exchanges with particular partners, i.e. to impose trade (and other economic) embargoes and sanctions.

It is but a short step from acknowledging that governments can exercise market power (in the sense of influencing the terms of trade) to assuming that this power also permits the extraction of political concessions from trading partners. Indeed, this assumption has been the conventional wisdom ever since Albert Hirschman asserted in 1945 that 'the influence effect of foreign trade' affords 'an effective weapon in the struggle for power'.[2] For these reasons alone, the assumption that economic power leads to political leverage would be an important element in any discussion of the political economy of interdependence. However, the validity of the assumption has recently been called into question and this renders its closer examination essential. This examination will be conducted in two stages. First, it will be helpful to clarify some aspects of the nature of the economic instruments used by governments as foreign policy tools in circumstances of economic interdependence. Second, the relationship between economic power and political leverage will be discussed.

The lessons of economic statecraft

David Baldwin has coined the term 'economic statecraft' to describe the practice whereby governments intervene in international economic relations for political motives. Seen in this light, 'economic statecraft could be said to lie between diplomacy and military statecraft so far as its degree of forcefulness is concerned.'[3]

Hanson, in turn, has suggested that such interventions for foreign policy reasons can be classified into three domains. First, he distinguishes the domain of national security, where governments may restrict economic relations with a potentially hostile trading partner for strictly defensive reasons. The Western strategic embargo on export of goods and technologies which might have enhanced the Soviet Union's military capabilities is the prime example of this category of intervention. The second domain is occupied by 'measures adopted with a view to making a foreign government take some specific foreign-policy decisions which it would not otherwise have done'. Into this category fall economic sanctions and other 'linkage' and 'leverage' measures which, at least ostensibly, carry some message to the target state about some aspect of its political behaviour. The third domain comprises very long-run strategies in pursuit of some 'grand design', of which economic warfare and economic detente are the two most extreme examples.[4]

Hanson's distinction between economic sanctions and economic warfare warrants further elucidation, not least because it does not always accord very closely with popular usage or understanding of the concepts. To some extent, of course, the distinction may be seen simply as one of degree in that comprehensive economic sanctions, which have as their objective the total economic isolation of the target state, clearly constitute a form of economic warfare. This is undoubtedly true of the mandatory and comprehensive UN sanctions imposed against Rhodesia and, most recently, Iraq, and is also true of the total sanctions which many long demanded (and some still demand) should be imposed against South Africa.

The two forms of statecraft can, however, also be seen as different in kind. Thus, for Hanson, sanctions constitute (limited) 'signalling' devices, which operate within the context of 'normal' trade relations.[5] Within this context, they seek to influence the target nation's behaviour in specific policy matters, and in so doing may or may not impose costs on the target country, on the imposing country, or on both. By contrast, economic warfare 'is a far more ambitious form of statecraft' which has the specific objective of limiting or reducing the target state's political and strategic power by weakening it economically, relative to the state or states prosecuting the war.[6] The rationale for a Western policy of economic warfare against the Soviet Union could thus have been put in the following terms:

The Soviet Union is an inherently expansionist power; unless the nature of Soviet society changes fundamentally, we must accept that it is an adversary and will act to our disadvantage; it can be prevented from doing so only by weakness, or a prudent fear of consequences, or both; it is therefore wise for us to do whatever we can to make this adversary weaker rather than stronger; the less its productive capacity, the less its power to threaten us and the greater the likelihood of internal dissatisfaction which might just possibly, in the longer run, force a change in the nature of the society.[7]

For Hanson, an important difference between economic sanctions and economic warfare is to be found in the distribution of costs between the imposing (or sending) nations and the target. Whereas sanctions – even 'effective' sanctions – may conceivably prove more costly economically to the imposers than to the target, economic warfare 'is ineffective if it costs the sender more than the target nation, since it is the effect on relative economic strength that matters'.[8] It follows from this that economic warfare does not necessarily require absolute reductions in the target's economic welfare – relative reductions will suffice. At the opposite extreme to warfare among Hanson's 'grand designs' in economic statecraft lies the pursuit of detente with a potential enemy. In its strongest form, detente 'would entail an active cultivation' of exchange relations, including especially the commitment of public resources to the creation of the necessary institutional frameworks and to an 'explicit . . . [and] deliberate taxpayer subsidy . . . [which would be] justified by the long-term political benefits to be gained'.[9] In its weaker form, a strategy of detente would see the relationship merely as one between normal trading partners, but tempered by a political wariness about national security interests which would be reflected in at least some level of control over trade in strategic commodities. Thus, the level of exchange relations would presumably be determined by the decentralized efforts of individual firms seeking to engage in such relations, albeit supported by the 'normal' availability of official export credits and conducted within the general framework of the country's trading institutions.[10]

Whether in its stronger or weaker form, a policy of detente towards a target nation rests on the opposite rationale from that which informs an economic warfare strategy. With regard to East–West relations, Hanson put the case for detente in the following terms:

It rests on a fundamentally different intuition about Soviet society: that it is not inherently expansionist. . . . [The USSR is] much like any other [power] in history: prepared to take any easy opportunities to expand its influence but open to the attractions of international cooperation and not incapable of being (or becoming) a status quo nation. . . . [A] more prosperous Bear is a Bear with a bigger paunch, not a bigger punch: . . . prosperity tends to soften all societies and Soviet society is no exception.[11]

As is evident, Hanson developed his classification of the forms of economic statecraft primarily in relation to East–West economic strategies. Yet many of the distinctions and conclusions that he draws can be carried over directly to other problem areas in international economic relations, including Southern Africa. For example, many observers would recognize a direct analogy between the rationale for detente with the Soviet Union and 'constructive engagement' with South Africa. Similarly, in the rationale for economic warfare quoted above, South Africa, or even Iraq, could be readily substituted for the Soviet Union. In this instance, however, the analogy may not seem quite as complete. Thus, for many advocates of the economic isolation of South Africa and Iraq, the objectives are seen to be much more than a mere 'relative weakening' of the target's economic strength; absolute reductions in economic strength and economic welfare are explicitly sought. Furthermore, the nature of the anticipated political impacts is frequently asserted to be much more extensive and the time-scale much shorter than Hanson's definition of economic warfare would seem to concede. Notwithstanding any such definitional differences over the particular categorization of statecraft techniques which Hanson has employed, at least three of his insights and conclusions do have more general application to states ensnared in apparently conflictual politico-economic relations.

The first two points relate to the dynamic impact which economic statecraft can have on the degree of economic interdependence between two states. First, Hanson notes that 'the exercise of influence through economic statecraft is not necessarily a zero-sum game: A's influence over B may increase by this means, while at the same time B's influence over A also increases.'[12] This is, of course, likely to be particularly true of efforts to achieve – in the terminology of the previous chapter – 'positive' interdependence (or detente), but it could also apply to thrusts towards 'negative' interdependence, such as the pursuit of economic warfare or the building of a balance of terror. Second, Hanson argues that East–West relations have afforded a 'special character' to Western economic statecraft. This is because

the relationship between the two superpowers is a continuing one, and of central importance to both sides. [Western] attempts . . . to influence Moscow are cumulative in their effects on a relationship that is constantly at the top of both sides' foreign-policy agendas. To analyse them as though they were a set of influence attempts whose outcomes were independent of one another is misleading.[13]

This special character surely applies to all 'influence attempts' between countries whose relationships are of 'central importance' to each other.

The third insight which can be generalized relates to circumstances where there are profound disagreements about the correct strategy to pursue. In such cases, there is likely to be no objective basis for discriminating between 'opposing intuitions . . . [which] are influential and irreconcilable' and no capacity to assemble the empirical evidence which might permit such discrimination.[14] The risks attaching to the choice of one strategy in preference to another will therefore be very high, and the need to pursue a middle course, though likely to be scorned by adherents of the competing theories, will be enhanced. This requirement applies particularly in cases where it is necessary to maintain an alliance of countries in implementing any strategy against the target.

As will become apparent, all three of these conclusions can be applied with considerable force to the Southern Africa region in the past decade, and especially to relations between South Africa on the one hand and its neighbours on the other. First, however, we must consider the nexus between economic power and political influence.

Economic power and political leverage

The concepts of economic power and of economic interdependence are clearly intimately linked. In Michaely's words, 'one is the precise reverse of the other. "Power" is the "dependence" of *others* on the home unit.'[15] Furthermore, as we have noted, pure market power permits manipulation of the terms of trade, and hence of the gains from trade. The interdependence which is the unavoidable concomitant of bilateral trading relations thus confers on each partner the power to deprive the other of the gains from trade (albeit at the cost of losing one's own gains as well).

The question remains, however, whether the connection between economic (i.e. market) power and the economic terms of trade simultaneously establishes a similar connection between economic power and the 'political' terms of trade. The foregoing discussion of economic statecraft took for granted the assumption that economic power in fact can be used to exert political influence in a direct manner. This was wholly in line with the tradition in the literature on asymmetrical bilateral economic interdependence.

The implications of this conventional wisdom can be stated thus: the fact that B 'needs' its economic exchanges with A more than A needs them implies that A can manipulate (or threaten to manipulate) the exchange relations so as to induce B to change its behaviour in respect of some variable unrelated to the exchange relations. To put the point another way, since B is more dependent upon A than vice versa, A has the capacity to force B to give up some preferred policy stance in order to retain the benefits which B derives from its economic links with A.

This argument is commonly heard in the Southern African context. For example, in the words of the report on the 1986 mission to South Africa by the Commonwealth Eminent Persons Group, 'the evidence is clear . . . South Africa [has] enormous power to exercise economic pressures on [the neighbouring] countries, which it has not hesitated to use for political ends.'[16] That governments do indeed use economic instruments in pursuit of foreign policy goals is not in question. Moreover, the assumption that economic power affords political leverage, and conversely that economic dependence is associated with weakness in political bargaining strength, appears entirely plausible in the light of the many practical examples in international relations of the coupling of political demands with the prospect of an increase, or the threat of a reduction, in economic benefits. The attempt by the US to secure a Soviet withdrawal from Afghanistan via a partial embargo on grain exports; the fear of an OPEC threat to curtail oil supplies to the US on account of the latter's support for Israel; and – as we have already seen – South Africa's manipulation of economic relations with its neighbours to discourage, *inter alia*, the latter's support for the international sanctions campaign and the granting of military bases to the ANC – these are but a few commonly cited examples of the phenomenon.

However, as R. Harrison Wagner has recently pointed out, the conventional wisdom that B's economic dependence upon A enables A to coerce B politically actually conflates two logically distinct implications of the 'influence effect' assumption.[17] The first implication is that A has the capacity to alter the existing distribution of the gains from trade in its own favour (and hence to B's disadvantage); and the second implication is that B's welfare can be further reduced (and A's further increased) by virtue of B being forced to make the political concession demanded by A. B's loss, in other words, is twofold. Wagner's contention is that this conflation, which dates back to Hirschman, is invalid and is not borne out by systematic analysis grounded in modern bargaining theory.[18] His argument can be summarized in three stages.

Wagner notes first that it is wrong to assume – as Hirschman implicitly did – that there is no distinction between the determinants of a government's market power, especially as reflected in its ability to influence the terms of trade through changes in its commercial policy, and the determinants of its general bargaining power, were it to engage directly in negotiations with another government over the terms of trade. The source of market power lies predominantly in the capacity to manipulate the quantities of imports and exports of goods by altering their prices through the use of tariffs and subsidies. In technical terms, therefore, this power rests with the market elasticities of demand and supply for the goods in question. By contrast, a government's general bargaining power derives from its 'relative evaluation ... of the consequences of interrupting trade'.[19] Governments are generally concerned with the impact of trade upon a wide range of policy objectives (including aggregate employment, income distribution, the effect on political constituencies, etc.), and the factors influencing these will likely be more wide-ranging than those which determine market elasticities alone.[20]

Second, and more fundamentally, Wagner argues that even if market power and bargaining power over the terms of trade were essentially the same, it is not legitimate to assume that bargaining power over economic linkages translates into bargaining power over (say) political or foreign policies. The reason is that governments' relative valuations of the latter will generally be different from their valuations of the former. As Wagner puts it,

The intuition behind [Hirschman's argument] is that bargaining power derives from the relative value that bargainers place on what is at stake in their negotiations. But if governments are bargaining over some political concession that one government has demanded of another, their evaluations of their trading relationship tell us nothing about their evaluations of the political concession that is at stake in their negotiations. Thus any inference from market power to political influence must assume that the governments' evaluations of this concession are irrelevant. But this is contrary to the very intuitions that are the basis for Hirschman's analysis. In fact, the commonsense ideas underlying ... the political significance of economic dependence ... are useless in telling us when one government can use the threat of interrupting trade to extract political concessions from another.[21]

Third, Wagner then makes systematic use of bargaining theory to demonstrate that, even in circumstances of asymmetrical bilateral economic interdependence, the less dependent country does not have the capacity both to improve the terms of trade and to coerce the more dependent country into making political concessions.[22] If B is economically more dependent on A, then A can only exact political concessions from B by itself making concessions over the terms of trade.[23]

The obvious question which arises from this conclusion is how to explain the evident capacity of so many governments to achieve political concessions from other governments without – apparently – making economic concessions. Wagner's answer is that the extraction of both political concessions and an improvement in the terms of trade can only happen if the 'coercing' government, A, has not already fully exploited its bargaining power within the economic side of its relationship with the 'coerced' government, B.[24] This unexploited potential is most likely to exist in circumstances in which A has hitherto left the determination of its terms of trade with B largely to market forces and, in consequence, has received a lesser share of the gains from trade than it could otherwise have obtained. In Wagner's words, the more dependent country has already been conceded better terms of trade than it could have won through direct bargaining, and the government of the country attempting to exercise influence is, in effect, trying to collect the bargaining gains it had earlier forgone, though in the coin of political concessions rather than improved terms of trade.[25]

A simple hypothetical example from Southern Africa will serve to illustrate the point. Lesotho exports migrant labour to South Africa. Most of the migrants work on the mines. Within the constraints imposed by various governmental regulations and policies, both the number of Basotho miners employed, and the wage rate they receive, are determined primarily by the mining companies. To this extent, the terms of trade are determined by the market, not by government-to-government negotiation. Suppose now that the South African authorities, disapproving of Lesotho's stance on a political issue, threaten to impose a higher tax on migrants' earnings, unless Lesotho changes its stance. Wagner's analysis implies that it is only if South Africa has 'reserves' of market power which it has not hitherto utilized that it can extract the political concession. In other words, the crucial factor is that, despite having had the (market) power to impose the higher tax, it is only by virtue of having hitherto refrained from imposing it that South Africa can induce Lesotho to change its behaviour in respect of a completely unrelated matter. The fact of Lesotho's concession appears – misleadingly – to suggest that South Africa has used its economic power to manipulate Lesotho politically. However, had the South African government itself previously negotiated all aspects of the employment of migrant workers from Lesotho with the Lesotho government, and had it already achieved the maximum benefits possible, it would not have been able to extract the political concession from Lesotho without having to make a compensating economic concession to Lesotho (e.g. by reducing the existing tax).[26]

Indeed, Wagner's conclusions are even more general – and more startling – than this in two respects. First, regardless of the relative economic dependence of the two countries, neither side can obtain political concessions from the other without having to offer compensation in the form of improved terms of trade. Thus, at least in principle, the argument above would hold equally were it to be Lesotho which was seeking to extract the political concessions. (In practice, of course, it is much more likely to be the stronger of the two countries which has failed to exploit its economic power to the full – countries with relatively little economic power would be unlikely to settle for less than they could get.)[27]

Second, 'such influence is possible only if the exchange of better terms of trade for political concessions makes both parties to the transaction better off than they would have been had they bargained only over the terms of trade.'[28] Thus, if B accedes to a demand from A for a political concession, in order to preclude A from appropriating a higher share of the gains from their mutual economic relationship, both A and B will still be better off than if A had simply exploited its economic bargaining power to the full. A clearly prefers to forgo some of its (potential) economic gains to obtain B's political concession; and B clearly prefers to yield the political point rather than forgo the extra economic benefits which it has hitherto enjoyed. Were this exchange not regarded as mutually beneficial, it would not take place. Thus, 'even if there is unexploited bargaining power in an existing economic relationship, there may be no way to convert it into political influence.'[29] Conversion requires that both governments prefer the exchange to the alternative outcomes on offer.

In the above example, this result implies two things: first, that Lesotho will only accede to the political demand if it values the economic gains which it would stand to lose, were South Africa to impose the higher tax, more highly than it values the political policy stance it is being asked to give up; and second, in acceding to the demand, Lesotho creates a situation which both governments prefer to the alternative of the higher tax being imposed. The Lesotho government will consider itself better off than if the tax had been increased; and the South African government has achieved a political gain which is more important to it than the higher tax. The latter point is self-evident because, despite having the market power to do so, South Africa has not in fact increased the tax.[30]

Wagner is at pains to emphasize that his analysis gives formal theoretical reinforcement to the assumption that asymmetrical interdependence in respect of a specific aspect of a relationship affords greater power to the less dependent country in bargaining over the relevant gains.[31] The essence of his argument however is that market power should not be automatically equated with bargaining power because 'governments [may] value the gains from trade less than does the market'.[32]

Wagner's contribution will doubtless not be the last word on this controversial subject. However, his analysis reinforces the conclusion adduced earlier in this study about the need for great care in interpreting the meaning of the term 'economic dependence' and in defining the many components of dependence. Equally, the foregoing analyses have underlined the complexities of the concept of economic interdependence and, thanks to Wagner, have suggested that the (invariably negative) normative connotations assigned to the relationship between economic power and political influence should not be taken for granted. Understanding and analysis of relationships of dependence and interdependence between countries requires instead a dispassionate and systematic approach. Such an approach is seldom easily achieved and, especially when the relationships are accompanied by political tensions and conflicts, great vigilance is needed to ensure that it is not squeezed out by normative and emotionally charged arguments. The latter, though superficially persuasive, run a greater risk (in the words of Arad et al., quoted at the beginning of this Part of the study) of 'applying the wrong image and wrong rhetoric to problems . . . [and hence leading] to erroneous analysis and bad policy'.

PART THREE
THE DYNAMICS OF ECONOMIC CONFLICT IN SOUTHERN AFRICA

The states of Southern Africa are joined by more than their geographic proximity. Extensive . . . [economic] interdependencies underpin an organic unity. Yet politics deeply divides these states. As a result, Southern Africa is caught in a structural paradox: growing economic interdependence has been accompanied by intensifying partisan conflict, frequently involving cross-border violence. – Peter Vale (1989), p. 98.

10 Dependence, destabilization and sanctions

The theoretical discussions in Part Two have generated a number of important conclusions about dependence and interdependence in international economic relations. First, interdependence and conflict are by no means mutually exclusive. Greater interdependence certainly brings increases in the (mutual) gains from trade. But, at the minimum, there may be dissatisfaction over the distribution of the benefits. Beyond that, interdependence brings costs as well as benefits, reflected partly in the costs of dissociation and partly in the loss of political autonomy. The costs of dissociation, in turn, are determined partly by the technical composition and structure of trading relations, but partly also by the probability of dissociation. For any given country, the latter depends not only upon its own behaviour but also to a significant extent on the actions and intentions of its trading partners. Consequently, the scope for suspicion and uncertainty is considerable, the more so when political relations are less than enthusiastic. The problem facing each country's policy-makers is thus to determine the optimum level of bilateral relations with each of its trading partners by balancing the costs and benefits.

Second, where interdependence is (or is perceived to be) highly asymmetrical, there is the added problem of the fear on the part of the 'more dependent' partner that it may be subject to the exercise of unwelcome political leverage. Analysis of this issue suggests that the conventional wisdoms about it may reflect a misunderstanding of the nature of economic power. In particular, it suggests that one country cannot costlessly 'extract' political concessions from another. In the final analysis it has to pay a price for it in terms of a reduction in its actual or potential market power. However, where the stronger country's market power is both very large (in comparative terms) and not yet fully exploited, this price is unlikely to act as a major deterrent to it. But whatever the analytical niceties, the fear and resentment of this power can be real enough in the minds of policy-makers in the weaker countries.

Third, for these reasons, economic interdependence requires to be actively managed via appropriate institutions and policies. In the absence of such management, it can come to be viewed predominantly in a negative light, and can lead to the creation of a 'balance of terror' rather than a 'balance of prosperity'. Instead of an increase in interdependence being assessed according to the net benefits which it brings, it becomes associated almost exclusively with increased costs and hence becomes potentially destabilizing.

Fourth, whether a particular bilateral economic relationship should be regarded as one of dependence or interdependence can be determined, at least in principle, by the relative sizes of the costs of dissociation facing the two parties. Indeed, the extent of balance or imbalance in dissociation costs can lead to a taxonomy of states of relative dependence and interdependence.

Fifth, where the relationship is judged to be one of 'dependence', it is unhelpful – from the perspectives both of analysis and of policy – to view the condition predominantly in ideological terms. The focus should rather be on examining both the extent of the consequent vulnerability, as reflected in the size of the gains from trade and in the probability of dissociation, and the nature of the dependence, as reflected in the composition of the relevant exchange relations.

Finally, bilateral economic relations, whether dependent or interdependent, are frequently affected by the practice of economic statecraft, in which economic instruments are employed by governments in pursuit of political objectives ranging from the achievement of 'grand designs' to the conveyance of mere political 'messages'.

Until now, Southern Africa's policy-makers have not thought expressly in the conceptual terms outlined in the foregoing summary. Instead, they have – variously – held deeply entrenched beliefs in ideological concepts of dependence; regarded economic power as conferring almost unlimited political leverage; and emphasized either the benefits or the costs of economic interdependence to the exclusion of the other. But this does not mean they have not been deeply concerned – even if only implicitly – about many of the issues underlying these concepts. On the contrary, their implicit views about such matters as the relative costs and probabilities of dissociation have had profound consequences for regional relations, not least through their exercise of economic statecraft.

Some illustrations have already been given in Part Two of the potential application to Southern Africa of these more systematic conceptual frameworks. But their relevance can be seen most prominently in the attitudes to, and the management of, regional economic relations during the past fifteen years and in discussions about the prospective relations between a 'new', post-apartheid South Africa and its regional neighbours. These points will be taken up in the remainder of this study, beginning in this chapter with consideration of the way in which these attitudes and beliefs brought the region to the brink of outright economic warfare in the mid-1980s.

The political context for regional economic warfare

Clearly, there were legitimate political grounds for concern on the neighbours' part about the state of their bilateral relations with South Africa well before the advent, in the late 1970s, of the 'destabilization era'. Both the increasingly bitter racial dimension to the conflicts in the region in the 1960s and 1970s, and the associated problems of the politicization of economic relations with Rhodesia and with South Africa, aggravated the inherent tension between the costs and benefits of interdependence.

However, the decisive political context for the headlong descent into economic conflict in the 1980s was provided by the interaction between two new policy imperatives. One was dictated by the belief on the part of South Africa's neighbours in 'ideological dependence'; the other was reflected in the harsh reality of the exercise of military, political and economic power by South Africa in the region. Together, these forces added further interlocking strategic and political dimensions to the management of regional economic relations – dimensions which rendered it increasingly difficult for governments to define and pursue rational policies towards such relations.

As will be seen in the next chapter, the almost exclusive focus on 'dependence' as the relevant framework for analysis of the political economy of Southern Africa had significant implications for evaluations of economic relations between South Africa and its neighbours. On the one hand, the objective fact that trade, financial and labour flows to and from South Africa occurred on a considerable scale, that institutional links existed, and that the contributions of all these linkages to macroeconomic magnitudes were often proportionately large was generally, if not universally, acknowledged. On the other hand, the prevailing ideological conception of 'dependence' resulted in a disinclination on the part of the neighbouring states to view these linkages in anything other than negatively normative terms.

At the same time, through their growing political and material support for anti-apartheid forces, the neighbouring states became inextricably enmeshed in the internal political conflict in South Africa. In South Africa's eyes, this involvement demanded retaliation, leading inevitably to the 'export' of aspects of the conflict to the region. The scars inflicted on the neighbours simply reinforced their concern about their economic dependence on South Africa. The belief therefore spread that regional economic relations could not be viewed in isolation from the struggle for political power in South Africa. Consequently, economic links with South Africa came to be evaluated almost exclusively in terms of two political criteria: their (supposed) impact on the anti-apartheid struggle, and their implications for the neighbouring states' dependence on South Africa.

Indeed, via the intensifying campaigns for economic sanctions against, and disinvestment from, South Africa, the internal political struggle became not merely regionalized, but internationalized, with the battles being waged as keenly in Europe, North America and elsewhere, as in South and Southern Africa itself. Even so, it was economic relations in the region, and particularly the 'dependence' issue, which became the key strategic focus in the campaign to isolate South Africa internationally.

There were four mutually reinforcing reasons why the regional states felt drawn into the internal South African conflict and why that conflict came to be 'exported' to the region. Two – the political and military campaign against apartheid and the South African response – were primarily strategic in nature; the other two – the formation of SADCC and the sanctions campaign – had significant economic dimensions.

Destabilization and the anti-apartheid struggle

In Robert Jaster's words, 'the overriding objective [of destabilization was] to bring about a regional detente on terms imposed by South Africa . . . ; in short, nothing less than a *Pax Pretoria*.'[1] Great volumes have been written on destabilization, analysing its sources, its nature, its coherence and its consequences. It must suffice here merely to summarize some of its key features, to indicate why and how the philosophy and strategy of destabilization came to dominate Pretoria's regional policies, and to outline its impact on regional relations.

Against the background of the continuing repression of virtually all political opposition in South Africa, the neighbouring states felt a moral and political obligation to support international efforts to end apartheid and white rule, and particularly to assist exiled South African and Namibian guerrilla forces in prosecuting their military campaigns. Though the nature and extent of this commitment varied significantly from country to country and from time to time, there was no doubting the regional states' overt political hostility towards Pretoria.

Meanwhile, Pretoria's own intentions towards the region grew increasingly suspect and its actions increasingly hostile. The political ascendancy of the military and of the 'securocrats' in South Africa increased in the late 1970s. From their perspective, the growth in the number of Marxist regimes and liberation movements in the region, armed and funded by Eastern bloc countries, gave credence to their thesis of a communist-sponsored 'total onslaught', with its concomitant requirement of a countervailing 'total strategy'. The region therefore acquired a greatly enhanced significance for South Africa's national security objectives. This significance, and the vehemence of Pretoria's wrath, grew in proportion to the succour afforded by the neighbouring countries to anti-South African forces. From this potent mixture emerged the strategy of destabilization.

On the crucial military level, destabilization had several dimensions.

Most importantly, Pretoria afforded continuing support to the UNITA movement in its civil war against the Angolan government, and to the brutal dissident Mozambican organization, RENAMO. Admittedly, the involvement of US and Soviet/Cuban forces in Angola gave that conflict a particular global strategic context which, at least arguably, impinged on South Africa's interests.

However, South Africa's support for RENAMO could claim no such justification. Taking advantage of the economic depredations and political disaffections resulting from calamitous economic mismanagement by the FRELIMO government (and aggravated by severe drought), RENAMO set about wreaking further havoc throughout the greater part of Mozambique. For a considerable period it operated from bases inside South Africa. Though its prior and subsequent history belie the popular view that RENAMO was largely a creation and a puppet of the South African government, or at least of the South African military, the fact that it for so long both served South Africa's interests by disrupting the transport corridors to Zimbabwe, and received extensive South African logistical support, identified it as such in many observers' minds.[2]

At a much lower level, South African forces made a number of sporadic, but limited, military incursions into the neighbouring states, with the primary objective of denying the ANC the capacity to establish a presence on its borders. But these actions also carried a wider political message to the various regional governments about South Africa's capacity and willingness to project its power into the region and to defend its interests.

Destabilization also had its economic aspects. As already noted, apart from the general devastation wrought by the conflicts in Angola and Mozambique, the activities of UNITA and RENAMO also resulted in the continued closure of the transport routes to Lobito in the former and to Beira, Maputo and Nacala in the latter. Though not widely recognized, these closures pre-dated South African destabilization. The Mozambique–Zimbabwe transport corridors had been closed by Mozambique itself during the latter stages of UDI, and – like the Benguela routes – had suffered both on account of internal guerrilla warfare and poor maintenance.

The closure of these routes had resulted in the landlocked countries – Botswana, Lesotho, Malawi, Swaziland, Zambia and Zimbabwe – being denied access to routes other than those which traversed South Africa. This had had the useful effect, from South Africa's point of view, of increasing its market power in the region – power which it had not hesitated to exploit during the UDI period. Though not initially responsible for the situation, South Africa continued to benefit from the inoperability of these routes during the destabilization era, in that it was able to perpetuate significant political and economic pressures on these countries.

The situation was complicated by the fact that destabilization gave added impetus to internationally backed and funded programmes to rehabilitate the regional transport system and, hence, to restore the neighbours' access to alternative routes. Successful implementation of these programmes would have redressed part of the imbalance in market power in the region. To the extent that destabilization helped to inhibit these programmes, it effectively thwarted achievement of these objectives. Not surprisingly, however, all this merely reinforced both the belief that the neighbours' dependence upon South Africa was 'unnatural' and the pervasive suspicion, if not fear, of South Africa's motives and intentions in the region.

Thus, whether or not these outcomes were consciously intended by Pretoria in the first instance – naturally, they were viewed as such in the region – they undoubtedly suited South Africa's purposes, the more so as, with the passage of time, transport was to become a crucial weapon in the growing confrontation. In this respect, the formation of SADCC and the rising clamour for sanctions were to play central roles.

The political role of SADCC

The third interlocking element in the regionalization of the conflict was provided by the formation in 1980 of SADCC (The Southern African Development Coordination Conference). SADCC continually emphasized that, in its 'urgent task . . . [of] economic liberation', it was concerned with a reduction in the general 'dependence' of the SADCC economies.[3] However, there was never any doubt but that it was their 'dependence' upon South Africa which was the main problem to be confronted.[4]

It was self-evident that the *sine qua non* of giving real content to SADCC's hopes of reducing the neighbouring states' 'dependence' on South Africa was to relieve their almost total reliance upon South Africa's transport system for overseas trade. Very sensibly, therefore, SADCC's practical priorities were with the logistical and financial difficulties of rehabilitating and extending the region's transport infrastructure. To this end, it concerned itself predominantly with the raising of foreign aid contributions from the international community.[5]

Beyond this essentially practical role, however, SADCC was widely conceived of as having a central political role in the struggle against continued white domination in South Africa and Namibia.[6] Initially, this was limited largely to the recognition that SADCC was the political foil to South Africa's own hopes of creating a 'Constellation' of Southern African states. Pretoria's desire was for a voluntary regional association based, in the first instance, on economic cooperation but leading subsequently to mutual security pacts and ultimately to political cooperation.[7]

In the light of South Africa's dominant economic role in the region, and of the high levels of economic interaction between South Africa and its neighbours, there can be no doubt that there was merit in the concept of a regional economic organization within which economic relations could, at the minimum, be discussed, if not necessarily managed or regulated. However, in the increasingly conflictual circumstances in the region, neither the SADCC nor the 'Constellation' concept had any prospect of real success in this respect. Given the overweening manner in which South Africa was wont to conduct itself in the region, even the economic objectives of the Constellation were bound to have been regarded warily by the neighbours. But its political objectives, which expressly included recognition of the 'independence' of South Africa's tribal homelands, absolutely guaranteed its rejection. Equally, since SADCC expressly excluded any notion of participation by South Africa in any of its deliberations – indeed, in much of the literature on SADCC, South Africa either appeared not to exist at all or was exclusively an object of criticism – it necessarily consigned itself to play at best a marginal role in the conduct of regional economic relations.

The official disappointment in South Africa at the formation of SADCC, and particularly at the participation of the more 'moderate' regional states, such as Botswana, Lesotho, Malawi and Swaziland, was tempered for some by the recognition that, without South African involvement, SADCC (as an institution) would have little economic relevance, at least in the short term. Others saw it as part of a longer-term strategy by which Zimbabwe hoped to recapture some of the regional markets which it lost to South African exporters as a result of sanctions during the UDI period.[8] Either way, it appeared initially as a development with which South Africa could live. However, in so far as Pretoria hoped still to find a way to involve its neighbours in some form of South African-led association, it continued to misread the regional mood on the issue.

Indeed, in political terms, the fact that it was SADCC, rather than the Constellation, which saw the light of day proved to be highly significant. SADCC gradually became a focus for international efforts both to provide development assistance for Southern Africa and to register political solidarity with the SADCC member-countries, who were widely viewed as the David to South Africa's Goliath. In both of these political roles, SADCC's achievements were, by any standards, impressive.[9]

In these senses, therefore, SADCC was regarded as an instrument not merely for 'development coordination' among its member-states, as its title implied, but also for the exercise of economic statecraft against South Africa. As we have said, as an institution for the coordination of the regional states' economic development, SADCC was seriously flawed by virtue of its deliberate and total exclusion of the 'senior partner' in that development. But, notwithstanding its above-mentioned successes, SADCC was even more ill-suited to being an explicit economic instrument of its members' foreign policy objectives, particularly *vis-à-vis* South Africa. Indeed, in finding that economic cooperation did not always mesh with foreign policy cooperation, SADCC proved to be not unlike the European Community.

In particular, it was in their divergences of interest over the question of imposing economic sanctions on South Africa that SADCC's weaknesses were most seriously exposed.

The sanctions issue

Pretoria's underlying chagrin at the formation of SADCC and the associated rejection of its overtures for economic cooperation was gradually reinforced by the role played by SADCC, whether wittingly or unwittingly, in the widening international political campaign for economic sanctions against, and total international isolation of, South Africa.

The sanctions issue presented SADCC with a virtually insoluble problem. On the one hand, it was self-evident from the scale of the dissociation costs which they would incur, that none of the SADCC countries (other than Angola and Tanzania) were in a position to sever their economic ties with South Africa in a way that would be consistent with the implementation of the mandatory, comprehensive and universal economic sanctions which were so widely demanded in the mid-1980s. This was not solely a matter of their lack of choice over transport routes to the outside world; it was also a reflection of the breadth and depth of the economic linkages – in visible and invisible trade, in investment and other financial flows, in labour services and in infrastructures and institutions – which they had with South Africa. As had been the case with Zambia and Rhodesia twenty years earlier, the dissociation costs would have been unacceptably high.[10]

In some circles, there was a belief that unilateral reduction, even severance, by some SADCC countries of selected economic relations with South Africa was feasible, even in the short term. Air transport links were frequently mentioned as one such possibility.[11] The difficulty with this argument was that it overlooked the potential impact of such actions on the probability that South Africa would retaliate with partial – or even total – acts of dissociation of its own. Recognition of this point undoubtedly inhibited precipitate implementation of such actions.

On the other hand, both the regional and the international political pressures for sanctions were becoming almost irresistible. SADCC was not immune from these pressures, not least because the governments of some of its individual member-states publicly proclaimed both the necessity for the implementation of sanctions and their willingness to bear the consequent dissociation costs.

As a multilateral body, SADCC generally sought to avoid an official stance on sanctions, emphasizing instead that its objective of reducing dependence upon South Africa was a long-term process, and that total severance of economic relations with South Africa was not contemplated. At the same time, it was unable to avoid the political legacy of the Front

Line States alliance which had spawned it. It therefore affirmed that it was also politically fully committed to all international pressures to end apartheid.

This attempt to steer a middle course was consistent with Hanson's conclusion, noted earlier, concerning the likely strategies to be pursued in circumstances where there are 'opposing intuitions' about the appropriate forms of statecraft to pursue and no objective grounds to distinguish between them. On the one hand, being no more than a loose association for economic cooperation between independent states, SADCC itself had no capacity to implement sanctions or to pursue any other form of statecraft directly and on its own account. Organizationally, therefore, it had neither a mandate nor the mechanisms for articulating the political interests of its member-states, particularly on an issue on which they were, in fact, deeply divided, other than at the rhetorical level. On the other hand, particularly in order to attract development assistance, SADCC had to represent its member-states' views and interests to an international community which was also profoundly and irreconcilably divided on the wisdom and efficacy of sanctions.

Eventually, however, SADCC was constrained by overwhelming political pressures, including those emanating from some interest groups within South Africa itself, to give explicit support to calls for the imposition of sanctions. In doing so, by virtue of the above-mentioned circumstances, it inevitably proved unable to avoid a degree of sophistry. This was reflected in two claims: first, that the difficulties which would preclude some of the individual SADCC states from imposing sanctions against South Africa did not constitute an argument against the imposition by the international community at large of mandatory and comprehensive sanctions; and second, that the member-states of SADCC would avoid doing anything which might undermine the effectiveness of sanctions.[12]

SADCC's difficulty was that some of its member-governments were much less reticent than the others in calling for sanctions and, indeed, in threatening to impose them – in some instances even unilaterally. These differences stemmed from divergent views among the regional states about their economic relations with South Africa. Implicitly, destabilization not-withstanding, some governments perceived themselves as being in a state of 'irrevocable dependence' on South Africa. In other words, they derived such high levels of benefit from their dependence upon South Africa that dissociation was unthinkable for them, whereas (in their view) it would have been thinkable for South Africa. The problem for them was that their costs of dissociation were much too high relative to South Africa's costs.

For these countries – among whom might be numbered Botswana, Lesotho and Swaziland – the policy imperative was not to sever their links but rather to reduce this imbalance. Consequently, they were not averse to deepening their economic links with South Africa in important, but selective, respects. Lesotho, for example, embarked on the development of the Lesotho Highlands Water Project – a joint venture with South Africa of truly major proportions. Since this project involves the sale by Lesotho of its abundant water supplies to an increasingly water-constrained South Africa, it is bound to raise the future costs of dissociation for South Africa significantly more than it will raise them for Lesotho. On a smaller but still significant scale, the joint diamond venture between the Botswana government and De Beers, and the efforts by Swaziland to attract South African investment capital represent thrusts in a similar direction. In essence, these countries, building on their existing strong institutional and other links with South Africa were employing their economic statecraft to move the relationship further in the direction of detente, at least in economic terms.

Some other SADCC member-countries – most notably Zimbabwe and Zambia – responded to their economic relationship with South Africa in a different – and internally contradictory – way. Implicitly, they saw their dependence upon their more powerful neighbour almost exclusively in terms of costs, both economic and non-economic. They therefore heavily discounted the economic benefits from the relationship. In so far as they recognized any such benefits, they viewed them as accruing only in the short term, whilst they saw the costs as persisting in the longer term. But when they sought to view the relationship from South Africa's perspective, they – again implicitly – reversed the rankings. They accorded greater weight to what they saw as the long-term economic benefits derived by South Africa, and they discounted South Africa's costs of dissociation. Their net perception was that economic relations with South Africa were virtually all benefit to South Africa and all cost to themselves. For them, the thrust of these relations was in the direction of 'negative' interdependence, and their instinct was to employ their economic statecraft in pursuit of economic warfare. Thus, not only did they conclude that sanctions – i.e. dissociation – would relieve them of a major cost burden, but they also considerably overestimated the scale of the net benefits of which South Africa would thereby be deprived.

The contradictions inherent in this approach were brought to the fore in these two countries, and ultimately resolved, by a conflict between the public and private perceptions of the relative costs and benefits of economic transactions with South Africa. After much brinkmanship, individual economic actors, for whom the costs of dissociation would, of course, have been both immediate and very large in proportion to the actual benefits which they derived from such transactions, successfully dissuaded their governments from attempting to impose sanctions on any significant scale.[13] In the event, therefore, the economic statecraft which these countries actually practised emitted conflicting signals.

From Pretoria's perspective, however, the distinction between SADCC as an institution on the one hand, and its individual member-governments on the other hand, was sometimes blurred. So also was the distinction between those governments who actively favoured sanctions and those whose support was at best rhetorical. Hence, in South Africa, SADCC was increasingly seen as a vehicle not (or not only) for the promotion of economic development in the neighbouring states, albeit via the reduction of economic links with South Africa, but rather for the prosecution of the 'total onslaught' on South Africa. Certainly, the perception that some of the SADCC member-governments, if not necessarily SADCC itself, were intent upon pursuing full-scale economic warfare generated a grim determination in Pretoria to reinforce its leverage, both economic and non-economic, over its neighbours.

In all this, as noted earlier, transport links – and the economic transactions underlying them – became a critical political weapon. With the passage of time, it became Pretoria's express objective to hold its neighbours hostage, in the sense of constraining them to use the South African transport routes. This it achieved by its machinations to inhibit rehabilitation of the other regional routes. Having secured the constraint, South Africa also drew on some of its unexploited reserves of market power to shift the terms of trade further in its favour. This it did partly through the prices it charged and partly through the exercise of 'railway diplomacy', in which the availability of transport facilities to the neighbouring states was manipulated in ways calculated to remind them of their vulnerability.

Indeed, the greater the growth in the threat of sanctions, the greater became the importance for Pretoria, from a national security perspective, of control over the region's transport infrastructure. This, in turn, greatly reinforced the neighbours' equally natural desire to exercise a greater range of choice in the conduct of their trading relationships. In short, independent transport links began to acquire a life-or-death importance for all the regional states with the result that normal economic considerations were increasingly overridden by the political imperatives of national security.

All this was reflected in an inexorable drift – at times even a headlong plunge – by both sides towards outright economic warfare. Put crudely, as seen from Pretoria, the neighbouring states had no option but to conform to the demands of, and submit to the power wielded by, South Africa. If, by reason of the triumph of hostile political motives over economic self-interest, they were reluctant to recognize this reality, then they would have to be reminded of it from time to time, via a combination of threats and demonstrations of political, economic and military power. In this, Pretoria was ultimately successful. In effect, by virtue of its having considerable reserves of still unexploited market power, South Africa was extracting both more favourable terms of trade for itself and achieving the political concessions it was seeking, namely that the regional states should draw back from the imposition of sanctions. For the neighbours – indeed, for much of the rest of the world – South Africa's actions confirmed the belief that regional economic relations were inherently undesirable. Consequently, some of the neighbours at times seemed intent upon inflicting proportionately large costs of dissociation upon themselves, in return for the satisfaction of inflicting proportionately smaller costs upon South Africa.

The example of Zimbabwe

The dilemmas which were generated by the 'structural paradox' of growing economic interdependence and growing political conflict in the region were generally applicable to all South Africa's neighbours. However, some of them can be particularly well illustrated by the case of relations between Zimbabwe and South Africa.

Following its independence, and the victory for the Zanu-PF party led by Robert Mugabe, Zimbabwe's new government lost little time in marking out the elimination of the apartheid system and minority rule in South Africa as prime political objectives. To this end, it also committed itself to promote South Africa's total economic isolation. The increase in political tension was mutual. South Africa had been banking on a victory for the more moderate – and potentially cooperative – party led by Bishop Muzorewa. Indeed, it was primarily on the expectation of this outcome that Pretoria exerted such strong pressure on the government of Ian Smith to negotiate an end to the war. It did not therefore prove easy to adjust to the existence of an avowedly Marxist and hostile government.

However, because the Zimbabwean economy had become even more closely interlinked with the South African economy during the UDI period, the costs of dissociation for both countries had increased substantially. On the other hand, except in the mid–1970s, when South Africa had used the threat of trade sanctions to pressure Ian Smith to agree to a transition to majority rule, the probability of dissociation had always been relatively low.[14]

The new government's objectives raised the risk of dissociation between Zimbabwe and South Africa to unprecedented levels. Given the magnitude of the costs which would be incurred, this now posed the problem for all parties concerned of distinguishing between political rhetoric and real intentions. This problem was to recur frequently in different guises in subsequent years.

One side of the problem concerned the question of Zimbabwean exports to South Africa, including manufactured goods and migrant labour services. On migrant labour, the Zimbabwean government refused in 1981 to renew the operating licence for TEBA (the recruiting agency for migrant workers) in Zimbabwe, and closed its labour representatives' office in South Africa. Subsequently, upon the expiry of the contracts of existing Zimbabwean migrants, the South African authorities began to repatriate the workers on the grounds that this was a requirement of the Zimbabwean government. The latter protested against the repatriations saying that it was not opposed to Zimbabweans working in South Africa; it would not, however, act as an agency for recruitment.[15] Although a substantial number of the deportees reportedly returned illegally to work in South Africa, in the absence of adequate institutional mechanisms for recruitment, the total number of Zimbabwean workers (officially) in South Africa declined sharply from more than 20,000 in 1980 to less than 8,000 in 1983 and subsequent years.[16] In this instance, therefore, Zimbabwe displayed a clear willingness to accept the logical implications of its principled opposition to the migrant labour system.

By contrast, the Zimbabwean government was at pains not to abrogate the bilateral trade agreement with South Africa which it inherited from the UDI period. The agreement gave Zimbabwe privileged access to a number of South African markets. In 1981, it was the South African government which gave notice of its intention to terminate the agreement. However, the agreement was in fact renewed and retained over subsequent years despite numerous pledges by President Mugabe to break off all trade relations with South Africa.[17] The difficulties of finding alternative markets for its exports were doubtless a major factor in preventing Zimbabwe from implementing these promises; another would have been the retaliatory measures which South Africa might have taken. Indeed, the greatest problem for Zimbabwe was surely the uncertainty over the point at which action and counteraction would cease were it to initiate any major severance of economic links.

Of course, in addition to these considerations, the regional transport system embodied several components of the conflict between the political and economic imperatives facing Zimbabwe, particularly where imports were concerned. One component was naturally the lack of access to alternative transport routes. Following independence, there was, in fact, some resumption by Zimbabwe of trade via the regional transport routes which did not traverse South Africa itself. However, reversion to these alternative routes was severely limited for two main reasons. First, poor maintenance of, and operational inefficiencies along, the alternative transport infrastructures had rendered them less than satisfactory carriers of traffic. This was especially, but not only, applicable to the Tazara route. Second, most of the alternative routes (other than Tazara) had been effectively closed for extended periods of time by sabotage and by other security problems arising out of the conflicts in both Mozambique and Angola. Thus, notwithstanding urgent plans for the rehabilitation of these routes, it was clear that heavy reliance on the South African transport system was going to be unavoidable for the foreseeable future.

Another important, but less obvious, component lay in the fact that, even if the alternative routes had been functioning and accessible, it was far from clear that diversion to these routes of all trade with and via South Africa would have made economic (as opposed to political) sense. Indeed, it is highly probable that a significant number of the deeper and more extended trade links which had been developed during the long Rhodesian crisis and which utilized the South African transport system would probably have persisted for the simple reason that they were, in practice, the most cost effective and competitive links.

In this respect, much was made, of course, of the legitimate point that the routes to Beira, Maputo and even Lobito, were much shorter than any of the South African routes, and hence were the 'natural' outlets for Zimbabwean trade. On these grounds, it was argued that, given efficient operation, the shorter routes, with their lower freight charges, would be more cost-effective. This argument was reinforced by the fact that, in the absence of alternative outlets, the South African transport system had a high degree of monopoly power, and the terms of trade which were established for freight services between South Africa and Zimbabwe naturally reflected this imbalance in market power. The conclusion drawn by many from this argument was that most, if not all, of Zimbabwe's imports from third countries (such as Japan) could be obtained more cheaply by importing them directly from the original suppliers instead of via South Africa. The argument was extended also to imports of South African origin. South Africa, it was argued, was a high-cost producer of manufactured goods and substitutes could be obtained more cheaply on the world market.

These arguments were, however, flawed in several respects. First, overall freight costs are not solely determined by distance travelled, but also by the speed, handling capacities and qualitative facilities of the transport system. For all the political objections to using it, the South African transport system did have some residual cost advantages in at least some of these respects for at least some commodities. Second, in the presence of competing routes, South Africa's market power would have been reduced and this would undoubtedly have been reflected in lower freight charges. Whilst this would have shifted the terms of trade in Zimbabwe's favour it might none the less have retained the competitive advantage of the South African routes for some commodities. Third, price is not the only factor which determines trade. Zimbabwe may well have been able to import (say) spare parts for its German machines or its Japanese vehicles direct from the original suppliers, but the capacity to pick up the telephone and obtain the goods much more quickly from stocks held in (say) Johannesburg could well have been much more important to the Zimbabwean firms. Fourth, in the case of goods of South African origin, in addition to the questions of proximity, speed of delivery, local knowledge, etc., the question of their competitiveness was much more complex than suggested simply by South Africa's status as a high-cost producer. On a long-run view, many South

African goods may well have been internationally uncompetitive in the Zimbabwean market. But, on a number of occasions in the 1980s, South Africa's currency depreciated not only against the major international currencies but also against the Zimbabwean dollar, with the result that many of its exports actually became significantly more competitive in the short term.

In short, even the economic issues underlying the transport question were much more complex than many seemed prepared to acknowledge. Moreover, the fact that the alternative transport routes were not actually available rendered – or rather should have rendered – much of the argument largely hypothetical until Zimbabwean economic agents were actually in a position to exercise a choice.

Instead, all these economic issues were undercut by the political pressure for Zimbabwe to impose sanctions by cutting, or at least reducing, some or all of its economic links with South Africa regardless of the consequences or of the availability of alternative export markets, import sources and transport facilities. At the minimum, this pressure, together with the aggressive rhetoric which accompanied it, had unsettling effects upon the existing trade links between Zimbabwe and South Africa. Even more important, however, was the fact that political criteria were being put forward as the major, if not the only, basis on which to determine whether economic linkages, both general and particular, between the two countries should continue. Whether the primary reason for this was to reduce Zimbabwe's 'dependence' on South Africa, or to help bring down the edifices of white minority rule, had by now become irrelevant. The *raison d'être* of all economic relations is the economic benefits they bring to the participants, yet political imperatives were now threatening to impose very high dissociation costs on both countries.

In the event, as we have noted, Zimbabwe finally drew back from the brink and the region was saved from the vortex into which it might otherwise have been sucked.

11 Evaluating economic relations

Even before the issue of sanctions and its consequent political imperatives began to dominate the political economy of Southern Africa, the tendency to question the value of economic relations between South Africa and its neighbours was already well-established. This was largely the result of the almost exclusive focus on 'dependence' as the relevant framework for analysis. 'Dependence' was seen as inhibiting 'economic liberation' and a reduction in the range and scale of 'dependent' economic relations was thus a priority. The politicization of regional economic relations on account of their racial dimension inevitably reinforced this tendency.

As the conflict deepened, it was widely and variously asserted that the logic of all regional relations involving South Africa was necessarily a conflictual one; that the *raison d'être* of economic links between South Africa and its neighbours was the exercise (or potential exercise) by the former of a stranglehold over the latter; and that, by virtue of the very existence of apartheid, economic relations with South Africa could be neither complementary nor beneficial for the neighbours.

In the face of such assertions of this kind, arguments that economic relations did indeed generate considerable mutual benefits appeared to carry little weight. At best, they were dismissed on the grounds that they were derived from purely 'economistic' principles, and that no amount of such questionable economic benefits could compensate the neighbouring states for the political costs and depredations occasioned by South Africa's actions in the region. At worst, because economic links with South Africa were viewed as being 'all cost to the neighbours and all benefit to the apartheid state', arguments against delinking were regarded as apologies for, and support of, both apartheid and the political regime which sustained it.

That South Africa did impose severe costs on its neighbours in numerous – and reprehensible – ways is not in dispute. However, the belief that there is very little that is beneficial for the neighbours from their economic relations with South Africa involves a confusion of ideological, normative, positive and logical reasonings which require careful and systematic disentanglement.

The problem of weighing non-economic against economic issues is by no means confined to situations of exceptional hostility and conflict, although it is clearly most acute in such circumstances. Policy evaluations, especially in regard to international economic exchanges, are a continuing and universal problem for policy-makers in all countries and in all circumstances. They

merely become more apparent when ideological and normative considerations acquire an exceptionally high profile. In these circumstances,
emotional arguments tend to cloud rational analysis. The objective of this
chapter is to seek to disentangle the issues.

The principles of evaluating exchange relations

Achieving this objective requires first an understanding of the general principles underlying the evaluation of international economic linkages. As we
have seen, economic relations between countries consist partly of a highly
complex set of disaggregated linkages and transactions between 'individual'
economic agents in the countries concerned, and partly of an equally complex set of more aggregative influences, infrastructures and institutions
which link together the 'national' economies. The establishment of wide-
ranging exchange relations between any two countries requires considerable
investment of both private and public resources. If only because the costs
of dissociation are significantly increased by these investments, once trading
and institutional linkages are established, they are likely to be enduring.
Ultimately, however, voluntary exchange relations will endure only if they
are positively valued by all the parties involved.

This assertion still begs the question of how to evaluate the worth of
cross-border economic relations. Economic theory answers this question in
an appealingly simple way by extending, to the country level, the 'gains
from trade' analysis which applies at the individual level to exchanges
between economic actors.

When any two individual economic agents engage in a process of bilateral
exchange they do so because both consider that the process renders them
'better off'. The source of this 'welfare' improvement is that the act of
exchange increases the total quantities of goods which are available to each
party for consumption. In principle, the exchange process continues until
all possibilities for mutual gains have been exhausted. The consequent
enlargements of both parties' 'consumption sets' represent proximate
measurements of their respective total gains from trade. However, the
measurement of the increases in economic welfare which accrue to each
party, and which constitute their ultimate gains from trade, is a matter of
purely subjective valuation.[1]

None the less, whatever the measurement difficulties, because the
exchange relations are voluntary, they necessarily confer (net) benefits on
all the parties involved: if, on balance, any participants did not gain, they
would not voluntarily engage in the relevant transactions. Trade is thus a
positive sum game which leaves all parties considering themselves better off
than if they had not participated.

It is particularly noteworthy that this result imposes no requirement that the gains from trade should be equally distributed between the parties. This requirement would actually be difficult to impose for the reason that subjective valuations of welfare gains are not readily susceptible to interpersonal comparisons, i.e. to judgements as to whether one party has gained more or less than the other party. But this aside, the theory expressly leaves unresolved the issue of the extent to which each party's consumption set is enlarged. The distribution of the gains depends instead on factors external to the trading model. These factors – which, as we have seen, include the participants' market power – may be summed up under the heading of the relative 'bargaining strengths' of the parties. In other words, whilst trade is indeed a positive-sum game, it is these relative strengths, rather than any normative considerations, which determine the actual 'terms of trade' – and, hence, the division of the benefits – between the parties.

Economic theory translates this argument about trade between individuals *mutatis mutandis* to the case of two countries engaging in trade. In doing so, the presumption is made that, because trade brings (net) benefits to the individual participants, it must also confer (net) benefits on the country (or 'society') as a whole. The underlying reasoning is entirely analogous to the individual case, except in one respect, namely that the evaluations of the economic welfare gains are no longer made by the individual gainers themselves. They are represented instead by increases in 'social welfare'. However, economic theory does not seek to specify either how, or by whom, these social welfare gains are evaluated.

Neither these omissions, nor the presumption that the individual welfare gains from trade must aggregate to an overall gain in social welfare, are in any way accidental. Quantifying or evaluating changes in society's overall economic welfare is an inherently difficult task and one which ultimately must involve value judgements. One of the most fundamental theoretical and philosophical issues to be addressed in reaching such judgements is the fact that they render inescapable the kind of interpersonal welfare comparisons which are eschewed by the 'gains from trade' analysis.

A simple example will serve to illustrate the point. Consider a proposed policy change – a tariff reduction (say) – which would lead a country to increase its imports of cheaper foreign coal. The change would benefit the domestic purchasers of coal, including the producers and the buyers of products in which coal features as a productive input. But the same policy would reduce the demand for domestically produced coal, to the detriment of the coal mines and miners and to others whose prosperity is linked to that of the mines. The change would thus lead to a fundamental conflict of interest between the beneficiaries of the welfare gains and the victims of the welfare losses. Economic theory can point to whether the total gains will or will not outweigh the total losses. However, it does not presume to judge which interest group is more 'worthy' of the benefits. Weighing –

and resolving – the conflict of interest is, in the final analysis, a matter for society at large.

This raises, in turn, the question of whose value judgements should be taken to represent those of society as a whole in deciding whether, and to what extent, particular economic policies do – or do not – benefit the country. The answer to this question is bound to be a matter of dispute.

Incorporating non-economic criteria

In principle, society's preferences can be and should be articulated through the political process. In practice, the representation of these preferences is, at best, highly imperfect. However, the only workable assumption which can be made is that the relevant judgements and evaluations are the ones made by those who effectively exercise the policy choices, namely national governments. Though it is individual economic agents who conduct (most) exchange relationships, it is governments who, through the legal, political and institutional frameworks which they create and support, validate the trades as having value to society. It follows that, where governments create or perpetuate trading relationships (including cross-border linkages), the presumption must be that – as in the case of individual economic agents – the overall net benefits to society are deemed to be positive. This applies regardless of whether the decisions result from deliberate policy choices or whether they are made simply by default.

A further difficulty presents itself at this point. It can reasonably be accepted that valuations of exchange relations at the individual level reflect only changes in economic welfare (albeit broadly defined). At the societal level, however, this assumption breaks down. Governmental decisions reflect not only economic welfare, but also a range of non-economic considerations which do not apply to individual economic agents. In particular, questions of (party) political interests and of the wider 'national interest' inevitably enter into governmental estimations of social welfare, in addition to the more strictly economic costs and benefits of any course of action. Explicit political and social considerations are thus injected into the equation. But the difficulties inherent in attempts to evaluate the strictly economic issues pale into insignificance when seeking to assess the impact of the non-economic considerations on the welfare of society.

It follows from all this that to criticize the choices thus made, or the preferences thus revealed, by governments is merely to imply that different actors might place different valuations on the relationships; it does not imply that the choices or the relationships are, in any objective sense, undesirable. It is, of course, no more true that they are objectively desirable. Even in cases where governments enjoy both general domestic and international legitimacy, it may be questioned whether every judgement they make accurately reflects society's preferences and whether every decision enhances social welfare. Even leaving aside the definitional problems of determining 'legitimacy', it is clear that these issues are bound to become much more questionable when legitimacy is lacking. None the less, it is difficult to see what other method can be used in practice to make such judgements. It may be possible, in respect of particular exchange relationships, to undertake cost–benefit analyses and to seek to use the results to confirm or refute their desirability from society's perspective. But this approach has its own shortcomings and, in any event, it cannot, in general, provide a practical alternative to the presumption that governments are the appropriate arbiters of society's interests.

In this sense, therefore, the continued existence of economic relations between any two countries must – in the absence of overwhelming and irrefutable evidence to the contrary – generally be taken to confirm their social desirability. The relationships would become undesirable only if the relevant decision-makers' perceptions of the relative magnitudes of the costs and benefits involved were to be altered, either through the political process, or through market processes (especially changes in relative prices), or both.

One other point also needs to be emphasized: as in the case of individual exchange relationships, the judgement that mutually beneficial gains can be derived from international economic relations is independent of the distribution of the gains, Again, the distribution will depend ultimately on the complex determinants of the relative bargaining strengths of the trading partners. However, even a highly unequal distribution of the benefits from trade cannot invalidate the fact that mutual benefits exist. Of course, there will always be grounds for arguing that a different – perhaps less 'unequal' – distribution would be more appropriate and that policies should be adjusted to this end. That is, however, a different matter from the fact that trade between countries, like trade between individuals, is not a zero-sum game.

The results of the foregoing discussion can be summed up as follows: first, voluntary international exchange relations lead to net benefits for both countries; second, the benefits will be distributed in accordance with the two countries' relative bargaining powers; third, evaluating the associated 'social' benefits and costs necessarily involves value judgements; fourth, there is no practical alternative to vesting these value judgements in the choices and preferences of national governments; and fifth, disagreements with these value judgements do not, in themselves, invalidate them – instead, the onus is on those who disagree with them to change them via the market and/or the political process.

On the one hand, therefore, the theoretical framework for evaluating the costs and benefits to any country of its economic links with other countries is, at best, weak. Conceptually valid though it may be in assisting individual economic agents to evaluate the outcomes of their exchange relations, the framework has somewhat less validity when applied to exchange relations between national states. On the other hand, no superior alternative analytical framework exists which could overcome these difficulties. Hence, barring clear evidence to the contrary, the perpetuation of bilateral trading relationships must be interpreted as confirmation of their mutual desirability.

The problem of adverse side-effects of exchange relations

For all its shortcomings, the framework outlined above – and the principles underlying it – can also accommodate arguments which lead governments to reduce, or even to sever, particular components of bilaterial relations on grounds of conflict with explicit non-economic policy objectives. Thus, within a continuing overall economic relationship between two countries, it would not be inconsistent to question the desirability of some specific aspects of exchange on explicit social, political or strategic criteria.

For example, consider the Western strategic embargo on exports of particular categories of goods to the Soviet Union in the post-war period. Though the scope of the embargo was widened and narrowed from time to time, in essence it reflected the political belief that the strategic dangers which might arise from Soviet access to particular technologies and equipment outweighed the economic welfare gains accruing to both sides from these transactions. Moreover, the fact that the scope of the embargo was altered periodically illustrates the effect of changing evaluations of the issue by different political actors in different political and strategic circumstances.[2]

Non-economic objections to particular aspects of exchange relations between South Africa and its neighbours can be handled in a similar way. For example, the discontinuation by the Zimbabwean government of South African recruitment of migrant labour, mentioned in the previous chapter, clearly can be explained – and justified – by arguments that its economic benefits to Zimbabwe were considered too small to offset its adverse social consequences. Furthermore, this judgement represented a reversal of that made during the pre-independence years.

By contrast, the export to South Africa of migrant labour from Lesotho generates adverse social consequences which undeniably are far more pervasive for Lesotho than they ever were for Zimbabwe. Yet, the willingness of successive Lesothan governments, post- as well as pre-independence, to perpetuate these links must be taken to imply that, on balance, the net economic benefits have always been adjudged to outweigh the net social disbenefits. Similarly, Namibia's post-independence decisions to remain – at least for the time being – within the Southern African Customs Union (SACU), to retain the South African rand as its currency and to welcome new investment by South African corporations signal the same judgement, even though all these linkages will, in their own ways, act as constraints upon a whole range of Namibian economic and political policy options. Against this, Namibia's decision to invest in the infrastructure required to reroute its international telecommunications traffic via Botswana instead of South Africa indicates that a different judgement has been made in respect of this link. None of these judgements will, however, be immune to future reconsideration.

The list of other such examples would be endless, but they all illustrate the point that, within the context of the total set of exchange relations, non-economic considerations, as articulated by national governments, can be, and are, taken into account in determining the neighbouring states' policies towards individual linkages with South Africa. Moreover, each judgement may be subject to periodic or even regular review and the assessed balance between the economic and non-economic costs and benefits can alter with the passage of time and with changing political and economic circumstances. These circumstances clearly include current attitudes towards economic statecraft. In other words, they are not limited to judgements in respect of domestic issues alone; attempts to influence the policies and behaviour of other governments also enter into the equation.

It is worth stressing that precisely the same sort of reasoning applies in the reverse direction. For example, with high unemployment in South Africa, the recruitment of Basotho and Mozambican workers deprives indigenous workers of job opportunities, but the South African government evidently judges the balance of interests to lie in continued recruitment. But even here, from time to time shifting political judgements have altered this balance, thus inducing expansion or contraction of the scale of recruitment. Moreover, a future government may take a fundamentally different view of the balance and, regardless of the preferences of the governments of Lesotho or Mozambique or their citizens, may place South African workers' interests above those of workers from neighbouring states.

In short, there is nothing unusual in the 'objective' economic benefits of specific international economic relations being weighed against, and qualified by, 'normative' and non-economic criteria, and so leading to decisions to alter the scale of, or even to discontinue, the relationships concerned. Provided both sets of costs and benefits are taken into account, and provided the underlying principles of the evaluation process are not obscured, the resultant decisions are explicable and defensible on rational grounds.

The hypothesis of 'unnatural' economic relations

In Southern Africa, however, emotional and ideological issues have been allowed to obscure these underlying principles and evaluative processes. In its reluctance to admit of much that is positive or desirable in the structure or content of economic relations between South Africa and its neighbours, the literature on the region labelled virtually all such relations as 'unnatural', 'involuntary', 'undesirable' and 'costly' from the neighbours' perspective, and as being inconsistent with the long-term interests of all the peoples of the region. In doing so, the literature, in effect, gave precedence to the non-economic, and ignored the economic, costs and benefits involved. The evident objective was to alter the judgements, if not of individual economic actors in the neighbouring states, then at least of their governments, about the value of economic links with South Africa. In consequence, the processes of evaluation excluded proper consideration of the inherent characteristics of exchange relations, and thus had a severely distorting impact upon the conduct of regional economic relations.

Within the framework of the 'dependence' analysis of the functioning of the international political economy, the argument that economic relationships with South Africa are 'unnatural' does have its own internal logic. Viewed from this perspective, it is axiomatic that all the peripheral, colonized countries of the world have been incorporated, deliberately and to their detriment, by the metropolitan and colonial powers and by the regional 'agents' of these powers, such as South Africa. In this sense, 'dependence' in the political economy of Southern Africa is neither more nor less 'unnatural' than in any other region of the world which is subject to the stranglehold of imperialism and of international capitalism.

Notwithstanding the declining currency of global 'dependence' as a satisfactory analytical framework, the view that economic relations and structures in Southern Africa are, in some way, particularly reprehensible, has acquired deep roots. This is reflected in claims (such as those quoted in Chapter 5 above from the Lusaka Declaration) that the characteristics of the regional economy are neither 'a natural phenomenon nor ... simply the result of a free market economy'; that 'the development of national economies as balanced units ... played no part' in their determination; and that the regional economy had been left 'fragmented ... and subject to economic manipulation by outsiders'.

This legacy of the 'dependence' approach cannot be left unchallenged, if only because its perpetuation could inhibit acceptance of any alternative approaches to regional relations. Some common-sense observations on the issue would therefore not go amiss.

On the one hand, to the extent that they were determined by the location of resources, the regional economic structures which emerged were indeed 'natural'; and they were undoubtedly the outcome of the 'free market' in so far as they resulted from the largely unfettered and decentralized decisions of large numbers of individual economic actors, both inside and outside the region, to engage in exchange relations with each other. On the other hand, it is clear that social and political forces and governmental policies also played a major role in generating the exploitation and development of those resources, and were themselves shaped and influenced by the patterns of resource development which emerged. It is also undeniable that the notion of creating 'balanced units' out of the region's constituent national economies played little role in the development process; that the regional economies are, in consequence, 'fragmented'; and that, in so far as South Africa's neighbours are significantly lacking in market power, they are subject to 'manipulation' over their terms of trade.

But it is important to recognize that these terms – 'unnatural', 'unbalanced', 'fragmented', manipulated', etc. – are merely descriptive terms which have been invested with a specific value-laden content in an attempt to render them analytically significant. It is therefore necessary to divest them of this content. Consider for example, the criticism that no effort was made to create 'balanced' national economies in the region. Three comments are relevant here. First, as we have seen in Chapter 1, the main outlines of the regional economic structures were set in place long before most of the national economies, in their current form, were even conceived of. Indeed, in so far as there was any presumption in this regard, it was for a single economic entity encompassing at least six of the current eleven national economies.

Second, as the discussion in Chapter 2 showed, to the extent that, through their economic policies, the various national governments sought to diversify their economic structures and to alter the development patterns which emerged from the minerals revolution, they did indeed seek to achieve a 'more balanced' outcome.

Third, whilst the notion of 'imbalance' has a clear negative connotation, it is entirely vacuous for analytical purposes unless and until it is given explicit definition and provided with a bench-mark against which it can be measured. This requirement must be met whether the criticism refers to the sectoral structure or output or the occupational structure of employment or the commodity structure of external trade, or to the distribution of income and wealth. Employing the term 'balance' solely in a normative sense distorts understanding both of the nature of the structures under investigation and of the implications for future policy.

It remains true, of course, that – measured against reasonable criteria – the regional economy has numerous shortcomings, of which the extreme distributional inequalities discussed earlier undoubtedly are the most severe. It does not follow, however, that these shortcomings render its structures and institutions valueless in absolute terms, with the implication that the world would be a better place if they did not exist. It follows only that the value of the net benefits delivered by the existing structures, including their distributional consequences, must be compared with those which would flow from realistic alternative structures, and that the appropriate policy conclusions should be drawn from that comparison.

The problem of involuntary economic relations

Against all this it has to be acknowledged that some elements of economic relations between South Africa and its neighbours are 'unnatural', in the sense of being involuntary. In particular, the landlocked – and in some instances even the coastal – countries of the region have been constrained, to a greater or lesser extent, to use the South African transport routes, rather than alternative routes independent of South African control. As a result of this constraint, the neighbouring states' foreign transport and trading linkages have certainly exhibited a lesser degree of geographic diversity than would otherwise have been the case. This is especially true for Zimbabwe, Zambia and Malawi for whom the diversion of traffic to South African routes, on account of the non-functioning of the transport corridors to Maputo, Beira, Nacala and Benguela/Lobito, has been greatest.

In so far as this constraint has arisen for reasons not of the neighbours' own making, the consequent increase in their economic involvement with South Africa undoubtedly has been involuntary. However, both the nature of the constraint itself and the extent to which the relations are involuntary need careful formulation.

First, the constraint applies only in so far the denial of access has been the result of factors wholly beyond the control of the neighbouring states. This point holds regardless of whether the denial is attributable to actions by South Africa or by other parties. In the latter case, however, responsibility for the denial cannot be laid at South Africa's door. In this respect, it must be recalled that South Africa was responsible neither for the original closure of the routes, nor for their poor operating condition. The widespread assumption that, had South Africa not embarked on its subsequent strategy of destabilization, all the routes would have been both open and functioning normally is therefore at least debatable. Second, it is only the increase in traffic over and above that which would have utilized the South African routes in any event, that can be classed as involuntary. The traffic volumes associated with the large range of normal economic links with South Africa cannot be so classed.

As this formulation makes clear, the implication that all economic links with South Africa are, in some sense, enforced is patently false. Indeed, the reverse clearly applies: Southern Africa may be far from being a common market, but – as we have seen – it functions in many respects as a coherent economic region with South Africa as its hub. Furthermore, the range and volume of economic transactions between South Africa and its neighbours, both historically and contemporarily, is so vast that the notion that more than a small proportion of them are involuntary is simply not sustainable. To argue (as some do) that virtually all links are involuntary because the historically determined transport routes – the legacy of the colonial era – locked the region into the South African transport network, is to stretch the point. The non-existence of alternative transport infrastructures does not make trade which utilizes existing routes involuntary, except in a wholly tautological sense. The only relevant consideration is the extent to which there is exogenous denial of access to alternative infrastructures which do exist.

The costs of destabilization

An alternative approach often adopted to establish the claim that, in the aggregate, economic relations with South Africa are both politically undesirable and economically costly for the neighbouring states, has been to point to the devastating consequences of the policy of regional destabilization pursued by Pretoria over the past fifteen years, but especially in the period 1980–8. Again, however, there has been considerable blurring of logical boundaries.

Various estimates have been made of the costs of destabilization to the SADCC countries. One estimate, published by UNICEF, has put the cumulative costs of destabilization during the period 1980–8 at '1.3 million lives and more than $60 billion (at 1988 prices) in damage and destruction'.[3] The figure for economic damage is cited as being 'more than double the initial estimates of GDP for the entire SADCC region for 1988'; furthermore, 'the GDP of Angola and Mozambique was [estimated to be] roughly half of what it would have been had it not been for the war'.[4]

Whether the costs imposed by South African destabilization are anything like as large as these estimates suggest is – to say the least – open to question. On the one hand, both SADCC as an organization, and analysts such as Hanlon, consider that their estimates in fact have 'erred on the side of caution',[5] thus suggesting that the true figure may be even larger. Against this, however, the validity of even these 'cautious' estimates is questionable, if only because their scale is counter-intuitive.

World Bank calculations indicate that the weighted average growth rate of real GDP for the whole of sub-Saharan Africa between 1980 and 1987 was only 0.4 per cent per annum.[6] In this light, the claim that, had it not been for South African destabilization, real output (GDP) in Angola and Mozambique in 1988 would have been double their actual levels becomes, at the minimum, improbable. Indeed, it is apparent that the estimates of the costs attributable to South Africa's actions in the region simply overlook the key variables which determine economic performance in any country, namely the nature and efficacy of domestic policies of resource allocation and economic management. That Angola and Mozambique have suffered dreadfully from their respective wars is not in question; nor is the fact of South African involvement in these wars. But the above estimates imply first that there would have been a complete absence of civil war without

South African involvement – a highly questionable assumption – and second, they overlook the devastation wrought by the Marxist economic policies pursued by the Angolan and Mozambican governments themselves. These estimates are therefore misleading in the extreme.

To illustrate the point further, Botswana achieved an annual growth rate of real output of no less than 13 per cent in the same period – the highest growth rate of any country in the world. Yet Botswana was also a victim of South African destabilization. Similarly, Malawi, Zimbabwe and Lesotho – all major sufferers from destabilization – each achieved growth rates of around 2.5 per cent per annum, or six times the average for sub-Saharan Africa. If one were to ignore the domestic policy context, it would be as legitimate, on the basis of actual performance in the 1980s, to conclude that South African destabilization was a distinct advantage for these countries as to argue the reverse!

Whatever the true costs of destabilization for the neighbouring states, the argument that, by virtue of these costs, all economic relations with South Africa are undesirable, again conflates several logically distinct issues. First, as Shaw and Carlsson have pointed out, every regional power, including South Africa, harbours normal and legitimate 'regionalist aspirations'.[7] The objection to destabilization cannot be that South Africa has sought to project its economic and political power and influence in its regional domain. This projection is an inevitable consequence – indeed a defining characteristic – of being a regional power. The objection lies with the abnormal – and often illegitimate – influence which South Africa has sought to exercise, primarily through the deliberate and excessive use of its military power.

Second, the argument overlooks the substantial flows of additional foreign aid which the SADCC countries have attracted on account of South Africa's heavy-handed behaviour in the region. These inflows may have been less than the recipients would have wished, given their development objectives. But any increase in assistance which was prompted by destabilization logically – if reluctantly – must be offset against any calculations of the costs of destabilization.

Finally, as has been repeatedly pointed out in this chapter, a judgement on the value of all economic links with South Africa cannot be made on the basis of the costs of destabilization alone, since this would discount the benefits which accrue to the neighbouring states from all their normal trade and financial transactions with South Africa.

In short, the fact that the political relationship between countries is sometimes hostile and conflictual does not mean that dispassionate evaluation of their economic relationships is impossible. On the contrary, we have shown that explicit social and political considerations can be and should be incorporated into the evaluative process. Indeed, it is only when the latter is consciously inclusive of all relevant factors that a fully considered judgement can be made. Rightly or wrongly, however, in a global system based on the concept of national sovereignty, the only definitive judgement on the issue in respect of any country is the one made by its government of the day.

12 The economic role of SADCC

The advent of SADCC in 1980 generated hopes of a significant restructuring of economic relations in the region. This was to be achieved partly by means of the rehabilitation and extension of the regional transport network, thereby restoring the *status quo ante*, in which most of the overseas trade of Zimbabwe, Zambia and Malawi was carried via Mozambique instead of South Africa. It would have brought an increase in choice – and hence a likely reduction in costs – in the conduct of their foreign trade relations. These hopes were shared unreservedly by all of South Africa's neighbours.

But SADCC appeared to have in mind a much more fundamental restructuring of the region's foreign trade relations than could be achieved by the wholly desirable, but limited, objective of restoring the transport network. SADCC's central and oft-stated objective was a reduction in the 'dependence' of its member-countries, especially – but not only – on South Africa. In SADCC's view, and in the view of the intellectual sources from which SADCC largely drew its inspiration, this 'dependence' was a structural problem which was inherent in both the international and regional economies. As we have seen from Chapter 5, this was not a view derived from any general belief in the gains from trade; on the contrary, free trade was seen to lie at the root of the 'dependence' of the SADCC countries both on South Africa in particular and on the international capitalist system in general.

Against this background, SADCC rejected the standard approaches to regional economic integration, such as common markets or customs unions, the conceptual frameworks for which were also based on the general hypothesis that trade is mutually beneficial. SADCC sought instead to replace its 'dependent' trade structures with a system of trade relations based on the 'collective self-reliance' of its member-states.

The objective of 'collective self-reliance'

At one level, SADCC's objective of collective self-reliance was little different from that underlying any proposal for regional economic cooperation. In essence, the aim is to generate higher levels of trade among the member-countries themselves and to reduce, for each member-country, both the proportion of its import demand and the proportion of its export sales accounted for by non-member-countries. On these objectives, too, there was clear unanimity.

At another level, however, SADCC's primary concern with 'dependence' gave an entirely different meaning to its concept of collective self-reliance. SADCC wanted these structural changes to be sufficiently large to give meaningful content to its 'dependence'-reduction objective. It also wanted to achieve this through 'balanced' or 'equitable' development processes. Whilst all SADCC members would have subscribed to these objectives at the rhetorical level, they did not – as will be seen – subscribe to the full implications which this interpretation of the concept carried at the actual policy level.

An index of the magnitude of the task SADCC was setting itself is provided by the fact that, in 1979, intra-SADCC trade accounted for less than 3 per cent of the SADCC countries' total foreign trade. (With Namibia included in SADCC, the proportion was little more than 2 per cent.) Of the remaining 97 per cent plus of SADCC's foreign trade, slightly less than one-fifth was directly with South Africa and slightly more than four-fifths with the rest of the world. Differentiating between exports and imports, only about 6 per cent of all exports from SADCC countries went to South Africa, but South Africa supplied nearly 29 per cent of all SADCC imports. (Again, the inclusion of Namibia would have raised these proportions to 7 per cent and 33 per cent respectively.)[1]

These averages disguised very wide country-to-country variations. Tanzania, for example, had no measurable trade with South Africa at all, whereas more than 91 per cent of all of Lesotho's trade was with South Africa. There were also very wide differences in the geographical distribution of imports compared with exports. Thus, except for Lesotho, South Africa generally purchased less than one-fifth – and in several instances less than one-twentieth – of the SADCC countries' exports. By contrast, South Africa accounted for 88 per cent of Botswana's imports, 87 per cent of Swaziland's, 42 per cent of Malawi's, 38 per cent of Zimbabwe's, 14 per cent and 12 per cent respectively for Mozambique and Angola, and 6 per cent for Zambia.

Admittedly, the 3 per cent figure for intra-SADCC trade in 1979 was an historically low figure: the proportion had been almost 5 per cent in 1970 and, by virtue of the Central African Federation, may well have been even higher prior to UDI.[2] The decline had clearly been due in part to the closures of Rhodesia's borders with Zambia, Malawi and Mozambique during the 1970s. It was also due to the virtual cessation of the relatively substantial trade between Angola and Mozambique following their independence. This suggests that, given more propitious circumstances, the scope for increased intra-SADCC trade certainly existed. On the other hand, even starting from 5 per cent, achieving an increase which would really constitute a meaningful reduction in such overwhelming external 'dependence' was, to say the least, an ambitious objective. Moreover, all the above figures relate only to merchandise trade; all other economic linkages, including trade in invisibles and in factor services, are excluded.

The profound nature of SADCC's declared ambition of 'dependence' reduction was underlined by the slogan which it adopted to characterize collective self-reliance: 'Let production push trade, rather than trade push production.'³ Again, this could be interpreted at two levels. In prosaic terms, it merely pointed towards policies of import substitution and of state support for various 'strategic' investment projects. Strategies of this nature – intended to conserve scarce foreign exchange and to diversify and enlarge the domestic market – were still commonplace in Third World countries at the beginning of the 1980s. Notwithstanding growing criticisms of their theoretical foundations and mounting empirical evidence of their capacity to produce perverse consequences, such strategies could still command intellectually respectable support in appropriate, if limited, circumstances.

However, the interpretation favoured by SADCC's more radical members and advisers, and the one reflected in the supporting academic literature, was that SADCC did not want the allocation of resources to productive activities to be determined primarily by way of response to market forces, especially where these were dominated by export opportunities in South Africa or in the major industrialized countries. Rather, investment should occur in accordance with domestically determined non-market policy criteria. Among these criteria were the need for self-sufficiency, the need for production to be oriented towards the consumption requirements of the domestic population, the need to eschew reliance on 'dependence'-reinforcing foreign capital, and the need to minimize any consequent distributional inequalities both within and between the SADCC member-states.

In any economy, a switch of this nature in the mechanisms for resource allocation would indeed bring about major structural changes in both production and trade. But achieving such changes clearly requires state intervention in, and centralized direction of, resource allocation decisions on a major scale. In short, if this were the correct interpretation of SADCC's collective self-reliance strategy, then it would have implied the need for radical and fundamental transformations of all the member-states' economies along the lines of the (differing) strategies already implemented in post-independence Tanzania, Angola and Mozambique and then contemplated (in the early 1980s) by newly independent Zimbabwe.

The determinants of the SADCC model of economic cooperation

It needs to be emphasized that SADCC's scepticism about the value of the traditional conceptual approaches to regional economic cooperation was not without good cause. The history of attempts at such cooperation, let alone integration, in the Third World had been – and remains – a depressing one. The African experience has confirmed this: the East African Community and the Central African Federation both foundered within a decade of their inception, and neither the several different attempts over the past thirty years at regional economic cooperation in West Africa nor the slightly more recent Preferential Trade Area (PTA) for Eastern and Southern African countries have yet demonstrated a capacity to achieve significant and enduring advances.

SADCC was therefore well advised to be wary of such schemes. Moreover, in purely practical terms, the SADCC countries were anxious to avoid a repetition of others' mistakes. Part of the explanation for the earlier failures lay in their adoption of grandiose objectives, complex and inflexible structures, and bureaucratic and inefficient supra-national institutions. In many instances, the requisite technical conditions for the success of these arrangements were, at best, not fully present. SADCC therefore opted, as a matter of deliberate policy, for a pragmatic step-by-step approach to regional cooperation. The fact that it created flexible and almost minimalist institutional arrangements, including only a small central bureaucracy and widely devolved responsibilities to national governments, thus encouraged the hope that unrealistic schemes would be avoided.

But SADCC's pragmatic approach was also a matter of necessity: its member-countries were not only politically and economically diverse; they also had conflicting economic and political interests. They had widely diverse production structures, resource endowments, land ownership patterns, development priorities, institutional affiliations and resource allocation systems. On the last-mentioned point, for example, they ranged across the spectrum from Botswana, which was leaning progressively towards market-based mechanisms and liberal trade policies, to Angola and Mozambique, who espoused Marxist-Leninist ideologies and central planning on the Soviet and East European models.

Politically, they also had much less in common than might generally be supposed. Granted, they had a shared heritage of experience of colonialism and of white rule and, except for Mozambique and Angola, all of them were members of the Commonwealth. But they differed widely in their strategic and ideological orientations, their political systems, the composition and interests of their ruling elites, and in their attitudes towards regional integration. Having struggled long and hard to achieve their political independence, they were in no hurry to submerge their newly acquired sovereignty in any supra-national body. They were, of course, united in their opposition to white minority rule and in their concern about South Africa's overwhelming power. Furthermore, as destabilization proceeded, their solidarity on these issues was greatly reinforced. At the same time, they also had wide-ranging attitudes towards, and differing interests in, their economic links with South Africa, which were also highly varied in scope and content.[4]

The advantages of the minimalist approach

In this light, SADCC's pragmatism was to prove crucially important in preventing it from breaking up in the face of its internal contradictions. On the one hand, there was its official and formal objective of collective self-reliance which has been summarized by Hanlon in the following terms:

SADCC set itself the target of weaving 'a fabric of regional cooperation and development' based on 'equitable regional integration' . . . SADCC argues that 'the key to regional cooperation in production is rationalisation of productive capacities and their support services and deliberate avoidance of unprofitable competition and duplication'.[5]

On the other hand, it was abundantly clear that the political commitment to the radical interpretation of collective self-reliance simply did not exist. Indeed, in practice, the political capacity to sustain and implement even the relatively modest sectoral responsibilities which were devolved to the member-governments was not always forthcoming.

In a more formal institutional structure, these political weaknesses would have led to the early demise of any attempt at regional cooperation. As Hazlewood has pointed out, whatever the contribution made by technical and institutional shortcomings to the failure of earlier integration schemes, the lack of political will among the partner-states to maintain the alliance undoubtedly was the single most important factor.[6]

In fact, however, given SADCC's loose organizational structure, and its inability to impose any collective will in respect of resource allocation decisions, there was never any realistic prospect of the objectives of collective self-reliance being met. Since all real decisions remained vested in national governments, SADCC was able to reconcile and survive the inherent tension between its 'collectivist' formal objectives on the one hand, and the highly individualist political and economic interests of its member-states on the other hand. As will be seen, this applied equally to decisions affecting intra-SADCC economic relations and those affecting economic relations with South Africa.

The lack of political capacity to implement the fundamental restructuring of regional economic relations which SADCC appeared to espouse proved fortunate for two other reasons. First, it spared the remaining SADCC members from the economic consequences which such policies had already visited upon those countries – such as Angola and Mozambique – which had adopted them. These policies included the wholesale nationalization of productive assets, including land, and the replacement of decentralized economic decision-making on the part of individual economic actors with a system of centralized economic planning. Whatever the merits or demerits of the reasons for the adoption of these policies in the first instance, their consequences were undeniably disastrous. By 1984, recognition – even if only implicit – of this fact was becoming increasingly apparent within SADCC, at both the collective and individual member-state levels. Particularly noteworthy was the acknowledgement of the potential role of the private sector. The Lusaka Declaration had made no reference to private capital investment (from whatever source) and, in its early years, SADCC continued to pay no attention to the issue. In 1984, however, SADCC took its first tentative steps towards addressing what Hanlon called 'this . . . newer and less comfortable area'.[7]

Second, had SADCC indeed gone down its proposed route it would have proved even more difficult than it did to get international political and economic support. As it was, not least because of its espoused aims, the major industrialized countries, especially the UK, the US, West Germany and Japan, showed less than wholehearted enthusiasm for SADCC in the early stages. This was reflected especially in the willingness to provide development assistance for SADCC projects. By 1984, only some $700,000 had been firmly committed by the international community towards proposed projects with a total cost amounting to $2.9 billion. Moreover, the bulk of these pledges came from relatively few sources, most notably the Nordic states, a few EC countries and some of the more developed Commonwealth members, especially Canada.

It was perhaps therefore also fortunate for SADCC that, by the time South Africa's destabilization campaign, combined with the growing international pressures for action against apartheid, engendered greater international sympathy and support for the organization, some of its more radical members had already begun to turn their backs on their earlier ideological political and economic dogmatism. The evident shift in the direction of pragmatism helped SADCC to gain wider international political sympathy and financial support. In particular, greater support was forthcoming from the EC as a multilateral donor, in addition to increased bilateral subventions from individual EC member-governments. Consequently, the cumulative total of firm funding commitments virtually quadrupled to $2.7 billion by mid-1988.[8]

The impact of the sanctions issue

But if the issues of destabilization and of sanctions had some compensating consequences for SADCC in the form of increased political and financial support, they also almost proved to be the death-knell for the organization's pragmatic and realistic approach to the diversification of regional economic relations. As discussed in Chapter 10, by the middle of the 1980s, destabilization and sanctions had brought to the fore an underlying combination of mutually reinforcing beliefs, imperatives and policies which appeared to place economic relations in Southern Africa under unprecedented threat of severe and arbitrary disruption and interruption.

There was, for example, still deep resentment among at least some of South Africa's neighbours at the poor economic hand which they considered they had been dealt during the colonial era, and of which the grotesque racial inequalities in living standards and political power had been both cause and consequence. There was also genuine anger and a sense of humiliation at what they felt – and at what the prevailing academic wisdom seemingly confirmed – to be their involuntary manipulation and exploitation by neo-colonial forces and agents. There was the widely espoused desire for 'economic liberation' and for the capacity to exercise self-determination in creating more 'equitable' and 'balanced' economic structures. There was outrage at the violations of their political and territorial integrity and at the human and economic costs which they suffered, both directly and indirectly, on account of South Africa's policies. And, perhaps most decisively, there was the political need to stand up and be counted – and if necessary to pay a heavy price – to secure for the black peoples of South Africa (and of Namibia) the rights and freedoms which they were denied.

Against this background, it understandably proved progressively difficult to maintain a sense of perspective with regard to the question of economic relations with South Africa. Instead, such relations became widely and popularly regarded as being among the key instruments for maintaining both the 'dependence' of the neighbours and the subjugation of the black peoples of South Africa and Namibia. Only by confronting, and by fundamentally altering, such linkages could these injuries be assuaged, these injustices redressed and these ambitions realized.

For several years, therefore, but especially from 1985 to 1988, the region stood on the brink of catastrophe as threats of sanctions and countersanctions were uttered and weighed. That it did not, in fact, topple over the brink was due, in the final analysis, to the unwillingness of the government of each individual SADCC state to bear the costs which would be consequent upon any attempt at large-scale economic disengagement from South Africa. Given all the above-mentioned causes for anger and outrage, they could not easily have arrived at these decisions. None the less, the decisions which they reached, however reluctantly, clearly reflected their ultimate judgement of the balance between the political pressures and the economic realities which they faced.

SADCC and the structure of regional economic relations

Consequently, the pragmatic approach to regional economic relations, including relations between South Africa and its neighbours, endured. Indeed, in relative terms, it is remarkable how little the underlying structures of these relations were in fact affected by the overt political hostility between South Africa and the SADCC states during this period. Inevitably, of course, some disruption to economic linkages did occur. But compared with the disruption occasioned first by Rhodesian sanctions after 1965, and second by the civil wars in Angola and Mozambique, and by the mismanagement of economic policies in these and several other SADCC countries after independence, the impact of the South African sanctions issue on the broad structures of intra-regional economic relations was limited.

This fact can be illustrated in four ways. First, in 1987, despite seven years of effort in pursuit of collective self-reliance, intra-SADCC trade still accounted for a mere 4.4 per cent of the SADCC countries' total foreign trade.[9] Thus, not even the ground lost during the Rhodesian sanctions period had yet been fully recovered. In value terms, intra-SADCC trade, at $631 million, was little more than double the $310 million recorded in 1979.

Second, there had also been very little change since the advent of SADCC in the proportions of SADCC exports and imports accounted for by South Africa. In 1986, South Africa was still purchasing 5 per cent of the SADCC countries' exports and supplying 26 per of their import requirements.[10] Third, in 1987, in volume terms, some 58 per cent of the 'dry goods' overseas exports of Botswana, Lesotho, Malawi, Swaziland and Zimbabwe were still being conveyed via South African ports.[11] On the one hand, at this stage the Mozambique routes were still operating well below their normal capacity, indicating that further switching of routes could be anticipated in the future. On the other hand, in a number of instances, and especially in the case of Botswana and Lesotho, the continued use of the South African routes was a reflection of their relative cost-effectiveness, indicating a likely limit to the switching process.

Finally, as we have noted on several occasions, one of SADCC's key objectives was to generate a more 'balanced' and 'equitable' structure of economic relations in the region. There is no doubt that one of the 'imbalances' that SADCC hoped to rectify was the dominant role of the Zimbabwean economy in relation to the other SADCC economies. Even at SADCC's inception, despite the fact that sanctions had severely distorted its economic relations away from Zambia, Malawi, Botswana and Mozambique and towards South Africa, Zimbabwe still accounted for a significant proportion of intra-SADCC trade. Thus, in 1979, Zimbabwe accounted for 28 per cent of intra-SADCC exports and 23 per cent of intra-SADCC imports.[12] It was clear that, with the lifting of sanctions, the sheer size and the level of industrialization of Zimbabwe's economy (relative to the other SADCC economies) would ensure an increase in these proportions. By 1987, they had in fact risen to 54 per cent and 27 per cent respectively.[13]

From an analytical perspective, none of these outcomes are unduly sur-

prising. The creation of cross-border economic linkages requires considerable investment of both private and public resources. Much of this investment is specific to bilateral trade with particular countries, and in some
instances even to particular transactions. For the individual economic agents
concerned, the sunk costs associated with this investment militate against
their willingness to initiate rapid, non-marginal changes in bilateral exchange
relations. This is especially true of attempts to substitute trade with new
partners for trade with existing partners when neither the requisite infrastructure nor the appropriate institutions for the new trade yet exist.

On the other hand, exchange relations are not, of course, immutable.
Large (and anticipatedly permanent) changes in (say) relative prices or other
market conditions will naturally bring behavioural changes in their wake.
Equally, exogenous factors, such as wars, explicit political decisions, or
even extreme climatic conditions, can force individual actors to endure the
costs of dissociation and to undertake investments in new and different
linkages. In the absence of such inducements, however, existing linkages
are likely to persist. A hostile political atmosphere may inhibit their expansion, or even gradually erode the mutual benefits which they bring. However, arguments which suggest that trade relations between particular countries can be expanded or contracted virtually at will in pursuit of (say)
political or strategic objectives simply overlook the fundamental and decentralized role played by individual market participants.

Seen in this light, the expectation that an organization such as SADCC,
lacking the capacity to create substantive new infrastructures and institutions for fostering cross-border exchange relations, should have been able
rapidly to achieve major structural changes in economic relations in Southern Africa was clearly unrealistic. Furthermore, given the unwillingness of
the individual SADCC governments to dissociate their economies from
South Africa, the exogenous shocks (in the form of political decisions to
dissociate) which might instead have effected such changes were also lacking. Trade relations in the region have thus continued to be shaped largely
by market forces in which there have been few developments of a magnitude
sufficient to disturb the underlying patterns of trade.

SADCC's achievements and limitations

None of the foregoing comments are intended to denigrate SADCC's practical achievements in diversifying regional economic relations. On the contrary, within the limitations of its institutional framework, SADCC has
made not inconsiderable progress in this direction.

In practice, SADCC's primary economic role has been to provide a
framework for setting and discussing desirable targets for 'development
coordination' among its member-states. This function has been particularly

valuable in the context of negotiations for external development assistance for projects involving or affecting more than one member-state. It has assisted the various donor agencies in identifying and in ranking the priority projects for assistance, and it has provided the recipient countries with an enhanced capacity to articulate their own needs and interests in their negotiations with the donors. Together, these functions have contributed to a more rational and coordinated programme of aid disbursements to the SADCC countries. In the highly imperfect world in which aid programmes normally function, these have been no mean achievements.

SADCC's efforts were naturally concentrated in the first instance on the urgent task of rehabilitating the existing transport network for the benefit of overseas traffic. In this respect, their progress has been impressive. The two key projects have been the rehabilitation and upgrading of the ports of Beira and Maputo, and of the Beira and Limpopo transport corridors to Zimbabwe. These have reached advanced stages, although operational efficiency remains below potential, partly because of continuing (if reduced) security problems, and partly because of capacity constraints, either in the form of rolling stock or port facilities.

But these projects were by no means the only focus of SADCC's efforts. Considerable attention was also paid to plugging the gaps in the articulation of transport and communication links within and between the member-states, via projects to improve intra-SADCC road, air, telecommunications and postal links. SADCC was thus helping to extend the infrastructure in ways which would enlarge the trade choices open to economic actors in its member-countries and which would make possible the achievement of greater diversity in exchange relations. Such projects have meant, for example, that it is now no longer necessary for international telecommunications traffic between the SADCC countries themselves, or between a SADCC country and the rest of the world, to be routed via the South African network. The need for air traffic, whether passenger or freight, within the region, or between the region and the rest of the world, to be routed via South Africa has similarly been reduced, at least in principle.

For all these (and other) achievements, however, the shortcomings of SADCC's minimalist institutional structure are plainly evident. In the case of air links, for example, Hanlon has complained that despite improved airport capacities and facilities, and despite coordinated schedules,

SADCC has so far failed to achieve any deeper levels of cooperation. National airlines are symbolic of national pride. They all lose money and managers and transport ministers are reluctant to concede any potential loss of traffic or independence. The most glaring failure from the point of view of regional integration is SADCC members' reluctance to concede traffic rights ... which allow carriers to transport passengers between intermediate stops .... The effect is that there are many fewer options for passengers than there are actual flights. ... This discourages intra-SADCC travel while ensuring nearly empty, loss making flights. . . . A joint SADCC airline [would be] a way of saving money and generating new traffic; but national pride means 'SADCC Air' is just a pipedream.[14]

Practical multilateral difficulties of this nature are by no means insoluble within the SADCC framework, but they are far more difficult to resolve than when the decision-making authority is more centralized. On the other hand, if the existence of SADCC has done relatively little to further formal multilateral linkages among its member-states, it has none the less high-lighted opportunities for increased bilateral relations, including trade agreements and cooperation on infrastructural projects. In the latter case, the emphasis has again been on foreign aid-funded public sector investment projects which have been modified to provide benefits for more than one SADCC member-state. Apart from transport and telecommunications projects, there have also been important cooperative developments in the energy sector. Energy has been another sector in which enhanced cross-border cooperation between two or more SADCC member-governments has been achieved.

At the same time, it is noteworthy that individual SADCC governments have proved as likely to enter into such agreements and arrangements with South Africa as with each other. Given that SADCC's official objective remains the reduction of 'dependence' on South Africa, and that claims about the depredations suffered by its members at the hands of South Africa have been a key factor in eliciting international support, this situation has generated some interesting and anomalous situations. For example, a significant part of the rehabilitation work at the port of Maputo is being undertaken and funded by South Africa and is taking place alongside the SADCC projects. Similarly, for several years, the South African Electricity Supply Commission (Eskom) has been engaged in wide-ranging discussions with a number of SADCC member-governments about the prospects for rationalization of regional energy supply arrangements.

These growing intra-SADCC infrastructural linkages will undoubtedly facilitate additional increases in other exchange relations, including at the levels of merchandise and invisible trade. A number of studies have identified some of the specific areas and commodities for which greater intra-SADCC trade potential exists. The fact remains, however, that bilateral trade agreements and other formal and informal expressions of intent not-withstanding, the figures cited earlier demonstrate that progress on these wider fronts has been disappointingly slow.

In this respect, the fundamental problem remains the small number of private sector economic actors in the SADCC countries who are engaged in exchange relations with each other. A number of factors have contributed to this outcome. These include continuing concern with national self-sufficiency (for example, in food production); continuing hostility to private investment and deep suspicion of the concept of profit; chronic shortages of foreign exchange allocations; non-convertibility of national currencies; onerous and inefficient bureaucratic procedures; and persistent gaps in infrastructures and support services. Against this, the relative ease with which transactions can be conducted with economic agents in South Africa militates against the investment of the time, effort and resources necessary to overcome these obstacles.

In short, the SADCC model for regional economic cooperation imposes considerable limitations on efforts to affect resource allocation other than via the aid coordination function. Even the latter operates far from perfectly, but its saving grace is that it is concerned with the allocation and distribution of additional investment resources emanating from outside SADCC. However, SADCC's member-governments are much more jealous of their sovereignty over their own internal – and exceptionally scarce – investible resources with the result that SADCC has very little capacity to influence their disposition.[15]

None the less, SADCC has made, and continues to make, a small, but positive impact on the scale and shape of intra-regional economic relations. Furthermore, notwithstanding the difficult and protracted issue of sanctions, in practical terms SADCC has functioned in largely non-confrontational ways. For this reason, the impact of the highly confrontational rhetorical and political stances of some SADCC member-governments has been much less damaging to cross-border relations than might otherwise have been the case.

13 Dependence and interdependence revisited

As we noted at the outset, most contemporary analyses of economic relations in Southern Africa have taken as their starting-point the allegedly undesirable and unacceptable dependence of the SADCC countries upon South Africa. The only alternative starting-point has been the supposedly benign and desirable interdependence between South Africa and its neighbours. A key purpose of this study, however, is to show that neither of these approaches has so far proved to be a satisfactory or fruitful point of departure.

The limitations of the 'dependence' approach

The 'dependence' hypothesis has, at best, limited value and validity. As noted in Chapter 5, the global theory on which it is based reflects reasoning which verges on the tautological and the fallacious, and is unable to provide operational definitions and measurements of economic dependence.

The intellectual confusion which the hypothesis has sown in respect of both theoretical analysis and policy formulation has been especially prevalent in Southern Africa. In its global form, the hypothesis suggested that the ultimate source of these problems was the international capitalist system. In Southern Africa, however, the focus has been predominantly on the role played by South Africa. One-way 'dependence' of the neighbouring states upon South Africa has been taken as axiomatic, as has the one-sidedness of both the resultant benefits and the resultant behavioural constraints. In Tostensen's words, 'dependence' means that '[the] *status quo* does not represent a neutral point of departure, but a series of burdens and threats . . . [in which] the costs and sacrifices are high', and the basic premise has been 'that whatever happens in the region is attributable to [South Africa's] action or inaction'.[1] In such circumstances, it is perhaps unsurprising that some policy-makers in the region came to be convinced that economic links with South Africa were 'all cost and no benefit' to the SADCC countries.

It is also not surprising that the policy options which have been informed and influenced by these premises have been seriously lacking in dispassionate analysis of the means, the ends and the consequences which they imply. Since the analysis confirmed the belief, recurrent throughout the literature on SADCC, that political independence is meaningless without economic independence, the presumption has been that policy should be directed towards achieving economic independence. However, in the absence of a definition either of 'economic independence' or of specification of the relationship (if any) between economic and political liberation, the policy implications of these key concerns of the founders of SADCC remained unclear.

As far as the SADCC countries' general external economic relations have been concerned, the broad policy objective has been the achievement of 'collective self-reliance'. If interpreted as seeking to build on the member-states' resource endowments and trade potentials to increase the proportion of intra-SADCC, and reduce the proportion of extra-SADCC, exchange relations, this objective would be unobjectionable in principle. In practice, however, it has manifested itself in damaging and self-defeating policies, including hostility to private investment, particularly foreign private investment, discounting of the value of foreign trade, and a misguided belief in the virtues of self-sufficiency.

In the specific case of economic relations with South Africa, SADCC has been hard put to avoid articulating its policy objectives in conflictive terms. The least conflictive formulation seemingly available has been the general one of seeking to reduce 'dependence' upon South Africa, whilst studiously avoiding discussion – sometimes even acknowledgement – of the extensive, continuing and often expanding relations which do exist. Some individual SADCC countries, however, have argued explicitly for confrontation and maximum economic disengagement.

The appeal of the 'dependence' hypothesis and of its policy implications has, of course, been greatly enhanced by the racial dimension to the political and economic conflicts in the region. For many observers, the axiom of 'dependence' meant that virtually all economic links between South Africa and its neighbours were to be regarded, at best, with suspicion, at worst, as giving succour to white minority rule and as perpetuating the system of apartheid. This argument, which reached its zenith at the time of the debate over the desirability of imposing international economic sanctions against South Africa, contributed to an entanglement of emotional and logical reasonings in the evaluation of regional economic relations. This entanglement meant that the political imperative of providing the SADCC countries with a wider range of choices in respect of their external economic linkages became confused with the distinct political imperative of needing to confront white rule in South Africa.

As we have sought to demonstrate, however, the 'dependence' approach has caused the neighbouring states to overlook many of the basic determinants both of international economic relations in general and of the distribution of the gains from trade in particular.

Our discussion of the historical background in Part One has shown that the spatial distribution of economic development within the region was initially and primarily the result of the location of the minerals deposits and of the interrelationship between the sequence and timing of their discovery and of the development of the transport infrastructure. This distribution was subsequently modified in important ways by the economic and political responses which the minerals revolution generated. It is clear that different responses would have brought different modifications, but the fundamental basis of the regional economy was – and still remains – its endowment of natural, and especially of mineral, resources.

One distributional aspect which could, in different political circumstances, have been fundamentally altered was the racial distribution of the benefits of economic development. The course of Southern Africa's economic development would also have been altered in important ways had its political development evolved in the direction of a single, unified state, as happened in (say) Australia, Canada and the USA, instead of towards the collection of distinct political entities which eventually emerged. The fact that the latter position obtained meant that exchange relations in the region took on an inter- rather than an intra-national character. This meant, in turn, that the share of the gains which accrued to each of the regional states from its external exchange relations in general, and its regional exchange relations in particular, became an express function of its individual bargaining power *vis-à-vis* its various trading partners.

It is entirely understandable that the post-independence political leaderships in the black-ruled states of Southern Africa were unhappy with the economic legacy which they inherited from the colonial era, and particularly with many of its distributional aspects. However, the 'dependence' hypothesis transmuted their underlying dissatisfactions into the twin ideological beliefs, first that these outcomes were an historical inevitability, and second that they could not now be altered except by opting out of, or by overthrowing, the existing order. A not untypical observation was that the SADCC countries' 'colonial legacy in infrastructure, production and distribution is not acceptable, economically and politically'.[2] The implication, of course, is that only 'fundamental [i.e. revolutionary] restructuring' can improve the development prospects for these countries.

As those countries which sought to take the revolutionary route to economic transformation quickly discovered, the experience was a painful one. The myriads of decentralized, voluntary and presumably beneficial resource allocation decisions made by individual economic actors were disrupted – in many instances discontinued – forcing them to bear significant dissociation costs. To cite but one example, in Mozambique, some 2,000 private companies had been involved in foreign trade at the time of independence in 1975; by 1979, an estimated 80 per cent of the country's external trade was being controlled by official state trading organizations.[3] It is not unreasonable to suppose that there was some connection between this 'transformation' and the substantial decline in Mozambique's foreign trade during the same period.

For those governments unwilling or unable to take the revolutionary route the outlook must have seemed exceptionally depressing. The 'dependence' hypothesis put them all in the same category: they had all, as the Lusaka Declaration graphically reminded them, been deliberately and involuntarily incorporated, fragmented, exploited and manipulated. Their only hope of 'economic liberation' was to escape the seemingly inescapable.

This outlook was seriously misleading in two key respects. First, as we have pointed out, all exchange relations involve some degree of economic dependence, and all countries engaging in international trade are necessarily vulnerable, in greater or lesser measure, to involuntary interruptions to that trade. However, the extent of this dependence varies according to the degree of openness of their economies, and according to the structure and composition of their trading relations.

The central message of our earlier discussion (in Chapter 6) of the theoretical and empirical issues involved in providing operational definitions and measurements of economic 'dependence' is that there is no single, satisfactory index of the state of dependence in specific instances. Were it possible to obtain the relevant data, and to apply the appropriate criteria, all the countries of Southern Africa – including, it should be noted, South Africa itself – would doubtless be found to have significant degrees of dependence in their external economic relations. However, both the extent of dependence and the nature of its sources would almost certainly vary greatly from one country to the next.

Moreover, in so far as the greatest source of concern has been the specific issue of the dependence of the neighbouring states upon South Africa, it is entirely meaningless to place Tanzania, which has virtually no exchange relations with South Africa, and Lesotho, the economy of which is intimately bound up with that of South Africa, in the same category of 'dependence'. Generalized assertions of 'dependence' are therefore essentially vacuous. Second, the belief that, by virtue of their dependence, the other countries in the region have merely been passive and impotent victims of South Africa's power, with no capacity to pursue independent domestic or foreign economic and political policies, is also not sustainable.

In Chapter 9, we discussed Wagner's bargaining theory analysis of economic and political power relations. Wagner's conclusion was that economically weak countries are not completely devoid of political bargaining power vis-à-vis economically strong countries, because the determinants of the economic and the political terms of trade are different. This point has also been addressed by Ronald Libby, who has argued that every state – even one which is very 'weak' – has some capacity both for 'independent political action in the context of severe economic constraints' and for manipulating its external economic links in pursuit of its own domestic and foreign policy objectives.[4] Dealing specifically with Southern Africa, Libby denies the necessity of a direct correlation between the scale of regional trade with South Africa and South African state power. Conversely, he denies that increased involvement in the regional economy is necessarily disadvantageous to Pretoria's independent neighbours and that it is necessarily viewed as such by them.

Indeed, Libby goes even further in arguing that the degree of each country's involvement in the regional economy is determined directly by the political and economic interests of its ruling groups. His argument is based on what he calls 'the autonomy of domestic politics', by which he implies that intra-regional economic relations cannot exist independently of domestic political interests. In each country, moreover, expansion or contraction of its regional economic links alters the balance of political power and influence among domestic interest groups and classes, and hence 'can have both positive and negative effects upon state power'.[5]

Through carefully documented and systematic analysis of the interests and actions of the ruling groups in each country, Libby concludes that in South Africa, Zimbabwe and Tanzania, the net effect of their strategies towards the regional economy in the late 1970s and early 1980s was actually to undermine the power of the state. By contrast, in Malawi, Mozambique and Zambia, the effect, on balance, was to bolster domestic political support for the ruling groups. Finally, in Botswana, Lesotho and Swaziland, the net impact upon state power was ambiguous.

In South Africa, for example, the government's post-1979 regional strategy incorporated an alliance with the large regionally-oriented corporations. However, the nature of this alliance contributed to right-wing discontent and so undermined state power.[6] In Zimbabwe, too, the power of the state was (inadvertently) undermined by its own regional economic strategy. Priority was given to restoring the performance of the inherited 'settler' economic structures, and particularly to maintaining the regional competitiveness of Zimbabwean manufactured exports. The government's electoral platform, however, had called for transformation to a socialist economy. The resultant internal conflict between the technocratic elites charged with carrying out economic rejuvenation and the populist factions intent on achieving transformation eroded the state's political support.[7] In Zambia, by contrast, Libby argues that state power was enhanced by participation in the regional economy because the beneficiaries were largely among the ruling party's own political constituencies.[8]

Again, Libby's analysis accords with our earlier view, discussed in Chapter 11, that evaluations of the desirability of particular sets of cross-border exchange relations cannot be made without reference to the revealed preferences of national governments. However, Libby's argument in effect makes the further point that, in revealing its preferences for an extension or contraction of specific exchange relations, and in exercising its capacity to give effect to these preferences, every state will engender for itself some domestic political and economic consequences.

Libby considers that 'the conventional orthodoxy that South Africa dominates the economies of other states in the region without, however, experiencing corresponding influence upon its own economy' has stultified analysis of the political economy of Southern Africa. Furthermore, it has led to a preoccupation with 'utopian strategies . . . for "disengaging" black African states from their ties with South Africa . . . and with visionary proposals for creating *de novo* a new regional economy that excluded South Africa'.[9]

In sum, Libby's views reinforce our argument that the 'dependence' axiom has afforded an inappropriate framework for analysis of economic relations in Southern Africa.

The limitations of the interdependence approach

The alternative hypothesis about regional economic relations – namely that South Africa and its neighbours are economically interdependent and that the mutuality of the consequent benefits is unambiguously desirable – has also had its shortcomings.

The fact of mutually beneficial interdependence has been misinterpreted as implying not only that limitations on further economic integration are irrational, but also that it renders closer political cooperation between the regional states ultimately unavoidable.

South Africa has long favoured a wider political basis for economic cooperation in the region. In the case of the BLS countries, for example, it sought from the outset to achieve their formal political incorporation. Even after this particular objective was made finally unrealizable by the political independence of the BLS countries, South Africa continued to seek *de facto* incorporation of its neighbours on functionalist grounds.[10] This was reflected in various ideas for regional economic cooperation, culminating in the still-born concept of the Constellation of Southern African States (CONSAS).

The essence of the functionalist argument was that economic self-interest in the neighbouring states dictated the need for closer economic cooperation with South Africa; and closer economic cooperation would create the institutional and behavioural conditions which would take the region inexorably in the direction of closer political cooperation. It was, of course, assumed that the latter would be predominantly on South Africa's terms. In that sense, the goal of incorporation remained.

This argument is, however, crucially flawed. It is true that economic cooperation does generate some of the necessary conditions for political cooperation, especially in the form of shared institutions and a common interest in economic prosperity. Moreover, where one partner is dominant, its economic fortunes clearly become a matter of common concern to all partners. But economic cooperation does not always create the sufficient conditions for political cooperation, let alone for incorporation.

The fallacy of this functionalist argument has been amply illustrated by the history of regional relations in Southern Africa. As we have seen, there has been no lack of commonality of economic interests. Yet, the plans of Rhodes (and others) for a much enlarged sub-continental state never materialized; the Southern Rhodesian settlers chose to eschew incorporation into South Africa; Rhodesia firmly defended its political independence from South Africa during the UDI period; the BLS countries (and, most recently, also newly independent Namibia) have opted for political independence even while retaining their formal customs union and monetary area links with South Africa; and it was recognized from the outset that the differing political interests of the SADCC countries would set clear limits to their capacity for economic cooperation.

In short, on the one hand, in the absence of a single political authority, there are severe limits to the achievement of any formal structures of economic union. On the other hand, there is no inevitability that common economic interests will lead to an ever-widening commonality of political interests. Clearly, in so far as closer economic integration is actively sought, a degree of closer political cooperation is required. But extension of the latter beyond the level required to give effect to the desired degree of economic cooperation remains a choice variable for each participating country.

These basic truths became obscured as the conflicts over economic relations with South Africa intensified, especially in the eras of destabilization and, subsequently, of sanctions. Initially, South Africa sought to overcome its neighbours' resistance to functional incorporation by offering, in effect, to 'buy' their cooperation. Extensive economic benefits, including promises of technical and financial assistance, in addition to new capital investment and more extensive trading opportunities, were held out as inducements to join CONSAS or some other similar arrangement. Since these blandishments seemed to imply a tilting of the terms of trade in favour of the neighbouring states, their rejection was a matter of some mystification to South Africa, where they were interpreted as the outcome of irrational political behaviour.

As was the case with the 'dependence' hypothesis, therefore, recognition was lacking that the neighbours' evaluations of their political terms of trade with South Africa were not determined by the same considerations as their economic terms of trade. South Africa therefore persisted in its belief that the prejudicial impact on the neighbours' long-term economic interests would eventually lead to more 'rational' behaviour. For the neighbours, however, the potential economic benefits were not judged to be a sufficient reason to surrender their political independence.

Subsequently, as internal and external developments led to changes in Pretoria's regional security objectives, and as the position occupied by the neighbouring states in the international sanctions campaign became increasingly critical, South Africa's need to exercise political influence over the region increased. Its functional approach to incorporation thus gave way to an increasingly coercive stance.[11]

In effect, whilst seeking to deny the validity of the 'dependence' hypothesis, on the grounds that regional economic relations were beneficial to its neighbours, South Africa was drawn increasingly towards acceptance of its fundamental tenets, and particularly to its assertion that the 'dependent' states had no room for independent manoeuvre. Put crudely, as seen from Pretoria, the neighbouring states' economic interests meant that, in the final analysis, they had no option but to conform to the demands of, and submit to the power wielded by, South Africa. Their reluctance to recognize this 'reality' arose primarily from hostile political motives. This had the unavoidable – if regrettable – result that they had to be reminded of the reality of their status from time to time. Destabilization, in all its manifestations, was the means by which they were so reminded.

The most significant fact, however, is that, for all its might, South Africa failed to achieve its larger objective of regional political cooperation beyond that necessary to perpetuate existing economic linkages. Neither the necessity for economic cooperation, nor the substantial benefits thereof, were translated into an enthusiasm or willingness on the part of the neighbours to accede to South Africa's vision of the regional political order. Their interdependence with South Africa certainly severely circumscribed and constrained their capacity to pursue wholly independent economic and political policies. Their evident desire (notwithstanding some of their rhetoric) to preserve the benefits of their exchange relations rendered this unavoidable. Furthermore, those SADCC countries, such as Zambia and Zimbabwe, who had threatened to impose sanctions were indeed dissuaded from implementing their threats. However, this was solely because they were not willing to bear the costs of dissociation which sanctions would bring. It did not in any sense signal a capitulation to South Africa's incorporationist ambitions.

Meanwhile, as we have seen, due to their own obsession with the problem of 'dependence', the SADCC countries also failed to appreciate the fact that bargaining over the terms of their economic exchanges with South Africa was not synonomous with bargaining over the political terms of trade. As a result, they sought to deny both the underlying coherence of the regional economy and the significant, if varying, extent of their own domestic interests in maintaining, even extending, their economic links with South Africa.

Thus, interdependence has hitherto also proved to be an inappropriate model for analysis of economic relations in Southern Africa because it has not acknowledged that divergent political interests can place limits on the capacity of common economic interests to lead to cumulative political cooperation and integration. The validity of this constraint has been repeatedly demonstrated by the history of economic relations in Southern Africa, but the continuing failure to appreciate the point has been especially evident in the past fifteen years.

14 From economic conflict to economic cooperation?

In essence, the problem with the application of the concepts of economic dependence and interdependence to the study of regional economic development in Southern Africa has been that, in its own way, each has failed adequately to address the difficulties of analysing cooperative economic relations in the circumstances which obtain in the region. Contrary to popular belief, these circumstances are not unique to Southern Africa. They include the existence of widely differing political interests in economic cooperation, very significant imbalances in economic and political power and influence and an atmosphere of hostility and suspicion concerning the conduct of exchange relations – all of which are widely, if not universally, present in the international political economy. That Southern Africa is distinguished by an underlying coherence in the structure of its regional economy and by the racial dimension to its political and economic conflicts in no way gainsays the need for analytical approaches which address the more general issues in appropriate ways.

The dependence approach started from the axiom of 'unnatural dependence' of the regional states, especially (if not only) upon South Africa, and proceeded to policy conclusions which are fundamentally at odds with the above requirements. It played down, even denied, both the coherence and the interdependence of the regional economy and the benefits which accrued to the neighbouring states from their economic relations with South Africa. This led to a wholly negative view of almost any form of economic cooperation with South Africa and to an increasing emphasis on the need for 'economic liberation' and 'collective self-reliance', both of which were presented – misleadingly – as substitutes for, rather than complements to, continuing, even expanding, voluntary exchange relations with South Africa. At the same time, against all the evidence, it seemingly denied that 'dependent' countries had any room for independent manoeuvre in respect of their political and economic destinies.

The dependence approach also became ensnared in the strait-jacket imposed by the false belief that, because of the apartheid issue, Southern Africa must be analysed in terms uniquely different from those applicable to the wider international political economy. This belief reinforced the failure to recognize the existence of significant differences in national interests among South Africa's neighbours vis-à-vis participation in the regional economy. Such differences, of course, not only undermined the

case, which was so forcefully impressed upon all the neighbours, for commitment of significant resources to disengagement from South Africa, but
they also underlined the long-term limitations of the SADCC-style
approach to regional economic cooperation.

By contrast, the interdependence argument sensibly stressed the region's
economic coherence, the origins of which lay in its historical pattern of
development, and recognition of which had extended into the post-colonial
period until the advent of the challenge from the dependence hypothesis.
However, the argument overlooked the complex manner in which interdependence impinges on the conduct of international economic relations,
and particularly the extent to which it limits and constrains the scope for
independent pursuit of both political and economic policies. It also failed
to take account of the fact that interdependence is not incompatible with –
indeed, may well be the source of – conflict between the interdependent
parties. Moreover, the standard forms of regional economic integration
towards which the hypothesis of interdependence pointed, such as common
markets and customs unions, were not well suited to structural economic
conditions in the region, not least because these integrative 'solutions' fail
to address the fundamental problem of the pervasive fear of South African
domination.

All these complexities of interdependence are widely acknowledged in
the contemporary general literature on the international political economy,
where the concern of policy, particularly in the economic sphere, is how
best to accommodate to, and to manage, interdependence between countries
and how to strike an appropriate balance between the resultant benefits and
costs. This concern is clearly particularly pertinent to regions in which one
country – the 'regional power' – dominates its neighbours. In Southern
Africa, the relationships between South Africa and its neighbours (and,
indeed, between Zimbabwe and most of its neighbours) are, beyond any
question, highly asymmetrical. The fact that the Southern African literature
overlooked these issues inhibited the interdependence argument from generating the positive approach to cooperative regional economic relationships
which its adherents expected.

Beyond dependence and interdependence

The criticisms we have made of the uses to which the concepts of economic
dependence and interdependence have been put in Southern Africa do not
constitute a denial of the existence of dependent or interdependent economic
relations in the region. All the countries of the region have open economies.
Hence, by definition, they are dependent to the extent to which they derive
gains from their economic relations with the outside world. Furthermore,
even the most casual observations reveal that there are a large number of

bilateral economic relationships between countries in the region which embody significant, if varying, degrees of interdependence.

To carry the debate about international economic relations in Southern Africa forward from the entrenched positions of the past, it is therefore necessary to address and surmount the concerns and criticisms of the two concepts which have been brought to light in the course of this study.

In principle, if the requisite data were available, the extent of dependence in the region would be measurable. However, each country would exhibit a different degree of dependence. This is partly because the overall extent of openness to trade and other international exchange relations would be found to vary from country to country (and, within each country, from year to year), and partly because the structures of their respective trade relations would show them to be vulnerable in significantly different measures to interruptions of trade. Each country's costs of dissociation would thus also vary greatly, as would the risk that they would be incurred.

Estimation of the size of these costs would be greatly complicated by the fact that several countries in the region are landlocked and that, at some times, their choice of transport outlets to the rest of the world has been more restricted than at other times. During these periods, which have sometimes been extensive, the probability of their being cut off from their external economic relations has clearly been increased. An even more complicating factor is that their own policies and attitudes have contributed significantly to these variations in the probability of dissociation.

In so far as each of the eleven countries of Southern Africa (including South Africa) is dependent upon any one of the other regional states, the variations in degrees of dependence are undoubtedly also large. In overall terms, some countries have extremely limited exchange relations with each other; others have very extensive relations. Again, however, the effective degrees of dependence would have to take account of the compositional and structural aspects of each set of bilateral relations, and of the differing probabilities that these relations would be interrupted. All these factors would suggest the likelihood of a very wide range of dissociation costs for each country.

In the absence of the relevant data, it is clearly not possible to measure these variables in practice. None the less, as and when the data becomes available, it will be in these respects and in these directions, rather than in the pejorative and normative senses in which it has hitherto been employed, that the concept of dependence will continue to have potential utility in examinations of cross-border economic relations in Southern Africa.

Whether or not the revelation of a high degree of dependence, as defined in the above terms, would be a cause for concern and action on the part of policy-makers cannot be deduced a priori (unlike the case when dependence is defined in terms of the global hypothesis). As we have stressed, in the final analysis, evaluations of cross-border exchange relations are a matter for the political process. Individual economic agents will respond to market opportunities and price incentives. Where governments consider that the existing structures of exchange relations embody unacceptable degrees of vulnerability, it is entirely open to them to pursue policies which restrict or enlarge the stock of opportunities and which alter the relevant incentives. In such circumstances, the availability of satisfactory estimates of the extent of dependence would not only reveal the nature and extent of the problem but provide pointers to the appropriate corrective policy measures.

Clearly, however, any perceived political necessity for embarking upon dependence-reducing policies will depend upon the context within which the relevant economic relations are viewed. It is in this respect that a more satisfactory understanding on the part of the region's policy-makers of the nature of mutually dependent economic relations – i.e. of interdependence – will be of particular value.

First, as we have suggested in Chapter 8, the fact that interdependence simultaneously involves both costs and benefits implies that, for each country, there exists an optimum level for its bilateral exchange relations with any other country. This is the level at which the net benefits of interdependence are maximized.

Second, when a bilateral relationship is asymmetrical, in the sense that one country's dissociation costs are much higher than the other country's, a SADCC-type strategy – in which the former country seeks to achieve a reduction in the absolute level of its dependence by reducing the scale of bilateral exchanges – is not the only feasible response. It is also open to the more dependent country to seek to push the relationship in the direction of greater interdependence by engaging in new exchanges which will raise the partner's dissociation costs by more than it raises its own. Indeed, if the existing level of exchanges is below the optimum level, this would make much more sense than seeking to reduce dependence because it would also increase the level of net benefits accruing to the more dependent country.

Third, there are lessons which can be drawn from our discussions of economic statecraft and of economic and political leverage in Chapter 9. These suggest that in cases where the relationship between two countries is of particular importance to both sides, and where the capacity to exercise political influence is an important issue, economic statecraft can be employed in ways that will bring positive gains to both sides.

In short, it is open to all the countries of Southern Africa, but particularly to South Africa on the one hand and its neighbours on the other, to move towards a structure of regional economic relations which is based on a positive, rather than a negative, conception of interdependence. In so doing, they would be moving from what Boulding has called the 'threat system' to the 'exchange system'.[1] An alternative way of putting it is that they would be taking advantage of the substantially unexploited scope for gains in trade between neighbouring states to build, in Arad's terminology, a balance of prosperity rather than a balance of terror.[2]

Towards a post-apartheid regional economy

Dramatic political changes have recently been taking place in Southern Africa. In South Africa itself, the institutional structures and the legal bases of the apartheid system have already been substantially dismantled, all proscribed political organizations have been unbanned, political prisoners – including, most importantly, Nelson Mandela – have been released and a (hopefully sustainable) momentum has been created towards real negotiations to achieve a peaceful political settlement. The goal of ending white minority rule may well now at last be in sight, in which case the racial dimension to the region's conflicts, and the associated problem of the politicization of economic relations with South Africa, may also be in the process of elimination and resolution.

These welcome and unprecedented changes were in fact preceded, and were almost certainly facilitated, by some no less remarkable moves towards a reduction in political and economic tensions within the wider region. Among the most important developments were the fundamental shifts in the character and the scale of the Soviet Union's involvement in the region; the consequent December 1988 tripartite agreement between Angola, Cuba and South Africa, which in turn made possible the South African and Cuban military withdrawals from Angola and which led directly to Namibia's long-sought independence; and the evident suspension – hopefully now permanent – by South Africa of its policy of deliberate political, economic and military destabilization of its regional neighbours. Also important have been the earnest, if still unsuccessful, multilateral endeavours to resolve the continuing bitter and intensely destructive internal conflicts in Angola and Mozambique.

On the economic front, there have likewise been some welcome signs in several countries – notably Angola, Mozambique, Tanzania, Zambia, Zimbabwe and, significantly, newly independent Namibia – of a shift away from a radical and ideological approach to economic policy, and particularly towards the role of private investment. There has been an evident softening of official attitudes in the region towards economic relations with South Africa, with the result that many exchanges which hitherto have been conducted covertly and often reluctantly, are now becoming more open. In addition, new exchanges are being less strongly discouraged, with some even being actively encouraged.

All these changes undeniably have altered a number of previously entrenched assumptions and perceptions not only about strategic and political parameters, but also about economic possibilities, in the region. The prospect that Southern Africa may now be standing on the brink of resolving its remaining major political conflicts, including the problem of apartheid, has led many observers to assume that economic renewal and prosperity will necessarily follow. In particular, the belief is again growing that the motive force of the South African economy will create a virtuous cycle of development in the wider region via a substantial extension of trade, investment and institutional links with the neighbouring states. Visions of common markets and other forms of economic union are once again emerging in some quarters.

The conclusions of this study suggest that it would be decidedly premature to regard these as probable, let alone inevitable, outcomes of any regional settlement. Desirable as they may seem, to take them for granted would be to overlook too many obstacles – political, economic, institutional and intellectual – which will have to be overcome before they can be realized.

On the one hand, to the extent that some of the political inhibitions on closer economic cooperation either have been, or are in the process of being, removed, more cooperation is bound to occur. The ending of apartheid and the formal lifting of economic sanctions are clearly key issues in this regard. The advent in South Africa of a government which is perceived to have greater political legitimacy would counter the misguided tendency to regard exchange relationships between economic agents in the neighbouring states and economic agents in South Africa as inherently undesirable. It would thus help to unravel the entanglement of normative with positive issues which has so severely distorted evaluations of these exchange relations. Restoration of the existing regional transport system is continuing, and new links are being developed, thereby affording the landlocked countries progressively wider choices in the conduct of their foreign trade. This is effectively removing the only valid justification for the argument that economic linkages between South Africa and its neighbours are unnatural and involuntary.

The obstacles to regional economic cooperation

On the other hand, there are several reasons why realization of this optimistic scenario for the regional economy is by no means assured. One reason for caution is that the future strength and prosperity of the South African economy itself is not yet assured. South Africa's economy faces its own structural – not to mention political – hurdles in securing a recovery from the growth-inhibiting forces which have constrained it, especially over the past decade. Conditions in the region may help or hinder, but are unlikely to provide the key to resolution of these difficulties.

Second, the future economic prosperity of Southern Africa, including the scale of cross-border economic relations will also depend both upon the existence of political stability in the other countries in the region and upon the domestic economic policies pursued by them. Here, too, there are no assurances to be given. Welcome pressures for greater democratization are currently being felt in several regional states in addition to South Africa. However, even leaving aside the still uncertain outcomes to the conflicts in Angola and Mozambique, the consequences for political stability of these growing pressures must still be considered an entirely open question. Similarly, on the matter of economic policy there can be no guarantee that past mistakes will not be repeated or perpetuated.

But beyond all this lies the general fact that, whilst peace and political stability in any region are, of course, necessary conditions for economic prosperity and economic cooperation, they are not – as we have demonstrated – sufficient conditions. Reconciliation and rapprochement in Southern Africa may now be common items on many agendas, but the conditions for translating these into an imperative towards economic integration are not strongly in evidence.

First, even when the regional states have put behind them the conflictual legacy of recent history and the mistrust which this created over intraregional economic linkages, the inhibitions to such linkages will not be overcome simply by political statements of intent. If the region's states wish to give effect to any such intent they will need to find ways of overcoming the propensity for economic conflict and of creating instead a propensity for cooperation. This will require the active development of an appropriate political and institutional framework within which confidence and mutual respect can be built. Effective economic cooperation universally requires politically difficult choices and adjustments, including surrender of some of that much-prized attribute, national sovereignty. The experience of SADCC has confirmed the evidence from the region's earlier history that sovereignty is not likely to be surrendered very readily in Southern Africa, with or without apartheid. It would therefore be prudent to discount grandiose ideas about a Southern African common market.

Second, the belief that, in the post-apartheid era, conflict between South Africa on the one hand, and the neighbouring states on the other hand, will evaporate, is too simplistic. This is only partly because the nature and duration of the transition to majority rule in South Africa, and the characteristics and strength of the post-apartheid economic system, are still too uncertain to chart the state of future political and economic relationships within the region. More fundamentally, it is because the problem of the imbalance of power between South Africa and its neighbours will remain. This problem would arise in any region in which there is a dominant regional power, but it is clearly especially acute in Southern Africa. Indeed, there is – and will remain – throughout Southern Africa a legitimate fear that South Africa, however governed, will always exercise overweening economic power over its neighbours. A key lesson to be drawn both from Southern Africa's history and from the theoretical literature is that this fear will need to be addressed and assuaged before there can be any prospect of creating a prosperous regional order.

There has always been an assumption that a post-apartheid South Africa will join SADCC. But SADCC's primary *raison d'être* was the need to reduce dependence upon South Africa. Whether or not the ideological belief in 'dependence' persists, South African membership of SADCC will pose serious questions about its future role. If SADCC were to retain its informal, decentralized, low-key organizational structure, South African membership would simply further diminish the organization's symbolic political significance as a front against economic domination. At best it would remain little more than an aid-coordinating body.

If SADCC is to give effect to its other intended role, namely that of coordinating regional economic development, then it must approach closer to the traditional institutional models. However, such regional organizations have had a dismal record, especially in Africa, and there is little reason to believe that a Southern African economic 'community' would be inherently more likely to succeed. Indeed, with the problem of apartheid disposed of, and on the further assumption that settlements are reached in Angola and Mozambique, even the limited cohesion of interests which has held SADCC together may begin to dissolve. For example, Tanzania, Angola and even Zambia may begin to find they have more (or at least as much) in common with Central than with Southern Africa, not least because their long-standing concern about Zimbabwean domination would be likely to resurface. In short, the long-term viability of any formal regional economic grouping will depend upon an underlying unity of political interests as well as upon the shared economic benefits.

In practice, the emphasis in regional economic cooperation is likely to remain on more *ad hoc*, and essentially bilateral, arrangements. This will apply not only to the neighbouring states *vis-à-vis* South Africa, but also to relationships between the neighbouring states themselves. This more measured approach to the management of both common and conflicting interests is already well entrenched in the region, and probably represents the most realistic path to the building of cooperative economic relations.

Some of these links will be foreign aid funded, largely infrastructural projects; others will be official joint ventures; but in the long run, the key determinant of the scale and scope of economic interdependence will be the willingness (and ability) of individual (private) economic actors to identify and exploit profitable opportunities for cross-border exchanges.

The scope for Western policy is regrettably limited. In so far as it exists, it lies in two directions. The first is obviously the provision of development assistance. However, the notion of Marshall-plan type schemes is probably now wholly unrealistic. ODA is likely to remain too scarce for such schemes. The second option is to encourage confidence-building measures between the regional states. Here, too, targeted aid flows could be of value: one possibility, for example, would be assistance with the availability of foreign exchange to finance trade flows between countries with limited resources. In the final analysis, however, the capacity to build a 'balance of prosperity' in Southern Africa will be determined within the region itself.

Conclusion

The purpose of this study has been to examine critically the tendency to view international economic relations in Southern Africa in terms different from those applicable elsewhere in the international political economy. We have sought to demonstrate that the core of the problem does not lie in the unique and specific features of the Southern African situation itself. Rather it lies in the fact that, for varying reasons, there have always been clear political limits to the willingness of the countries of the region to embrace more integrative and cooperative approaches to their mutual exchange relations. The situation has not been helped by the shortcomings of the traditional analytical frameworks employed for consideration of these relations. In particular, there has been misunderstanding of the meaning of the concepts of economic dependence and interdependence, the origins and the nature of the impediments to which they give rise and the actions and policies required to surmount these obstacles.

At the end of the day, Southern Africa may not be capable of the 'economic miracles' which, as our opening quotation from Peter Vale points out, (Western) Europe and the Pacific Rim have achieved through settlement of their differences. As in Eastern Europe, there has been too much economic dislocation and there remain too many political imponderables to give much certainty to predictions of unprecedented regional prosperity. Indeed, there are still many reasons to fear the alternative scenario in which the region would be consigned to increasing despair and decline. But, in so far as economic interdependence within the region can provide the basis for confidence-building measures, and thereby contribute to a reversal of the trend towards economic decline, the opportunity should certainly be grasped.

To achieve this end, however, it will not be sufficient – though it will be necessary – to eschew the pursuit of conflictive regional strategies in favour of more accommodative approaches. It will also be essential to address the economic and political realities underlying economic relations in the region, to demolish any myths which, for one reason or another, have become received wisdom and to assert (or reassert) any truths which have become obscured. This is one game which is definitely worth the candle, and this study has represented a preliminary attempt to take up the challenge.

Notes

Introduction

1. Some analyses of dependence and interdependence in the region have addressed these issues in a more sophisticated way. Thus, some adherents of the 'dependence' school have acknowledged that, even in highly asymmetrical relationships, the mutuality inherent in interdependent relations affords the more dependent partners greater freedom of action, politically and economically, than might seem apparent at first glance. See Tostensen (1982) and Libby (1987). Equally, Lewis (1988, 1990), writing from a more 'orthodox' perspective, points to the behavioural constraints which interdependence brings. Arguments along these lines have, however, been the exception rather than the rule.
2. The vilification of anyone who dared to dissent from this 'party line', and the efforts made to suppress their views, constitute a story, the eventual telling of which will reflect little credit on those who were responsible.

Chapter 1

1. Given the emphasis in this study on *economic* relations, it might have been more appropriate to exclude Tanzania from this definition and to include Zaire instead. On the one hand, Tanzania's economic linkages are stronger with East and Central, rather than with Southern, Africa. By contrast, as will become apparent, the important Katangan copper-producing region of Zaire might be considered an integral part of Southern Africa. On the other hand, Tanzania has played a formidable political role in Southern Africa in the past twenty-five years, whereas – at least until recently – Zaire's political involvement in the region's affairs has been limited.
2. The main sources for this section, and for subsequent discussions of the economic history of South Africa itself, are Attwell (1986); Horwitz (1967); Houghton (1973); Libby (1987); Nattrass (1981); and Smith (1990), Ch. 5.
3. Hollingsworth (1982), pp. 210–45, provides a comprehensive country-by-country introduction to the railway systems of Africa.
4. The main sources for this section, and for subsequent discussions of the political and economic history of the wider Southern African region are Franklin (1963); Hailey (1963); Hanna (1965); Libby (1987); and Smith (1990).
5. For a history of the interrelationships between the Protectorates (including the third territory of Swaziland), Britain and South Africa, see, e.g. Hailey (1963). The events leading up to the incorporation of Basutoland and Bechuanaland were particularly complex, but among them was a desire to limit the extension of Republican influence and power. In the case of Bechuanaland, part of the motive was to preclude the Transvaal from acquiring a westward outlet to the

sea through the German Protectorate of South West Africa. Not the least of British concerns was the boost this also would give to German (and, by virtue of the eastward route from the Witwatersrand through Mozambique, to Portuguese) leverage over the Transvaal. (See Hanna (1965) pp. 75 *et seq.*; Hailey (1963), Ch. 1.) In the case of Basutoland, it was the territorial ambitions of the Free State which were seen to be the problem.

6. Rhodes, in fact, had hoped to incorporate Katanga but, unbeknown to him, the British government had already recognized the Congo boundary. See Hanna (1965), pp. 114–15; Franklin (1963), Ch. 2.
7. Horwitz (1967), p. 58.
8. An account of the railways issue is provided by Horwitz (1967), pp. 60 *et seq.*
9. ibid. p. 61 (emphasis in original).
10. ibid. p. 111.
11. ibid. p. 65.
12. Much controversy was to be generated in subsequent years over the precise nature of this status. See, for example, Strack (1978), Ch. 1.

Chapter 2

1. These macroeconomic influences are by no means irrelevant to economic relations in Southern Africa – indeed, given the weight of the South African economy, they could be considered crucial in the sense that South Africa's economic fortunes (or misfortunes) would almost certainly have significant consequences for the rest of the region. None the less, these macro aspects of economic interdependence will not be discussed in detail in this study.
2. Stoneman (1982), p. 277 notes that the Company's initial forays into commercial agriculture were not very successful and that it was mainly the African farmers who benefited from the increased demand. White farming came into its own only after the achievement of settler self-rule, at which stage Africans became subject to discriminatory laws and restrictions.
3. The nature – and consequences – of the mines' demand for labour is discussed *inter alia* by Wilson (1972) and Houghton (1973), Ch. 4.
4. Over the subsequent decade, annual employment averaged only about 300,000, but by 1960 it had risen towards 400,000 again. See Wilson (1972), Table 8, p. 70 and Appendix 3.
5. See Wilson (1972), pp. 3–5 and 68–71 for summaries of the various revisions over the years of the Mozambique Convention and other provisions which regulated the recruitment of foreign (unskilled) labour to the mines.
6. Houghton (1973), p. 88.
7. Hanna (1965), p. 179.
8. Strack (1978), p. 101.
9. Details of relations between South Africa and the three High Commision countries are given in Hailey (1963), Ch. III.
10. SACU in fact had its origins in even earlier customs agreements between the Cape Colony and several other surrounding territories, some of which were later incorporated into the Cape.

11. Hanna (1965), Ch. 10 outlines the historical background to the Federation and gives details of the extent of both cooperation and conflict among the three territories. See also Franklin (1963).
12. See El-Agraa (1988), pp. 1–2 for definitions of the alternative forms of international economic integration.
13. Horwitz (1967), Ch. 15 provides an extended discussion of the economic and political arguments which raged over these policies.
14. Stoneman (1978), pp. 63–5 provides a brief outline of the early history of industrialization in Southern Rhodesia.
15. Horwitz (1967), p. 436, footnote 3 cites the following illustrative comment on this point by Brand: 'In a community whose main object is to develop resources hitherto untouched, and where the government's main work is to foster such development, freedom to adapt customs dues and railway rates to the rapidly changing needs of the community is a matter of life and death.'
16. In this instance, there was a happy coincidence between the prevailing economic arguments for differential pricing of agricultural and non-agricultural freight in the interests of geographic diversification of economic activities on the one hand, and the positive political benefits for the government on the other hand. Horwitz (1967), pp. 116 et seq.
17. Houghton (1973), p. 176. The inclusion of all the SACU countries within all official data on South Africa's foreign trade constitutes an abiding problem for analysis of the geographical origins and destinations of intra-regional trade in Southern Africa.
18. Strack (1978), p. 4.

Chapter 3

1. It was not in fact until 1964, when Zanzibar was merged with Tanganyika, that the country's name was changed to Tanzania.
2. An account of South Africa's foreign relations, including those with black African and other Third World countries, after the advent of apartheid is given by Geldenhuys (1984), Ch. 1.
3. For assessments of South Africa's trade with Africa, see inter alia Blumenfeld (1982), pp. 42–3; Burgess (1976); Houghton (1973), p. 176; and Johnson (1977), esp. Ch. 3. Again it must be recalled that the published data refer to SACU and hence South Africa's trade with the BLS countries (and with Namibia) is not reflected in these figures.
4. Blumenfeld (1982), pp. 43–4.
5. Guma (1985) provides an explanation of the workings of the Rand Monetary Area Agreement.
6. Johnson (1977), p. 49.
7. Hanna (1965), pp. 289–91 and 298–301 offers a flavour of the nationalists' views on the benefits which had accrued from Federation.
8. Strack (1978), pp. 177–8.
9. ibid., Table 4.5, p. 115.
10. Renwick (1981), pp. 46–7.

11. Strack (1978), Ch. 4.
12. Zambia's economic difficulties in the face of Rhodesian sanctions are discussed, *inter alia*, by Strack (1978), pp. 123–6 and 177–80.
13. See, for example, Morna (1988), Ch. 5.
14. The financial, and particularly the foreign exchange, complications arising out of Rhodesia's relations with South Africa during the sanctions period are discussed by Strack (1978), pp. 108 *et seq*.

Chapter 4

1. Michaely (1984), p. 4.

Chapter 5

1. The condition is frequently also called 'dependency' since much of the literature originated from the work of Latin American political economists who used the term 'dependencia'.
2. Dos Santos (1970), p. 231.
3. Such methods include transfer pricing and under- or over-invoicing.
4. One of the earliest and most influential extensions of this thesis to Southern Africa is to be found in Arrighi (1967).
5. For a brief, but clear, statement of these arguments, see Todaro (1981), pp. 79–84.
6. The relevant literature is extensive. On South Africa itself, a select bibliography and brief summary is given in Blumenfeld (1986). Lipton (1985) provides a detailed (and critical) discussion. Amin (1987) affords several classic examples of the largely uncritical application of this thesis to the study of the wider region in the form of the SADCC countries. Cliffe (1983) notes with regret a relative lack of connection between the two literatures.
7. Nsekela (1981), pp. 2–3.
8. Tostensen (1982), p. 15.
9. Lall (1975), p. 800.
10. Little (1982), pp. 218–19.
11. Loehr and Powelson (1981), p. 319.
12. Little (1982), pp. 220–1.
13. Loehr and Powelson (1981), p. 319.
14. Arad *et al.* (1983), p. 16.
15. Little (1982), p. 220.

Chapter 6

1. Michaely (1984).
2. ibid., pp. 7–8 (emphasis in original).

3. ibid., pp. 13 *et seq*. Technically, the cardinal measure of this welfare loss is provided by the sum of two component consequences of the reduction in trade, viz. a 'production effect' and a 'consumption effect' (pp. 14–15, and Figure 2.1).

4. ibid., p. 16. In the literature on international economic sanctions the argument for the imposition of selective sanctions against 'critical' imports required by the target economy (e.g. oil) is based on similar considerations. See Blumenfeld (1987), pp. 194–5.

5. For example, our hypothetical patient may be deprived of a wide range of other exchanges and yet still not have his/her welfare significantly reduced if supplies of the critical drug remain available.

6. The relationship between the trade ratio and welfare measures is loose, but almost certainly positive. As a general rule, the larger the gap between the closed economy relative price ratios and the international price ratios, the larger will be both the welfare gains from trade and the trade ratio itself. Michaely (1984), p. 15.

7. ibid., p. 24, Table 2.2. The ranges quoted here represent trade ratios measured at current prices. For more than four-fifths of the sample, the ratios were higher – in many instances, significantly so – in the later year (1978) than in the earlier year (1960), presumably reflecting the world-wide trend towards freer trade in the intervening period.

8. Calculated from World Bank (1989), Tables 3 and 14. Data for South Africa in fact refer to SACU. No data were available for Angola, which is not a member of the World Bank.

9. Michaely (1984), pp. 26 *et seq*. The problem is further complicated by the fact that there is both a direct and an indirect component to the import content of export production. The indirect component arises from the use in export production of domestically-produced inputs which themselves have some imported content. See pp. 28–30 and Table 2.3.

10. ibid., p. 30, Table 2.4.

11. This is partly because low income countries are more likely to be exporters of primary products and, in general, primary production is likely to have a relatively low import component (as compared with, say, manufacturing) (see ibid., p. 31, Table 2.5). But it is partly also because the overall import coefficient in less developed countries is likely to be low in comparison with more developed countries (see pp. 30–4).

12. It is, of course, only changes in relative prices which give rise to this familiar 'price-index problem'. The issues can be formally illustrated diagrammatically using the standard transformation-cum-community preference curve analysis for 'tradable' and 'non-tradable' goods. Michaely, pp. 16 *et seq*., and Figure 2.2.

13. ibid., p. 19.

14. Michaely notes (pp. 19–20) that, in the long term, as an economy moves from low-income to high-income status, there are a priori grounds for expecting that, in general, the relative price of tradable goods will fall. The presumption here is that, if the output of the tradable sector is assumed to consist predominantly of goods, and of the non-tradable sector to consist mainly of services, the growth process will lead to a relatively greater expansion of the tradable sector in production. On the other hand, on the assumption that the income elasticity

of demand for services (non-tradables) will ultimately be greater than that for goods (tradables), long-run growth will generate a bias in consumption towards the non-tradable sector. These two trends must, in principle, imply a fall in the relative price of tradables as growth proceeds. If this is so, then it follows that the use of constant prices would overstate any increase (or understate any reduction) in the degree of openness over time. Despite the paucity of appropriate empirical data, Michaely presents estimates which confirm this broad hypothesis. However, there are no grounds for expecting the process to be consistent over time for individual countries. In the case of developing countries, Michaely's evidence (pp. 23–5, and Table 2.2) suggests the distinct possibility of perverse results even over fairly extended periods of time. In other words, until an economy reaches a fairly advanced state of maturity, it is not unusual for the relative price of tradable goods to rise, rather than fall, over even fairly extended periods of time.

15. For a given aggregate volume of imports, the implied dependence is less the more evenly are the imports spread across the whole range of industrial sectors. The proxies for this weighted index which Michaely has calculated for a number of countries suggest that the weighted ratio is likely to reveal much greater trade dependence in this particular respect than the unweighted ratios might imply. In this instance, however, it is less clear whether any systematic differences can be anticipated between more and less developed countries (pp. 39–41, and Table 3.2).

16. This argument is based on the familiar distinction in the international trade literature between 'Kravis-type' and 'Linder-type' goods (Michaely, p. 41 *et seq.*).

17. Michaely developed a variety of estimates for over a hundred countries which suggested this factor could be of considerable importance for determining the extent of dependence, if only because the statistical spread of the ratios was very large (Table 3.4). Again, however, the question of systematic differences between industrialized and developing countries is unclear, both theoretically and empirically (pp. 46–9, and Table 3.5).

18. Michaely, pp. 35–6.

19. ibid., p. 38. Michaely also suggests that there is likely to be a relationship between the share of exports in the total sales of a particular industry and the overall share of exports in the economy. The proxy indices which he constructed for nineteen countries suggest that the extent of dependence implied by these export composition factors does tend to be significantly higher than suggested by the simple ratio of exports to GDP (pp. 36–9, and Table 3.1). Empirically, Michaely's data (mainly for developed countries) also suggest it is likely that a high weighted ratio on the export side will be accompanied by a high weighted ratio on the import side, but whether this conclusion can be extrapolated to developing countries is unclear.

20. Michaely, p. 35.

21. ibid., p. 51.

22. ibid., Chs 4, 5.

Chapter 7

1. Arad *et al.* (1983) (henceforth Arad), p. 13.
2. Equally, any loss of benefit, financial or otherwise, which Kariba incurs from the inability to continue employing Zomba is a cost of dependence to him.
3. Arad, p. 26.
4. Strictly speaking, this result assumes a static world, in which the initial allocation of resources is optimal. In circumstances where the existing allocation is not optimal, or where dynamic effects are allowed for, the possibility exists that the substitute trade may in fact bring higher benefits than the original transaction. However, even though existing transaction sets are seldom optimal in practice, and dynamics effects do exist, some non-zero cost is still likely to be present in most cases of this nature.
5. Arad, p. 28.
6. See Arad, pp. 39 *et seq.*
7. *Ex ante*, of course, it would be more accurate – given the relevance of the probability of dissociation – to speak of the loss of *expected* national income.

Chapter 8

1. Arad *et al.*, (1983) (henceforth Arad), pp. 10–11.
2. Arad, p. 11. See also Moon (1987) on the increasing complexity of relations between developed and developing countries.
3. Arad, p. 13. See also Keohane and Nye (1977).
4. Arad, p. 12.
5. ibid. pp. 23 *et seq.*
6. Wagner (1988), p. 463.
7. Arad, pp. 28 *et seq*, esp. Figure 2.3, p. 30.
8. ibid., p. 29. This definition is subject to the assumption that the dissociation costs exceed some minimum threshold for both partners. For costs below this threshold, the degree of mutual dependence would be so low that the two countries effectively would be 'independent' of each other.
9. ibid., p. 33.
10. ibid., p. 31.
11. Arguably, the relationship might have been classified instead as one of Zambian dependence upon Rhodesia, if only because the reduction in Zambian GDP during the UDI period was greater than the reduction in Rhodesian GDP: the former grew at an average of only 1.9 per cent per annum between 1965 and 1980, whereas the latter grew at 4.4 per cent per annum (World Bank, 1989, Table 2.) However, this difference reflects not only the costs of dissociation, but a number of other unrelated variables (including the quality of economic management, which was arguably stronger in Rhodesia). Hence, it seems unlikely that Zambia's dissociation costs were so much larger than Rhodesia's to warrant the relationship being described as one of dependence, rather than interdependence. The matter could be settled only by detailed estimation of the two countries' dissociation costs.

12. Arad, p. 33.
13. ibid., pp. 33–4.
14. The two concepts of a balance of terror and a balance of prosperity are defined and discussed by Arad, pp. 5–7 and 34–7.
15. As with 'positive' interdependence, there are numerous permutations of relationships of deterrence which can be classified according to the relative degrees of balance or imbalance in the capacity of each side to impose costs on the other party. For the relevant taxonomy, see ibid., p. 34 *et seq.*, esp. Figure 2.4.
16. Arad, p.8.
17. Boulding's views are summarized briefly by Arad, p. 4.
18. ibid., pp. 5–7.
19. ibid., p. 10.
20. ibid., pp. 9–10.

Chapter 9

1. The limiting case arises only when the 'small country assumption' is universally applicable, i.e. when all countries are price-takers in international markets. But even when market power exists, it needs to be stressed that the weaker partner loses out only in a limited sense. Even a price-taker realizes absolute – and positive – gains from trade. These gains are merely smaller than those which could have been acquired had market power been greater.

   Furthermore, the weaker partner's gains from trade may still be larger than those of the stronger partner in relative terms: it is conceivable that, as a proportion of its total economic welfare, the weaker partner's gains from trade may be larger than those of the stronger partner. This in itself throws some light on the nature of interdependence as a 'mutual' condition in which interruptions of trading relations would lead to losses on both sides. Since the original gains from trade are not normally equally distributed, the losses likewise will be greater for one party than for the other. Much more importantly, in relative terms, the party for whom the welfare gains from exchange relations comprise a larger share of total economic welfare – and this could be either the weaker or the stronger party in terms of market power – may appear to be more dependent upon the trade. Dependence in this sense thus becomes a relative, rather than an absolute, concept.
2. Hirschman (1945), p. 17; Wagner (1988), p. 462.
3. Baldwin (1985), pp. 13–14; Hanson (1988), p. 7.
4. Hanson (1988), pp. 3–4.
5. ibid., p.17 and pp. 38–9.
6. ibid., p. 57. See pp. 53–9 for an extended discussion of the concept of economic warfare.
7. ibid., p. 53.
8. ibid., p. 57.
9. ibid., p. 58.
10. ibid., p. 57.
11. ibid., pp. 55–6.

12. ibid., p. 7.
13. ibid., p. 15.
14. ibid., p. 58.
15. Michaely (1984), p. 7 (emphasis in original).
16. Commonwealth Secretariat (1986), pp. 127–8.
17. Wagner (1988), pp. 462 *et seq.*
18. ibid., pp. 462–5.
19. ibid., p. 463.
20. ibid., pp. 463–4.
21. ibid., pp. 464–5.
22. ibid., pp. 465 *et seq.*
23. ibid., p. 472.
24. ibid., pp. 472–3.
25. ibid., p. 473.
26. It is important to note that, by assumption, the only 'threat' being made by South Africa in this hypothetical example is to raise the tax on migrant earnings. Thus the argument would hold even if Lesotho were in South America, rather than physically surrounded by South Africa. The other sources of South Africa's economic power – for example, the capacity to cut off Lesotho's food imports – clearly give it far greater bargaining strength than is being supposed here.
27. Wagner (1988), pp. 472–3.
28. ibid., p. 472.
29. ibid., p. 481.
30. The argument here is in no way undermined if, in addition to extracting the political concession, South Africa also succeeded in changing the terms of trade over migrant labour in its favour by increasing the tax. This outcome would merely reinforce Wagner's argument, for it would demonstrate that South Africa indeed had sufficient unexploited market power to change the terms of trade even without demanding a political concession.
31. Wagner (1988), p. 474.
32. ibid., p. 483, footnote 37.

Chapter 10

1. Jaster (1986), p. 16.
2. ibid., p. 27.
3. Nsekela (1981), p. 3.
4. See, for example, Hanlon (1984), pp. 3–4.
5. ibid., Part 1.
6. See, for example, ibid., Chs 2, 3; and Green and Thompson (1986).
7. Jaster (1986), pp. 9–10.
8. SAIRR (1980), p. 628.
9. Hanlon (1990), Ch. 4, documents the extent of SADCC's successes in both these respects.
10. Hayes (1987), Ch. 4, gives one of the most comprehensive assessments of

the potential costs which sanctions would have imposed on South Africa's neighbours.

11. As late as 1990, Hanlon was still arguing that sanctions were feasible, affordable and desirable for the SADCC countries. See Hanlon (1990), Ch. 3.
12. The formal SADCC position is reproduced in Hanlon (1990), Appendix 5.
13. It will be clear that the high costs of dissociation which these economic actors would have faced were mainly a function of the 'sunk cost' element (see Ch. 7 above).
14. Renwick (1981), pp. 52–4 notes the importance of the role played by pressure from South Africa in the timing of the Rhodesian government's decision to negotiate an end to UDI.
15. SAIRR (1982), p. 88.
16. Leistner (1988), p. 123, Table 1.
17. Hill (1983), pp. 219–20.

Chapter 11

1. The formal demonstration of this result depends upon the two economic agents placing different relative values on the goods, given their existing endowments. Since the process of exchange alters the quantities of the goods which are available to each party for consumption, it necessarily also alters the relative values which they place on them. The exchange process continues up to the point at which both parties place the same relative values on the goods, at which stage the possibilities for mutual gains have been exhausted.
2. The nature of the Western strategic embargo against the Soviet Union is discussed by Hanson (1988), Ch. 4.
3. Hanlon (1990), p. 19 and Appendix 4.
4. ibid., p. 157.
5. Hanlon (1986), p. 270.
6. World Bank (1989), Table 2.
7. Shaw and Carlsson (1988), p. 2.

Chapter 12

1. These (and subsequent) data for 1979 were calculated from Sollie (1982), p. 5, Table 2.
2. For the 1970 trade matrix, see ibid., p. 4, Table 1.
3. Nsekela (1981), pp. 227 et seq; Hanlon (1990), p. 65.
4. The extent of this diversity is acknowledged in Nsekela (1981), pp. 15 et seq.
5. Hanlon (1990), p. 65.
6. Hazlewood (1988), p. 186.
7. Hanlon (1984), p. 11.
8. Hanlon (1990), p. 39, Table 3. Meanwhile, the total being sought had also more than doubled to $7.2 billion.
9. Hanlon (1990), p. 60, Table 6.

10. ibid., Statistical Annex 5, p. 131.
11. Calculated from ibid., Statistical Annex 10, p. 135.
12. Calculated from Sollie (1982), Table 2.
13. Hanlon (1990), p. 60, Table 7.
14. ibid., pp. 85–6.
15. The fact that SADCC governments frequently do not make optimum use of these resources – or, more accurately, do not permit the owners of the resources to utilize them effectively – in no way diminishes the relevance of this point.

Chapter 13

1. Tostensen (1982), p. 143 and p. 9 respectively.
2. Green and Thompson (1986), p. 263.
3. Sollie (1982), pp. 31–2.
4. Libby (1987), p. xvii.
5. ibid., p. 315.
6. The terms of the alliance were that the state would assist the corporations in securing the economic benefits of increased regional economic dependence upon South Africa. In return, the corporations would assist the government in securing the neighbours' 'co-operative' behaviour with regard both to sanctions and to sanctuary for the ANC. The alliance also had a domestic political purpose, namely the economic, social and political stratification of urban black society. However, the alliance threatened the interests of some of the National Party's traditional constituencies among conservative and less affluent and less secure whites (ibid., pp. 12–13, 62–88 and 313–15).
7. The implication is that arguments which focused on the need to reduce South African leverage over Zimbabwe through a strategy of economic disengagement completely missed the point about the crucial domestic political importance of regional economic links (ibid., pp. 11–12, 62–3 and 89 et seq.).
8. The government reversed its policy of disengagement from Rhodesia in 1978 and subsequently pursued a policy of sourcing imports from the cheapest sources, including South Africa. This was not simply because the sectors most closely linked to the regional economy – such as mining – were South African-dominated. It was also because these sectors provided the economic base for the ruling party's own major political constituencies, namely the trade unions and the urban middle classes (ibid., pp. 9–10, 229–45, 316–18 and 327–8). By means of similar analyses, Libby illustrates the cases both of other supportive and of ambivalent 'regional-domestic political economy relationships' in the remaining countries.
9. ibid., p. 3 and p. 5 respectively.
10. Vale (1987), pp. 180 et seq.
11. ibid., pp. 184 et seq.

Chapter 14

1. Arad *et al.* (1983), pp. 4–5.
2. ibid., pp. 5–10.

Bibliography

Amin, Samir, Chitala, Derrick and Mandazo, Ibbo (eds) (1987): *SADCC: Prospects for Disengagement and Development in Southern Africa*, The United Nations University and Zed Books, London.

Arad, Ruth, Hirsch, Seev and Tovias, Alfred (1983): *The Economics of Peacemaking: Focus on the Egyptian–Israeli Situation*, Macmillan for the Trade Policy Research Centre, London.

Arrighi, Giovanni (1967): *The Political Economy of Rhodesia*, Mouton, The Hague.

Attwell, Michael (1986): *South Africa: Background to the Crisis*, Sidgwick and Jackson, London.

Baldwin, David A. (1985): *Economic Statecraft*, Princeton University Press, Princeton.

Blumenfeld, Jesmond (1982): 'Economic relations and political leverage', in James Barber, Jesmond Blumenfeld and Christopher R. Hill, *The West and South Africa*, Chatham House Papers No. 14, Routledge and Kegan Paul for The Royal Institute of International Affairs, London.

Blumenfeld, Jesmond (1986): 'Class, race and capital in South Africa revisited', *The Political Quarterly*, Vol. 57, No. 1, January–March, pp. 74–83.

Blumenfeld, Jesmond (1987): 'The economics of South African sanctions', *Intereconomics*, Vol. 22, No. 4, July/August, pp. 190–8.

Burgess, Julian (1976): *Interdependence in Southern Africa: Trade and Transport Links in South, Central and East Africa*, Special Report No. 32, The Economist Intelligence Unit, London.

Cliffe, Lionel (1983): 'Zimbabwe: political economy analysis and the contemporary scheme', in *Southern African Studies: Retrospect and Prospect*, Centre of African Studies, University of Edinburgh.

Commonwealth Secretariat (1986): *Mission to South Africa: The Commonwealth Report* (The Findings of the Commonwealth Eminent Persons Group on Southern Africa), Penguin Books, London.

Dos Santos, Theotonio (1970): 'The structure of dependence', *American Economic Review*, Vol. 60, No. 2, May, pp. 231–6.

El-Agraa, Ali M. (ed.) (1988): *International Economic Integration*, Macmillan, London (2nd edn).

Fetter, Bruce (1983): *Colonial Rule and Regional Imbalance in Central Africa*, Westview Press, Boulder.

Franklin, Harry (1963): *Unholy Wedlock: The Failure of the Central African Federation*, George Allen and Unwin, London.

Geldenhuys, Deon (1984): *The Diplomacy of Isolation: South African Foreign Policy-Making*, Macmillan for The South African Institute of International Affairs, London.

Green, Reginald H. and Thompson, Carol B. (1986): 'Political economies in conflict: SADCC, South Africa and sanctions', in Phyllis Johnson and David Martin (eds),

Destructive Engagement: Southern Africa at War, Zimbabwe Publishing House for Southern Africa Research and Documentation Centre, Harare.

Guma, X. P. (1985): 'The Rand Monetary Area Agreement', *South African Journal of Economics*, Vol. 53, No. 2, June, pp. 166–83.

Hailey, Lord (1963): *The Republic of South Africa and the High Commission Territories*, Oxford University Press, London.

Hanlon, Joseph (1984): *SADCC: Progress, Projects and Prospects*, Special Report No. 182, The Economist Intelligence Unit, London.

Hanlon, Joseph (1986): *Beggar Your Neighbours: Apartheid Power in Southern Africa*, James Currey for Catholic Institute for International Relations, London.

Hanlon, Joseph (1990): *SADCC in the 1990s: Development on the Front Line*, Special Report No. 1158, The Economist Intelligence Unit, London.

Hanna, A. J. (1965): *The Story of the Rhodesias and Nyasaland*, Faber and Faber, London (2nd edn).

Hanson, Philip (1988): *Western Economic Statecraft in East–West Relations: Embargoes, Sanctions, Linkage, Economic Warfare, and Detente*, Chatham House Papers No. 40, Routledge and Kegan Paul for the Royal Institute of International Affairs, London.

Hayes, J. P. (1987): *Economic Effects of Sanctions of Southern Africa*, Gower for the Trade Policy Research Centre, London.

Hazlewood, Arthur (1988): 'The East African community', in Ali M. El-Agraa (ed.), *International Economic Integration*, Macmillan, London (2nd edn), Ch. 7.

Hill, Christopher R. (1983): 'Regional co-operation in Southern Africa', *African Affairs*, Vol. 82, No. 327, April, pp. 215–39.

Hirschman, Albert O. (1945): *National Power and the Structure of Foreign Trade*, University of California Press, Berkeley.

Hollingsworth, Brian (1982): *Railways of the World*, W. H. Smith, London.

Horwitz, Ralph (1967): *The Political Economy of South Africa*, Weidenfeld and Nicolson, London.

Houghton, D. Hobart (1973): *The South African Economy*, Oxford University Press, Cape Town (3rd edn).

Jaster, Robert S. (1986): *South Africa and its Neighbours: The Dynamics of Regional Conflict*, Adelphi Papers No. 209, International Institute for Strategic Studies, London.

Johnson, R. W. (1977): *How Long Will South Africa Survive?*, Macmillan, London.

Johnson, Phyllis and Martin, David (eds) (1986): *Destructive Engagement: Southern Africa at War*, Zimbabwe Publishing House for Southern Africa Research and Documentation Centre, Harare.

Keohane, Robert O. and Nye, Joseph S. (1977): *Power and Interdependence*, Little, Brown, Boston.

Lall, Sanjya (1975): 'Is dependence a useful concept in analysing underdevelopment?', *World Development*, Vol. 2, No. 11, pp. 799–810.

Leistner, Erich (1988): 'Labour migration', in E. Leistner and P. Esterhuysen (eds), *South Africa in Southern Africa: Economic Interaction*, Africa Institute of South Africa, Pretoria, Ch. 6.

Leistner, Erich and Esterhuysen, Pieter (eds) (1988): *South Africa in Southern Africa: Economic Interaction*, Africa Institute of South Africa, Pretoria.

Lewis, Stephen R. (1988): 'Some economic realities in Southern Africa: one hundred million futures', in Coralie Bryant (ed.), *Poverty, Policy and Food Security in Southern Africa*, Lynne Riener Publishers Inc, Boulder.

Lewis, Stephen R. (1990): *The Economics of Apartheid*, Council on Foreign Relations, New York.

Libby, Ronald T. (1987): *The Politics of Economic Power in Southern Africa*, Princeton University Press, New Jersey.

Lipton, Merle (1985): *Capitalism and Apartheid*, Gower/Maurice Temple Smith, Aldershot.

Little, Ian M. D. (1982): *Economic Development: Theory, Policy and International Relations*, Basic Books for Twentieth Century Fund, New York.

Loehr, William and Powelson, John P. (1981): *The Economics of Development and Distribution*, Harcourt Brace Jovanovich, New York.

Maasdorp, Gavin (1984): *SADCC: A Post-Nkomati Evaluation*, South African Institute of International Affairs, Johannesburg.

Michaely, Michael (1984): *Trade, Income Levels and Dependence*, North-Holland, Amsterdam.

Moon, Bruce (1987): 'Political economy and political change in the evolution of north-south relations', in Gavin Boyd and Gerald W. Hopple, *Political Economy and Political Change in the Evolution of North–South Relations*, Frances Pinter, London.

Morna, Colleen Lowe (1988), *The SADCC Ports Handbook*, Africa File Special Report, Africa File Ltd., London.

Nattrass, Jill (1981): *The South African Economy: Its Growth and Change*, Oxford University Press, Cape Town.

Nsekela, Amon J. (ed.) (1981): *Southern Africa: Toward Economic Liberation*, Rex Collings, London.

Renwick, Robin (1981), *Economic Sanctions*, Harvard Studies in International Affairs No. 45, Harvard University Center for International Affairs, Cambridge, Mass.

Robinson, Peter B. (1987): *Trade and Financing Strategies for the New NICs: The Zimbabwe Case Study*, Working Paper No. 23, Overseas Development Institute, London.

SAIRR (South African Institute of Race Relations): *Survey of Race Relations in South Africa*, SAIRR, Johannesburg (published annually).

Shaw, Timothy M. and Carlsson, Jerker (eds) (1988): *Newly Industrializing Countries and the Political Economy of South–South Relations*, Macmillan, London.

Smith, Alisdair (1986): 'East west trade, embargoes and expectations', Discussion Paper No. 139, Centre for Economic Policy Research, London.

Smith, Susanna (1990): *Front Line Africa: The Right to a Future*, Oxfam, Oxford.

Sollie, Gunnar (1982): *Trade Patterns and Institutional Aspects of Trade: An Empirical Study of Trade in Southern Africa*, DERAP Working Papers A267, Christian Michelson Institute, Bergen.

Stoneman, Colin (1978): 'Foreign capital and the reconstruction of Zimbabwe', *Review of African Political Economy*, No. 11, January–April, pp. 62–83.

Stoneman, Colin (1982): 'Industrialization and self-reliance in Zimbabwe', in Martin Fransman (ed.), *Industry and Accumulation in Africa*, Heinemann, London, Ch. 13.

Strack, Harry R. (1978): *Sanctions: The Case of Rhodesia*, Syracuse University Press, New York.

Todaro, Michael P. (1981): *Economic Development in the Third World*, Longman, New York (2nd edn).

Tostensen, Arne (1982): *Dependence and Collective Self-Reliance in Southern Africa*, Research Report No. 62, Scandinavian Institute of African Studies, Uppsala.

Vale, Peter (1987): 'Regional policy: the compulsion to incorporate', in Jesmond Blumenfeld (ed.), *South Africa in Crisis*, Croom Helm for The Royal Institute of International Affairs, London.

Vale, Peter (1989): 'Pretoria and Southern Africa: A pathological report', *International Affairs Bulletin*, Vol. 13, No. 3, pp. 96–105.

Wagner, R. Harrison (1988): 'Economic interdependence, bargaining power, and political influence', *International Organization*, Vol. 42, No. 3, Summer, pp. 461–83.

Whiteside, Alan (1985): *Past Trends and Future Prospects for Labour Migration to South Africa*, Occasional Paper, South African Institute of International Affairs, Johannesburg.

Wilson, Francis (1972): *Labour in the South African Gold Mines 1911–1969*, Cambridge University Press, London.

World Bank (1989): *World Development Report 1989*, Oxford University Press, New York.

Index

African National Congress see ANC
agglomeration economics 39
agricultural exports 31
agricultural workers 32, 33
  see also labour market
agriculture 14, 15, 24, 31–2
  commercial 14, 31, 39
  food supplies 32, 39
ANC 45, 111
Anglo-Boer War see Boer War
Angola 1, 13, 160
  and South Africa 45, 49, 111, 132–3
  colonial period 19, 22
  economic relations 31, 50, 163
  geography 36
  political independence 43–5
  railways 26, 31
anti-apartheid campaign 110–11
apartheid 1, 4–5, 45, 46–7
  and capitalism 66–7
  anti-apartheid campaign 110–11
  minority rule 42, 45
  post-apartheid systems 160–1,
    162–3
  unequal development 17
Arad, Ruth 90, 91, 93, 94
arms trade 47

Baldwin, David 96
banking system 35
barter 28
Basutoland see Lesotho
Bechuanaland see Botswana
Beira (Mozambique) 18, 37, 51, 144
Belgian Congo see Zaire
Benguela railway 26, 31, 51
bilateral trading relations 107–8,
  123–5
BLS countries see Botswana
                   Lesotho
                   Swaziland
Boer republics 14, 15, 19, 21–2
Boer War (1899–1902) 20–2, 23
Botswana 13
  and South Africa 115, 116, 133

colonial period 19, 20, 23, 35
  economic relations 31, 49, 151
  geography 36
  political independence 43, 45
boundaries see geographical boundaries
boycotts see economic sanctions
British Commonwealth 43, 47, 50
  UDI 43, 44–5, 50–7, 77
  see also Great Britain
British South Africa Company 19–20,
  22–3, 24, 31–2
Bulawayo (Zimbabwe) 18

Cairo (Egypt) 18
Cape Colony, the 20–1
Cape Town (SA) 14, 15, 18, 20
Cape-Free State Customs Convention
  (1889) 21
capital investment 33–4
  foreign 14–15, 27
  industrial development 38
  international 64–5
  monopoly capital 64
capital mobility 29
capital services 27
  see also trading relations
Central African Federation 35–6, 37,
  40, 43, 46, 50, 138
civilized labour policy 38–9
collective self-reliance 135–7
colonial rule 141
  and economic
    interdependence 26–41
  and mineral resources 17, 19–20, 21
  British 1, 13, 17, 19–25, 43, 64
  neo-colonialism 141
  Portuguese 43–5, 50
commercial agriculture 14, 31, 39
Commonwealth Eminent Persons
  Group 100
communications 34, 144
  see also transport systems
Congo see Zaire
CONSAS 112, 113, 152

Constellation of Southern African
    States *see* CONSAS
cross-border transactions *see* trading
    relations
Cuba   44, 111, 160
currency convertibility   35

De Beers   116
destabilization   46, 110–12, 132–4,
    140–1, 160
    see also economic sanctions
Dos Santos, Theotinio   63–4
Durban (SA)   15

East Griqualand   14, 18, 19, 21
Eastern African Community   138
Economic Commission for Africa
    (UN)   47
economic conflict   1–2, 5, 20–2, 46–7,
    92–3, 96–7, 107
    political context   109–10
economic cooperation   156–65
economic dependence   2–5, 7–8, 156–7
    and trading relations   71–80,
        128–30, 158–65
    consequences   66
    costs   81–7
    definition   61–2, 63–4
    measurement   70–80
    social costs   85–7, 158
    theory   63–9, 147–52, 154
economic integration   9, 22–5, 30–6
    limits to   36–7
economic interdependence   2–5, 7, 8,
    42, 107–8, 157
    and colonial rule   26–41
    and SADCC   137–8, 140–1
    and trading relations   89–94
    benefits   8
    consequences   95–6
    definition   61–2, 88
    negative   92–3, 107–8
    positive   92–3, 107–8
    theory   88–94, 152–5
economic power   99–104
economic relations   2–5, 46, 96–9
    and ideological differences   4, 6
    and SADCC   141–3
    and transport systems   30, 31, 36,
        51–2, 111–12, 116, 119–20, 144
    components   27–30
    disadvantages   127–8
    evaluation   123–5

gains from   124–6
history   6–7, 12–24
institutional framework   30, 35–6,
    145
involuntary   131–2
macroeconomic   29–30
non-economic criteria   125–7
politicization   47–51, 109–10, 125–7,
    133–4, 153–4
regional   22–5, 30–6, 42
South Africa   2–5, 31, 42, 48, 51–3,
    122–34
theory   3–4, 159–60
unnatural   128–30
see also trading relations
economic renewal   8–9
economic sanctions   43, 47, 49, 96–7,
    127
    and South Africa   110, 114–18,
        132–4, 140–1
    and UDI   51–7
    destabilization   46, 110–12, 132–4,
        140–1, 160
economic statecraft *see* economic
    relations
economic warfare *see* economic conflict
education   34
exports   27–8, 40, 49, 74
    agricultural   31
    industrial   77–8
    see also trading relations

factor services   27–8, 32
    unilateral   28
    see also trading relations
farming *see* agriculture
financial transactions   28
First World War (1914–18)   32, 38
food supplies   32, 39
    see also agriculture
foreign aid   28, 163–4
foreign exchange   35
foreign investment   14–15, 27
    see also capital investment
foreign loans   27
FRELIMO   44, 111
Front Line States   45, 46, 114–15
functionalist economics   152–3

geographical boundaries   17, 18–19
geographical distribution:
    of economic activities   17, 39
geographical influences   36

Germany 19, 22
global village theory 88–9
government policies see policy-making
Great Britain:
  and South Africa 47, 50
  Boer War (1899–1902) 20–2, 23
  colonial rule 1, 13, 17, 19–25, 43, 64
  Commonwealth 43, 47, 50
guerrilla warfare 44, 52
Gwelo see Gweru
Gweru (Zimbabwe) 18

Hanlon, Joseph 139, 144–5
Hanson, Philip 96–9
Harare (Zimbabwe) 18
harbours see ports and harbours
Hazlewood, Arthur 139
Hirsch, Seev 90, 91, 93, 94
Hirschman, Albert 95–6, 100, 101
historical survey 6–7, 12–24
Holland:
  colonial rule 14, 15, 19, 21

ideological differences 44, 46
  and economic relations 4, 6
  and economic theory 63, 64, 66–8
  Marxist theories 4, 6, 63, 64, 66–8
immigration 14, 15, 19–20, 32, 34
imports 27, 37, 38, 49
  intermediate goods 74, 77
  replacement of 76
  see also trading relations
independence see political
  independence
industrial development 17, 47–9
  impact of 38–41
  manufacturing industries 39–40
industrial exports 77–8
institutional framework:
  economic 30, 35–6, 145
intermediate actors 28
  see also trading relations
intermediate goods 74, 77
international capital 64–5
  see also capital investment
international relations 47, 49
  see also economic relations
investment see capital investment
invisible trade 27–8, 31, 48
  see also trade relations
involuntary economic relations 131–2

Jameson raid (1895) 23

Johannesburg (SA) 15
judicial system see legal system

Kariba hydroelectric station 36, 50
Katanga (Zaire) 18, 20
Kimberley (SA) 14, 18, 19
Kruger, Stephanus Johannes Paulus,
  President 19–20

labour agreements 35
labour market:
  agricultural 32, 33
  civilized labour policy 38–9
  migrant labour 16–17, 32–3, 35,
    81–5, 118–19
  mine workers 32, 33
  poor whites 38–9
  skilled 15, 48
  unemployment 128
  unskilled 16–17, 48
labour migration see migrant labour
labour services 27–8
  see also trading relations
legal system 34, 37
Lesotho 13
  and South Africa 115, 116, 127–8
  colonial period 19, 23, 35
  economic relations 49, 151
  geography 36
  political independence 43
Lesotho Highlands Water Project 116
Libby, Ronald 150–2
Limpopo railway 37
Limpopo River 18, 19–20, 23, 144
linguistic differences 17
living standards 17, 34
Lobengula, Chief 20
Lobito (Angola) 26
Lourenço Marques (Mozambique) 18,
  37, 51
Lusaka Declaration (1980) 67, 69, 150

macroeconomics 29–30
  see also economic relations
Malawi 13
  colonial period 19, 20, 23, 35
  economic relations 151
  geography 36
  political independence 43, 50
  see also Central African Federation
manufacturing industries 39–40, 47–8
  see also industrial development
Maputo (Mozambique) 144

market forces   38
Marxist theories   4, 6, 63, 64, 66–8
Matabele tribe   20
Michaely, Michael   70, 73–4, 79, 99
migrant labour   16–17, 32–3, 35, 81–5,
    118–19
  tropical   33
mine workers   32, 33
mineral resources   14–19, 30
  and colonial rule   17, 19–20, 21
  and regional development   17, 18–19
  discovery   14–15
  impact of   14–19
mining development   38
minority rule   42, 45
  see also political independence
missionaries   20
monopoly capital   64
  see also capital investment
Mozambique   1, 13, 15
  and South Africa   111, 132–3
  and Zimbabwe   53–4
  colonial period   18, 19, 21, 22
  economic relations   31, 51, 53–4,
    149, 151, 163
  geography   36
  political independence   43–5, 52
  railways   37, 51, 52
  transport system   54
MPLA   44
Mugabe, Robert, President   118

Namibia   1, 13, 48, 127–8
  and SADCC   112
  colonial period   19, 24
  railways   26
Natal (SA)   14, 15, 20, 21
the national interest   125–6
National Party (SA)   46–7
nationalism   47
  see also political independence
Nationalist-Labour Pact government
    (SA)   39–40
native reserves   20
Ndola (Zambia)   18
negative interdependence   92–3, 107–8
neo-colonialism   141
Northern Rhodesia see Zambia
Nyasaland see Malawi

OAU   47, 66
oil production   51
open economic systems   157–8

Orange Free State   19, 21, 22
Organization of African Unity see
    OAU

PAC   45
policy-making   45–6, 49, 107–8
political context:
  of economic relations   47–51,
    109–10, 125–7, 133–4, 153–4
political ideologies see ideological
    differences
political independence   42–57
  and economic conflict   46–7
  and economic relations   47–51
  nationalism   47
political power   99–104
political unification   26–7, 36–7
poor white problem   38–9
Port Elizabeth (SA)   14, 15
ports and harbours   14, 36
Portugal   18, 19–20, 22
  colonial rule   43–5, 50
positive interdependence   92–3, 107–8
postal services   34
Preferential Trade Area see PTA
price structure   74–5, 143
private sector companies   28, 145–6,
    149
PTA   138
public sector bodies   28
public utilities   36

racial inequality see apartheid
railway agreements   21
railway freight   39, 119–20
  see also trade routes
railways   15, 18, 20, 21–2, 34, 51
  Benguela   26, 31, 51
  Limpopo   37
  pricing policies   119–20
  Rhodesian   37
  Tazara   37, 53
  see also transport systems
Rand Monetary Area   49
regional development   17, 18–19
RENAMO   44, 111
repatriation   118–19
Rhodes, Cecil   18, 19–20, 23
Rhodesia see Zambia
                Zimbabwe
Rhodesian Railways   37
road transport   34
  see also transport systems

SACU 37, 40, 42, 48, 127–8
  membership 35, 49
SADCC 56–7, 167
achievements 143–4, 146
  and economic relations 141–3
  and economic sanctions 114–18,
    132–4, 140–1
  and South Africa 112, 113, 114, 117
  economic role 135–46, 147–8
  formation 67, 110, 135
  limitations 144–6
  Lusaka Declaration (1980) 67, 69
  membership 13, 163
  political role 112–14
Salisbury see Harare
Second World War (1939–45) 37, 39
segregation see apartheid
self-determination see political
    independence
self-reliance see collective self-reliance
service transactions see invisible trade
Sharpeville (SA) 47, 48
skilled labour 15, 48
social benefits:
  of economic relations 125–6
social costs:
  of economic dependence 85–7, 158
social development 17
South Africa 1, 13
  and Angola 45, 49, 111, 132–3
  and Botswana 115, 116, 133
  and Great Britain 47, 50
  and Lesotho 115, 116, 127–8
  and Mozambique 111, 132–3
  and SADCC 112, 113, 114, 117
  and Swaziland 115, 116
  and Zambia 49, 53–4, 116
  and Zimbabwe 51–3, 54–7, 116,
    118–21, 127
  apartheid 1, 4–5, 45, 46–7, 66–7,
    110–11
  destabilization 4–6, 110–12, 132–4,
    140–1, 160
  dominance of 34–6, 42
  economic relations 2–5, 31, 42, 48,
    51–3, 122–34, 147–8
  economic sanctions 110, 114–18
  geography 36
  government policies 45–6, 49
  history 20–2, 24–5
  international relations 49, 109–10

manufacturing industries 39–40,
    47–8
migrant labour 32–3
National Party 46–7
Nationalist-Labour Pact 39–40
regional development 18–19
South African Customs Union see
    SACU
South African Reserve Bank 35
Southern African Development
    Coordination Conference see
    SADCC
Southern Rhodesia see Zimbabwe
South-West Africa see Namibia
Soviet Union 44, 111, 160
Soweto (SA) 45
SWAPO 45
Swaziland 13
  and South Africa 115, 116
  colonial period 19, 20, 23, 35
  economic relations 49, 151
  political independence 43
  transport system 34

Tanganyika see Tanzania
Tanzania 13, 19, 22
  capital investment 34
  economic relations 151, 163
  political independence 43, 45
tariffs 37, 38–9, 124–5
Tazara railway 37, 53
TEBA 118
telecommunications see
    communications
tourism 27
Tovias, Alfred 90, 91, 93, 94
trade agreements 30, 49, 119, 137–8
trade disruption 79–80
trade embargoes see economic sanctions
trade ratios 73–5
trade routes 51–2, 119–20
  see also transport systems
trading relations 27–9, 31–2, 48–51
  and economic dependence 71–80,
    128–30, 158–65
  and economic
    interdependence 89–94
  and SADCC 135–46
  and UDI 51–7
  bilateral 107–8, 123–5
  exports 27–8, 31, 40, 49, 74, 77–8
  imports 27, 37, 38, 49, 74, 76, 77

see also economic relations
transport systems   14, 26, 54
  and economic relations   30, 31, 36,
    51–2, 111–12, 116, 119–20, 144
  railways   15, 18, 20, 21–2, 26, 31, 34,
    37, 51, 53
  roads   34
Transvaal Republic   18, 19–20, 21, 22
Transvaal-Natal Railway Convention
    (1894)   21
tropical workers   33
  see also migrant labour
Tsumeb area (Namibia)   26

UDI   43, 44–5, 50–7, 77
UNCTAD   66
unemployment   128
  see also labour market
unequal development   17
UNICEF   132
unilateral factor services   28
UNITA   44, 45, 110
United Nations   43, 47
United States   111
Unilateral Declaration of Independence
    see UDI
unnatural economic relations   128–30,
    156
unskilled labour   16–17, 48
urban development   15, 19

Victoria Falls   18
visible trade   27
  see also trading relations
Vorster, Balthazar Johannes,
    President   49

Wagner, R. Harrison   100–4, 150
Wankie area (Zimbabwe)   18
water supplies   116
Witwatersrand (SA)   14, 15, 18, 19, 20,
    21
  industrial development   40–1, 65

World Bank   132
World War *see* First World War
    (1914–18)
    Second World War
    (1939–45)

Zaire:
  economic relations   31
  mineral resources   18, 26
  railways   31
Zambesi River   18, 20, 36
Zambia   13
  and South Africa   49, 53–4, 116
  colonial period   18, 19, 23–4, 35
  economic relations   31, 51–2, 151,
    163
  geography   36
  migrant labour   32, 33
  mineral resources   18, 20, 26
  regional development   19
  see also Central African Federation
Zanu-PF party (Zimbabwe)   118
Zimbabwe   1, 13
  and Mozambique   53–4
  and South Africa   51–3, 54–7, 116,
    118–21, 127
  capital investment   34
  colonial period   20, 23–4, 35
  economic relations   31, 42, 43, 46,
    50–4, 142, 151, 163
  exports   77, 78
  geography   36
  industrial development   39, 47–8
  manufacturing industry   39–40
  migrant labour   32, 33
  mineral resources   18
  political independence   46
  regional development   19
  transport system   144
  UDI   43, 44–5, 50–7, 77
  Zanu-PF party   118
  see also Central African Federation

ES

10 30

'5 10 30